AF552581

MAHATMA GANDHI

OTHER LOTUS TITLES:

Aitzaz Ahsan	*The Indus Saga: The Making of Pakistan*
Alam Srinivas	*Storms in the Sea Wind: Ambani vs Ambani*
Amir Mir	*The True Face of Jehadis: Inside Pakistan's Terror Networks*
Bhawana Somaaya	*Hema Malini: The Authorized Biography*
Chaman Nahal	*Silent Life: Memoirs of a Writer*
Duff Hart-Davis	*Honorary Tiger: The Life of Billy Arjan Singh*
Frank Simoes	*Frank Unedited*
Frank Simoes	*Frank Simoes' Goa*
Hindustan Times Leadership Initiative	*The Peace Dividend: Progress for India and South Asia*
Hindustan Times Leadership Initiative	*Building a Better Future*
Hindustan Times Leadership Initiative	*India and the World: A Blueprint for Partnership and Growth*
M.J. Akbar	*India: The Siege Within*
M.J. Akbar	*Kashmir: Behind the Vale*
M.J. Akbar	*Nehru: The Making of India*
M.J. Akbar	*Riot after Riot*
M.J. Akbar	*The Shade of Swords*
M.J. Akbar	*Byline*
M.J. Akbar	*Blood Brothers: A Family Saga*
Meghnad Desai	*Nehru's Hero Dilip Kumar: In the Life of India*
Nayantara Sahgal (ed.)	*Before Freedom: Nehru's Letters to His Sister*
Neesha Mirchandani	*Wisdom Song: The Life of Baba Amte*
Rohan Gunaratna	*Inside Al Qaeda*
Maj. Gen. Ian Cardozo	*Param Vir: Our Heroes in Battle*
Maj.Gen. Ian Cardozo	*The Sinking of INS Khukri: What Happened in 1971*
Maj. R.P. Singh, Kanwar Rajpal Singh	*Sawai Man Singh II of Jaipur: Life and Legend*
Mushirul Hasan	*India Partitioned. 2 Vols*
Mushirul Hasan	*John Company to the Republic*
Mushirul Hasan	*Knowledge, Power and Politics*
Rachel Dwyer	*Yash Chopra: Fifty Years of Indian Cinema*
Shrabani Basu	*Spy Princess: The Life of Noor Inayat Khan*
Thomas Weber	*Gandhi, Gandhism and the Gandhians*
V. Srinivasan	*New Age Management: Philosophy from Ancient Indian Wisdom*
Veena Sharma	*Kailash Mansarovar: A Sacred Journey*
Verghese Kurien, as told to Gouri Salvi	*I Too Had a Dream*
Vir Sanghvi	*Men of Steel: Indian Business Leaders in Candid Conversation*

FORTHCOMING TITLES:

B.K. Trehan & Madhu Trehan	*Retirement Made Easy*
Leela Kirloskar	*Dealing with Divorce Made Easy: The Essential Handbook*

MAHATMA GANDHI
A Historical Biography

BIDYUT CHAKRABARTY

LOTUS COLLECTION
ROLI BOOKS

Lotus Collection

This edition published in 2007
The Lotus Collection
An imprint of
Roli Books Pvt. Ltd.
M-75, G.K. II Market, New Delhi 110 048
Phones: ++91 (011) 2921 2271, 2921 2782
2921 0886, Fax: ++91 (011) 2921 7185
E-mail: roli@vsnl.com
Website: rolibooks.com
Also at
Varanasi, Bangalore, Kolkata, Jaipur & Mumbai

Cover design: Nabanita Das
Layout design: Narendra Shahi
Production: Kumar Raman

ISBN: 81-7436-506-0

Typeset in Photina MT by Roli Books Pvt. Ltd. and printed at Anubha Printers, Noida.

CONTENTS

PREFACE

THIS HISTORICAL BIOGRAPHY IS A CRITICAL GANDHIAN response to those who tend to belittle the academic feats of any kind by referring to their 'pipe-line' publications. In this world of academia, these individuals flourish by networks drawing not on serious academic works, but on 'back-scratching' among those belonging to the so-called 'mutual admirer club'. In the name of academic excellence (justifying their academic pretensions) these individuals despite having devastatingly damaged the natural growth of our academia survive as 'parasites'. The aim of this biography is thus two-fold: first, to reiterate the basic dictum of academia: *Vidya Dadati Vinayam* (Learning makes people humble), and secondly, to uphold the spirit of fraternity among those in the academia who still believe that academics is not merely a profession, but also a vocation. Instead of a fraternal bond, factions seem to have ruled the roost now. The schism between factions is not 'principle-based' but 'personalized ideology', largely idiosyncratically defined self-seeking means.

Gandhi's life is instructive. In his fight against the mighty imperial power, he was guided by ahimsa, which he never compromised even in adverse circumstances. Following the Chauri Chaura, Gandhi, for instance, withdrew the Non-

Cooperation Movement despite opposition from his colleagues. To him, it was 'a Himalayan blunder' and yet, he defended his decision simply because the campaign had deviated from ahimsa. The same Gandhi did not, however, assert to the extent he was expected when the Congress stalwarts agreed to accept partition as a major condition for the final transfer of power. Gandhi was thus a true 'organic' intellectual who epitomized 'praxis' in its classical definition.

Formatted in 'life and times' perspective, the biography is both a tribute to this greatest Indian and an intellectual account of his ideas and deeds that he undertook in a specific historical context of British colonialism. I owe a debt of gratitude to my family, my peers, my teachers and those who interacted with me when I had an opportunity to speak on Gandhi. I am thankful to my colleagues in the South Asian Studies Programme of National University Singapore, especially Professor Peter Reeves for his personal care and intellectual support during my stay in the campus. In the completion of this work, Dr Ian Copland of Monash University, Melbourne, had a very significant role, which he played more as a true friend in the Down-Under and less as a sponsor. I fondly remember Professor Ronald Terchek for having kindled my sustained interest in Gandhi and ahimsa. Professor Bob Frykenberg contributed immensely to this project by providing relevant inputs as and when I had asked for. My colleague in the University of Hull (England), Professor Bhikhu Parekh remains a constant source of inspiration to my intellectual feat. Without Dipakda's uncritical support in my fight against those distorting the system for narrow personal gains, it would not have been possible for me to remain Gandhian in my response. Subratada and Dipa Boudi made my regular trip to their home in CR Park most interesting not only because they provided 'food for thought' but also for their fulfilling company.

I thankfully remember my students and my family. Sanchita contributes to my tenacity by expressing doubts in my ability to handle our children, Barbie and Pablo, and my academic works simultaneously. Barbie and Pablo have sustained my interests in creativity by their constant engagement in activities that are not stereotypical and hence require innovations while gauging their nature and impact. By her frugal lifestyle, my mother makes me believe in the natural beauty of simple life long before I was drawn to Mahatma's philosophy of life. My Calcutta-based sisters provide resources for life in circumstances, which are not exactly conducive for academic creativity.

Finally, I would like to remember those individuals pretending to be my friends when the cloud disappears and blue sky is visible with an earnest request to avoid indulging in *hara-kiri* for narrow personal gains. We survive if we appreciate academic excellence regardless of creed, colour and clan. We ruin ourselves if we do otherwise.

INTRODUCTION

MOHANDAS KARAMCHAND GANDHI (1869-1948), POPULARLY known as Mahatma Gandhi, continues to generate interest even more than half a century after his assassination in 1948. The much-hyped reenactment of the famous Dandi Yatra (march) in India in 2005, which Gandhi undertook in 1930 as part of his famous Salt Satyagraha is perhaps suggestive of the relevance of Gandhian technique in political mobilization in contemporary India. It is true that though Richard Attenborough's film on Gandhi immensely popularized him all over the world, Gandhi remains an important topic of research and discussion among those interested in exploring alternative ideological traditions. The task is made much easier simply because Gandhi's own writings on various themes are plenty and less ambiguous.[1] His articulation is not only clear and simple but also meaningful in similar contexts in which he led the most gigantic nationalist struggle of the twentieth century. Gandhi wrote extensively for the *Indian Opinion*, *Young India* and *Harijan,* the leading weekly journals of the era where he commented on the issues of contemporary relevance. Superficially they may not appear to be relevant now, but his writings frequently address matters of everyday importance to

Indians in the early and mid-twentieth century. Writing for the ordinary people, he usually employed metaphors and engaged in homilies to teach Indians about their abilities and also their strong cultural/historical traditions. This is one of the ways in which he involved his readers in non-violent struggles against the British imperialism, untouchability and communal discord.

This biography seeks to articulate the historiography of India's freedom struggle of which Gandhi was undoubtedly the central figure, by engaging with those key issues/themes that have been raised in the research conducted over the past few decades. This will serve two purposes: first, apart from situating Gandhi within the broad contour of the nationalist campaign, this exercise will acquaint readers with major theoretical premises on the study of Gandhi and his ideas which arose out of a specific context involving the nationalists and their *bete noire*, the colonial power. Secondly, by dwelling on people's perceptions of the Mahatma, the proposed biography aims to explore the relatively unknown dimensions of the life of perhaps the most popular nationalist leader of the twentieth century. The Mahatma became a metaphor that galvanized the masses into action even under most adverse circumstances. In the evolution of such a metaphor, the saintly image of Gandhi was as significant as his ideology of non-violence or ahimsa. While challenging many forms of 'domination', whether ancient or modern, in the subcontinent, he developed a comprehensive theory that transcended national boundaries about the basic contours of 'a good society' and the importance of 'non-violence'. Drawing upon 'ethnicity', 'religion' and other India-specific socio-economic characteristics, the Mahatma tried to articulate a distinctive 'cultural' vision of nationhood – a vision that immediately gained currency during the freedom struggle. Unlike his predecessors in the struggle for independence, Gandhi provided a multi-class nationalist model whereby even the contending classes were combined in his fight against imperialism. Gandhi, as a strategist fulfilled the aims and aspirations of those fighting for India's freedom. What is most striking is the success of Gandhi in articulating the 'local' grievances against the vested social, political and economic interests in a typical nationalist language. The movements that he launched and steered thus largely remained nationalist and never became isolated struggles either in terms of ideology or domain. These movements drew on anti-British sentiments and mobilized 'the nation' against an alien power in which the Mahatma remained supreme. An inspiration even in locations he hardly visited, Gandhi became a powerful symbol of protest for people in adverse circumstances. He became, as it were, a part of the mass psyche. Hence it would be wrong to simply identify Gandhi as a mere 'demagogue'. He was a mobilizer who redefined India's struggle for independence in a way as to solicit mass support for the cause. He was an ideologue as well who translated the age-old Indian tradition of 'ahimsa' into action. A mere philosophical principle became a plan of action. Gandhi stood out in the nationalist crowd simply because his ideology was not simply a sophisticated articulation of certain high 'philosophical' ideals, it was a well defined and perhaps the most appropriate plan of action. Swayed by Gandhi, Indian masses rose in revolt in most adverse circumstances.

One must be careful in delineating the features of the nationalist struggle in India that was not exclusively a Gandhi-led effort. For there were various other contending ideological currents mobilizing various strata of Indian society. As recent researches highlighting the 'subaltern' initiatives have shown the importance of ideologies other than non-violence in organizing anti-British protests during the period when the Mahatma was unquestionably the undisputed leader of the freedom struggle. What is striking is that none of these movements were hardly pan-Indian or had the capacity to generate any response beyond a relatively narrow geographical location. There is no doubt that these movements had also championed issues of massive social, political and economic significance. Their expanse was, however, very limited for historical reasons and hence these issues did not appear to be meaningful to the people at large. Gandhi may not have drawn on subaltern grievances, but he gave them a nationalist voice despite the so-called 'class limitation' of his approach. It was therefore not surprising that those identified as subalterns in the Gramscian vocabulary participated in the nationalist venture as and when the Mahatma gave the clarion call. The reasons for this are not difficult to seek. By taking part in the nationalist movements, the peripheral sections of Indian society also sought to realize their nationalist dream. Once the nation was liberated, they would accomplish their other goals. The logic is simple and easy to understand in a situation of colonial rule that thrived on exploitation. Masses participated in the Gandhi-led movements to register their natural protest against imperialism. With the defeat of the forces of alien administration, the situation would certainly improve and subaltern grievances would be effectively addressed. This is where Gandhi was unique. He succeeded in linking subaltern exploitation with the prevalence of an imperial power. As a result, the issues, potentially divisive of the multi-class model, were never allowed to prevail over the basic nationalist goal. It was thus possible for Gandhi not only to create but also strengthen the multi-class model despite obvious tension due to its contradictory nature. Indian National Congress remained committed to 'no tax campaign', but never endorsed 'no rent campaign' presumably because that would adversely affect the supportive landlords who Gandhi could hardly afford to antagonize. This resulted in obvious friction among those seeking to reach out to the subaltern masses. But such was the capacity of the Mahatma that they failed to alter the basic ideological thrust of the Congress under his stewardship. Subalterns were an important constituency in the nationalist politics with the well-defined nationalist boundary. In other words, subaltern issues were articulated in a typical nationalist vocabulary and were addressed in a way to make 'nation' prior to 'the peripheries'. The Gandhian non-violence was thus a nationalist response in which subalterns also found their expression and the Mahatma became a leader transcending narrow class characteristics.

Gandhi was a mass leader in the true sense of the term. The character of the national movement had undergone qualitative changes as soon as he became its leader. Unlike his predecessors in the freedom struggle, Gandhi brought in people from all walks of life. The Congress that he represented was a political platform articulating the voice of a nation that was fractured on various counts. Gandhi spoke the language of the masses. He dressed like them. In his vocabulary, there was a fine blend of both indigenous and Western traditions. Although he was inspired by ideas of stalwarts like Tolstoy, Emerson and Ruskin, he hardly talked in those terms. By creatively indigenizing the ideas, the Mahatma redefined them, which despite their Western roots became meaningful in the Indian context. Non-violence was thus not an alien concept, but was organically linked with India as a civilization. Furthermore, his language of politics was Indian in the sense that he always expressed his vision and strategy in vernacular. This is where Gandhi surpasses others in the nationalist struggle for independence. His social and political ideas acquired immediate salience presumably because they were supplemented by his pastoral style in daily life: travelling in third-class compartments, speaking in simple Hindustani, wearing self-spun khadi, using the imagery of Tulsidas' *Ramayana*, so deep-rooted in the popular religion of the north-Indian Hindu rural masses. Not only did he become the undisputed mass leader of the freedom struggle, he also became the most effective personality in the Indian National Congress that was famous for factional squabbles in the past. His role in the Congress was that of a senior colleague who ran the organization successfully by his ability to strike a balance among people of disparate views. The Congress became an umbrella organization in true sense of the term. Despite clinging to ideologies different from that of the National Congress, prominent ideologues of several other political outfits endorsed Gandhian means simply because of their capacity to motivate masses for the nationalist campaign. India's freedom struggle became nationalist and mass-based largely due to Gandhi's intervention. History was being re-written and the Mahatma became its architect. Ahimsa became a buzzword in political struggle even when the adversary was equipped with the most lethal weapons. Ahimsa was, as it were, an electrifying device, that awakened the moribund masses in a situation when the Indian nationalist movement was scattered and thus crippled due to historical reasons. The nationalist movement acquired completely different connotations both organizationally and ideologically during the Gandhian phase. Gandhi was thus a rare political symbol that was articulated differently by those participating in the national struggle for freedom. For the masses, ahimsa was inspirational and for his co-workers in the Congress it was an effective strategy to expand and strengthen the organization.

How did he view his enemies, namely the British? Gandhi's response to this question brings out the complexities of modern machine-based civilization. Like any other humanist, Gandhi hardly had any ill feelings towards the British people. He, however, was critical of the ruling authority that drew on 'brute force' to sustain its administration that was both inhuman and exploitative. Justifying his critique of machine civilization, Gandhi felt that machine makes everybody idle and if the craze for it continues, it will make everybody so incapacitated and weak that they shall begin to curse themselves for having forgotten the use of the living machine given by God. He believed that over-dependence on machine would take out the human creativity from human beings. In his own confession, 'it is possible to visualize a stage at which the machines invented by man may finally engulf civilization. If man controls machines, then they will; but should man lose his control over the machines and allow them to control him, then they will certainly engulf civilization and everything'.[2] What was his alternative? In response, the Mahatma defended the role of 'spinning wheel' by saying that 'when as a nation we adopt the spinning wheel, we not only solve the question of unemployment but we declare that we have no intention of exploiting any nation, we also end the exploitation of the poor by the rich'.[3] As explained, machine civilization was by nature not appropriate in a nation as large as India because of its inability to accommodate the growing labour force. It would not solve unemployment of the millions and hence would not be an effective strategy for India. A pragmatic Gandhi thus argued for spinning-wheel or charkha that would provide employment to the people and also would make them economically self-dependent. Whether spinning-wheel was an economically viable strategy, in terms of providing effective employment to all is debatable; but the idea of providing employment was certainly a refreshing one and acquired importance in the context of colonial rule. Charkha was thus not merely an economic strategy it was also a significant dimension of ahimsa. It was a device to make the nation self-dependent and thus confident about its existence. Undoubtedly, it was a masterstroke by a master-strategist who transformed charkha into a meaningful tool and perhaps the most powerful slogan in the nationalist campaign of India.

Charkha and ahimsa seem to be supplementary to each other in Gandhi's conceptualization of nationalist politics. Two arguments are crucial here. Gandhi never believed that East India Company captured India by the dint of physical force.

Instead, it was possible for the Company to establish its rule in India because of the support Indians extended to the British. In Gandhi's words, 'The English have not taken India; we have given it to them. They are not in India because of their strength, but because we keep them.' His logic was very simple. Indians fulfilled the Company's mercantile interests and hence the Company prospered. He explained this by drawing an analogy with the seller of 'bhang'. Unless one's habit was changed, the seller of bhang continued to remain. So, instead of blaming the seller, one should change one's habit. Similarly, if Indians decided not to cooperate with the Company, it would be difficult for them to survive even for a day. Furthermore, the communal schism among the Indians contributed to the strength of the Company. 'The Hindus and Mohammedans were,' argued Gandhi, 'at daggers drawn. This too gave the Company its opportunity, and thus we created circumstances that gave the Company its control over India'. Hence Gandhi concluded that 'it is truer to say that we gave India to the English than that India was lost.'[4]

After having discussed the root cause of India's enslavement, the Mahatma elaborated his strategy to get rid of the English rule. He was convinced that physical force was not an appropriate device to counter the English. We needed other means to be deployed. And Gandhi found his answer in passive resistance. In contrast with armed-resistance, passive resistance was a method of 'securing rights by personal suffering'. Drawn on 'soul-force', passive resistance involves suffering for breach of law. As Gandhi explained, 'When I refuse to a thing that is repugnant to my conscience, I use soul force. ... If, by using violence, I force the government to repeal the law, I am employing what may be termed body-force. If I do not obey the law, and accept the penalty for its breach, I use soul-force. It involves sacrifice of self.' Critical of physical force, Gandhi articulated a unique form of protest by drawing upon India's age-old traditions of ahimsa. Two ideas are important here: first, ahimsa became a creed for the Mahatma and he was persuaded to believe that it was perhaps the most effective 'weapon' in his fight against a mighty imperial power. Secondly, ahimsa involved self-sacrifice. Here too, the Mahatma drew upon philosophical tradition where self-sacrifice remained integral to human salvation. Indians remained instinctively 'non-violent' presumably because of these well-entrenched traditions in which they were nurtured. By articulating his approach in an indigenous way, Gandhi immediately struck a chord with those who gradually became part and parcel of the movements. Passive resistance was thus an Indian variety, informed by Western traditions as well. Unlike those movements in the past which had failed to mobilize 'the nation' against the British, the Gandhian response was structurally different and ideologically innovative: structurally different because the nation as a whole participated in movements against colonialism; ideologically creative because ahimsa-based passive resistance was neither transmitted from the past nor was negative in its content as was true during the revolutionary terrorist era of Indian nationalism. As evident, passive resistance is positive in its connotation. It is 'an all-sided sword' that draws its strength from 'control over the mind'. It does not require 'the training of an army'. Hence, even a man 'weak in body is capable of offering his resistance'. What is most important, as Gandhi himself underlined, is that 'passive resistance cannot proceed a step without fearlessness'. By fearlessness, Gandhi did not just mean free from fear of death; instead, he defined fear in a wider sense by including the fear of losing 'material possessions', 'honour', 'relatives', among others. What is clear is that the contour of passive resistance, as it was conventionally known, was radically altered and the participants were imbued with characteristics which were tuned to the context. Seeking to reach out to the masses and inspiring them by drawing their attention to the indigenous traditions of India, Gandhi provided a model that was a unique blend of India's philosophical traditions with what he derived from Tolstoy, Thoreau, Emerson and Ruskin.

Gandhi was an activist-theoretician who steered the nation against colonial rule. Politically appropriate and ideologically inspiring, ahimsa radically altered the complexion of the nationalist struggle. Not only was the nation redefined, its boundaries were also expanded by including the hitherto peripheral sections of society. The arrival of Gandhi on the Indian political scene was thus a clear departure from the past when the nationalist protest was narrowly conceptualized. There is no doubt that those who pursued the nationalist goal during the 'Moderate' and 'Extremist' phases of India's freedom struggle contributed immensely to nationalist cause. What distinguishes the Gandhian phase was the expanse of the nationalist constituencies and mass acceptance of ahimsa as an ideology. Interestingly, the Gandhian ideology was hardly stagnant and was constantly redefined in movements that drew on non-violence but had features challenging on occasions its basic ideological ingredients. Gandhi became a 'metaphor' shaping the nationalist campaign in accordance with what the participants deemed fit at a particular historical juncture. That is why, there is hardly a typical Gandhian response; instead, the response is contextual and thus it was not always possible for the leaders to translate the mass outbursts against the British strictly in Gandhian terms. The 1922 Chauri Chaura incident during the 1919-1922 Non-Cooperation Movement is illustrative here when the participants resorted to violence that led Gandhi to immediately call off the campaign.

WHO WAS MOHANDAS KARAMCHAND GANDHI?

The Mahatma was truly a child of his time. He was a loyalist, to begin with. He became perhaps the most staunch and effective critic of colonial rule in India. Born on 2 October 1869 in Porbander, Gujarat, Mohandas Karamchand Gandhi was the last child of his father's fourth and last marriage. Bania by caste, Gandhis were involved in petty trade. Gandhi's grandfather, however, rose to the position of dewan or chief minister of the princely state of Porbander. The family baton was passed on to Gandhi's father who later on became the dewan of Rajkot, another princely state in Kathiawar region of Gujarat. Despite his busy schedule, Gandhi's father took ample care for giving his children the comforts of an established home and the opportunities of education. At home, his mother, Putlibai, drew Mohandas to the rich civilizational traditions of India. Not only was he introduced to the religious and mythological texts, he was also influenced by his mother's 'saintliness' and 'deeply religious nature'.[5] The young Gandhi was inquisitive and kept asking questions to his mother who would patiently respond to him. These narratives had a deep impact on the young mind. Instead of being catholic in his religious preferences, the early influences on him made him realize the importance of 'an open mind' with regard to different religions that made India's civilization so rich and complex. Despite being Hindu, religious orthodoxy had no place in Gandhi's family. This was probably one of the reasons why Gandhi was sensitive to different and even contradictory faiths and practices that gradually loomed large, as Gandhi became the Mahatma.

Married at the age of thirteen to Kasturba, his marriage became a major turning point in his life. This was because of two reasons: first, marriage made him realize the importance of earning for sustenance. It was now humiliating for him to depend on his father's money. Secondly, he was disturbed with 'the shackles of lust', which, he thought, was responsible for diverting his attention away from other noble goals of life. He was in a dilemma, torn between his 'lust' and the concern for making life 'different and useful' for society. He expressed doubt as to whether his love for Kasturba was due to his physical lust. As he himself narrated, his passionate love for Kasturba did not allow him to even visit his father before his death. While describing his mental agony after his father's death, he thus lamented,

> I felt deeply ashamed and miserable. ... If animal passion had not blinded me, I should have been spared the torture of separation from my father during his last moments. ... The shame was this shame of my carnal desire even at the critical hour of my father's death, which demanded wakeful service. It was a blot I have never been able to efface or forget.[6]

He also attributed the death of his son after his father's demise as a curse, which he invited because of his reluctance and failure to see the dying father. This apart, Gandhi felt ashamed that he did not give ample attention to Kasturba's education. His resistance to her studies deterred Kasturba from pursuing her interest. Gandhi was perhaps aware of this, as he himself admitted by saying that if his affection for Kasturba had not been tainted with lust she would have become a learned lady. Not only that, his role as 'a cruelly kind husband' made Kasturba and their children suffer, as his son Manilal reminisced.[7] The epic character of Sita fascinated him and he wanted his wife to emulate the ideals for which Sita was venerated. We do not know how Kasturba accepted Gandhi's dictations. In her deep silence, the wife of Gandhi crafted a role for herself both in the family and later as his 'soul mate' when he plunged in the wider nationalist politics. For Gandhi, Kasturba became a symbol of ideal womanhood who would sacrifice for husband and children. Women's role was drafted as an appendage to their male counterpart. Gandhi was not gender-sensitive at least at the initial stages of his career. Here, he was clearly stereotypical in his ideas for he never reconciled to Kasturba's role beyond the familial boundaries.

After completing high school, Gandhi sailed for England seeking to obtain a degree in law. Gandhi was typical of his age when people tended to favour a law degree presumably because of social respectability of lawyers and the prospective pecuniary comfort it afforded. Sponsored by his elder brother, Gandhi was allowed to set out only after he promised his mother to avoid 'women, wine or meat'. In England, he left no stone unturned to adapt himself to the British society. He dressed like English man of that period by imitating the English dress code to the best of his ability. He got his three-piece suit stitched by a Bond Street tailor, bought a gold double watch chain, leather gloves, silver-mounted stick, burnished silk-top hat, starched stiff collars and flashy ties. He wanted to be a perfect English gentleman not only in terms of dress and linguistic skills, but also in terms of social respectability. He began playing bridge and also spent money in learning dance and violin. While he became a connoisseur of bridge, he had to abandon violin and dance for his 'lack of talent'.

After completing his studies in 1891, Gandhi returned to India in search of livelihood. What upset him most on his return was his mother's death during his stay away from home. He did not begin his professional life with a high note presumably because he had neither the gift of the gab nor had a firm grip over the technicalities of the legal profession. In view of a disappointing start with his career, Gandhi began searching for a job in legal firms, which would give him a steady monthly income. He left for South Africa on a legal assignment, and this changed the course of his life forever. Once in South Africa, Gandhi was tormented by the insult meted out to the Indians there but did not appear to have pondered over this until he was thrown out of a first-class railway carriage at the insistence of a white passenger during his journey from Durban to Pretoria. Whisked out of the carriage on a cold night, he understood what racism meant in real terms. Despite having a valid ticket, he was forced out simply because of his colour. This incident was a watershed in his life as he recounted later that without this bitter experience he would not have thought of fighting the cause of 'the coolies', an abusive expression for the Indians in South Africa. On finishing his assignment, Gandhi was preparing to leave South Africa when he decided to stay back on insistence of the local Indians who urged him to join them in their fight against a proposed Bill denying them the right to vote. A new era in Gandhi's life had begun. And a temporary visitor made South Africa his home for the next twenty years.

An experimentalist, Gandhi was always keen to try out new ideas and practices. For instance, when he was told that Indians could become as strong as the British provided they became non-vegetarian, he decided to give it a try. The idea was attractive and Gandhi, a strict vegetarian, had meat in his meal. The consequence was disastrous since he could not sleep the whole night, as he seemed to hear a goat bleating in his stomach! One can quote innumerable instances from his early life to demonstrate that Gandhi never accepted things uncritically. His tryst with experiments began at an early stage of his life. His stay and experience in South Africa were having a positive effect – Gandhi was evolving.

His early years in London were most crucial for his intellectual growth because it was here that he was introduced to the writings of two prominent social thinkers of the period, Tolstoy (1828-1910) and Ruskin (1819-1900). In articulating his social and political views, there is no doubt that these two thinkers influenced Gandhi. However, the importance of India's philosophical traditions cannot be undermined. In fact, it would be appropriate to suggest that Gandhi's views were the result of a perfect blend of Indian ideas and their western counterparts. Although Gandhi's concepts are fully in keeping with Indian tradition, they were probably 'developed from ideas which he absorbed in his childhood and youth, fertilized and brought to fruition by his contact with the West'. In this sense, the activist-theoretician Gandhi drew upon a unique model of political action, the roots of which can be traced back to both the Western and Indian civilizational traditions.

Gandhi read Tolstoy's *The Kingdom of God is Within You* in Durban, soon after its publication in 1894. This was a seminal text for Gandhi's theory of non-violent struggle. As he himself admitted, this text 'overwhelmed' him and 'left an abiding impression' on him. He was emotionally moved by Tolstoy's description of exploitation of the Russian peasantry during the reign of Tsar. He was outraged by the Tsarist torture of the peasants who contributed to the state exchequer by their labour. In course of time, he perhaps drew a parallel when he took up the cause of the Champaran peasants who rose against the authority for illegal exaction. Like Tolstoy, Ruskin also contributed to Gandhi's thought. After having read Ruskin's *Unto this Last* (1862) in 1904, while on a train journey from Johannesburg to Durban, Gandhi commented that the book brought about an instantaneous and practical transformation in his life. Whether Gandhi was persuaded by Ruskin's critique of laissez-faire utilitarian values of nineteenth century liberalism is not very clear. What Gandhi might have picked up was Ruskin's belief that 'all property is held in trust to God'. One sees imprints of this idea in Gandhi's conceptualization of 'trusteeship' in which Gandhi expected the property-owners to shoulder a social responsibility for the poor. In fact, Ruskin seems to have provided the foundational ideas of his *Sarvadaya*, a Gujarati tract, which provided a blueprint for social and economic welfare of the people. Apart from Tolstoy and Ruskin, Edward Carpenter's *Civilization: Its cause and cure* (1891) also inspired Gandhi. Like Gandhi, Carpenter was disillusioned with industrial civilization that caused devastation to human life. Both of them felt the need to harmonize private and public needs of individuals. Modern civilization had, they agreed, resulted in alienation between nature and community and also contributed to 'mechanization' of human life. Despite agreement on the nature of modern civilization, they, however, differed while suggesting the steps to cure civilization of its 'ills'. For Carpenter, the solution to distortions in human life lay in post-industrial socialist society because capitalism failed to bring about an equitable distribution of wealth. Gandhi was radically different. He was, it seems, a Luddite in his conviction since he appreciated the pre-industrial age. Rejecting capitalism as it flourished in India under the aegis of the colonial rule, Gandhi was supportive of a civilization that was critical of 'mechanization' of human life. One may argue that Gandhi was looking backwards and was thus utopian since it was not possible to reverse the civilizational cycle. What was unique in Gandhi's conceptualization that was similar to that of Carpenter was his effort at outlining a possible blueprint for future. While Carpenter insisted on 'a socialist society', Gandhi was critical of machine civilization, which, apart from causing alienation of various kinds, was also not a perfect device to fruitfully utilize India's vast population. Thus, Gandhi's solution was tuned to India's requirement and thus highly contextual.

Besides various intellectual influences, there were other larger socio-political processes in the nineteenth and twentieth century that had an imprint in his thought and action. The two most obvious ones are nationalism and democratization.

It is true that nationalist independence was Gandhi's primary goal. But, at the same time, he redefined nationalism in such a way as to avoid homogenizing the nation. For a specific political purpose, India was conceptualized as a nation underplaying those characteristics causing schism. Simply put, after the late nineteenth century the claim to any form of self-government was shelved so long as it was not articulated as the claim of a nation. Colonial sovereignty in part rested upon denying that India was a nation. The nationalist project was not simply something that elites dreamt up to define others in their image, it also sought to identify and highlight the distinctive features of a population to justify its claim for nationhood.

The belief in an Indian nationhood as a historical fact was based on Western models. But it 'was also an emotionally charged reply to the rulers' allegation that India never was and never could be a nation'. The construction of even a vaguely defined Indian nationhood was a daunting task simply because India lacked the basic ingredients of conventionally conceptualized notion of nation. There was, therefore, a selective appeal to history to recover those elements transcending the internal schism among those who were marginalized under colonialism. Hence, an attempt was always made in a concerted manner to underline 'the unifying elements of the Indian religious traditions, medieval syncretism and the strand of tolerance and impartiality in the policies of Muslim rulers'. So the colonial milieu was an important dimension of the processes that led to a particular way of imagining a nation in a multi-ethnic context like India, which is so different from the perceptions, based on Western experience. The political sensibilities of Indian nationalism 'were deeply involved in this highly atypical act of imagining'.

Apart from colonialism, the major factor that contributed to the formation of India as a political entity was the freedom movement. It is therefore no exaggeration to suggest that the Indian consciousness, as we understand today crystallized during the national liberation movement. So national is a political and not a cultural referent in India. This perhaps led the nationalist leaders to recognize that it would be difficult to forge the multi-layered Indian society into a unified nation state in the European sense. It is true that the non-Western leaders involved in the struggle for liberation were deeply influenced by European nationalist ideas. They were also aware of the limitations of these ideas in the non-European socio-economic context due to their alien origin. So while mobilizing the imagined community for an essentially political cause they began, by the beginning of the twentieth century, to speak in a 'native' vocabulary. Although they drew upon the ideas of European nationalism, they indigenized them substantially by discovering or inventing indigenous equivalents and investing these with additional meanings and nuances. This is probably the reason why Gandhi and his colleagues in the anti-British campaign in India preferred swadeshi to nationalism. Gandhi avoided the language of nationalism primarily because he was aware that the Congress's flirtations with nationalist ideas in the first quarter of the twentieth century frightened away not only the Muslims and other minorities but also some of the Hindu lower castes.

This seems the most pragmatic idea one could possibly conceive of in a country like India that was not united in terms of religion, race, culture and common historical memories of oppression and struggle. Underlying this lays the reason why Gandhi and his Congress colleagues preferred 'the relaxed and chaotic plurality of the traditional Indian life' to the order and homogeneity of the European nation state because they realized that the open, plural and relatively heterogeneous traditional Indian civilization would best unite Indians. Drawing values meaningful to the Indian masses, the Indian freedom struggle developed its own modular form, which was characteristically different from that of the West. Although the 1947 Great divide of the subcontinent of India was articulated in terms of religion, the nationalist language drawing upon the exclusivity of Islam appeared inadequate in sustaining Pakistan following the creation of Bangladesh in 1971.

The second broader context that appears to have decisively shaped Gandhi as a nationalist leader is democratization. What sort of 'unity' does democracy requires. After all, it was a staple of liberal discourse (J.S. Mill, for instance) that democracy could not flourish in multi-ethnic societies. The important thing about Mohammad Ali Jinnah and V.D. Savarkar is that they were deploying precisely the liberal argument about why a unitary nationhood is necessary for a modern polity. And then, they provided their own interpretations of how this was to be attained. Second, democracy complicates the problem of 'representation'. What is being represented and on what terms? After all, the divisions between the Congress and Muslim League turned on issues of representation. This is, however, not to suggest that the state created two monolithic communities and these communities came into being through 'the politics of representation' since the relationship between identity and democracy is far deeper and complex than it is generally construed in contemporary discourses on south Asia. Identity politics is about expressing one's agency and creating new forms of collective agency. In this sense, they are part of the democratic ferment – where people want to fashion identities for themselves. This process will happen at all levels with a complicated relationship between the levels.

Furthermore, democratization is both inclusive and exclusive as well. Inclusive because it unleashes a process to include people, at least theoretically, regardless of class, clan and creed; it is essentially a participatory project seeking to link different layers of socio-political and economic life. Excluded are those who are different in so many ways. We are introduced to a situation where a communal identity can be formed or malformed in contact with significant 'others', generally projected with 'an inferior or demeaning image'.

The 1919-1922 Non-Cooperation-Khilafat Movement is illustrative here. By a single stroke, both the Hindus and Muslims were brought on a single political platform submerging, at one level, their distinct separate identities. At another level, this movement is a watershed in the sense that these two communities remained separate since they collaborated as separate communities for an essentially political project. So, the politics of inclusion also led towards exclusion for the communities, which identified different political agendas to mobilize people.

Thus, Gandhi evolved in a peculiar kind of colonialism

that flourished in India. Both these forces of nationalism and democratization appeared to have played decisive roles. Nationalism as a concerted effort was not merely unifying, it was also expansive gradually in the sense that it brought together apparently disparate socio-political groups in opposition to an imperial power. The character of the anti-British political campaign gradually underwent radical changes by involving people of various strata, region and linguistic groups. The definition of nation also changed. No longer was the nation confined to the cities and small towns, it consisted in innumerable villages, which so far had remained peripheral to the political activities. Whatever the manifestations, the basic point relates to the increasing awareness of those involved in nation building both during the anti-imperial struggle and its aftermath.

Gandhi was born in an age that witnessed spontaneous protest against the ruling authority, first against the racist South African government and later against the Raj in India. What was significant in Gandhi was his ability to involve the people in both local and pan-Indian movements despite adverse consequences. Forces of nationalism and democratization were at work and created possibilities of different kind of protest movements when Gandhi emerged on the scene. Hence, it is possible to argue that had Gandhi appeared on India's political scene during the 'moderate' or 'extremist' phases of Indian freedom struggle simply because the nationalist ideology was co-terminus with the context. Once both the moderate and extremist means were exhausted, the Gandhian method emerged as probably the most appropriate, given the growing involvement of the people in the movements against the British and also various kinds of socio-economic interests. It was a radically different milieu in which the character of nationalism was bound to change. Gandhi not only understood the changing nationalist complexion, he also devised appropriate methods to meaningfully exploit the mass grievances in accordance with his own ideological predilections. Whether on the scene or not, Gandhi always remained the master of the movements that he spearheaded against the colonial ruler. A new phase of Indian nationalism began of which Gandhi was certainly the principal scriptwriter. There were undoubtedly contending ideologies and competitive leaderships. But they remained appendages to the Gandhian struggle strategically to sustain their existence. Gandhi gradually turned into 'a metaphor' guiding the nationalist movements at the grassroots on various occasions. Unlike his predecessors, Gandhi established an organic link with his constituencies and this is what resulted in gradual expansion of the contour of the nationalist politics in India. So, Gandhi evolved as Mahatma in a specific context of British rule that created an environment, which was conducive to the experiments that he conducted by involving masses in non-violent protest against perhaps the most devious empire.

GANDHI'S TEXT

Gandhi left an enormous wealth of his writings, hence one is better equipped to write about his ideas, though they were not always articulated in clear terms. There is no doubt that the *Hind Swaraj* is a seminal text in what is known as Gandhism in the sense that one easily finds a resonance of his thought that he developed later in this treatise. Hence a brief discussion of the *Hind Swaraj* will not be out of context.

Hind Swaraj is perhaps the most systematic exposition of Gandhi's ideas on state, society and nation. Although *Hind Swaraj* is an original tract, Gandhi while writing this, was heavily influenced by some of the leading Western thinkers. As he himself admitted, 'whilst the views expressed in *Hind Swaraj* are held by me, I have but endeavoured humbly to follow Tolstoy, Ruskin, Thoreau, Emerson and other writers, besides the masters of Indian philosophy'.[8] It contains a statement of some of the fundamental tenets in Gandhi's politics. In other words, Gandhi stated his position quite clearly in *Hind Swaraj* and held onto it all his life. *Hind Swaraj* laid in fact, the most crucial theoretical foundation of his entire strategy of winning swaraj for India. Aware that this tract revealed the foundational ideas of Gandhian thought, Gandhi, in a significant comment on the *Hind Swaraj* in 1921, explained the purpose behind the book by saying,

> It was written … in answer to the Indian school of violence, and its prototype in South Africa. I came in contact with every known Indian anarchist in London. Their bravery impressed me, but I feel that their zeal was misguided. I felt that violence was no remedy for India's ills, and that her civilization required the use of a different and higher weapon for self-protection. The Satyagraha of South Africa was still an infant hardly two years old. But it had developed sufficiently to permit me to write of it with some degree of confidence. … *[Hind Swaraj]* teaches the gospel of love in the place of that of hate. It replaces violence with self-sacrifice. It pits soul-force against brute force.[9]

The aim of *Hind Swaraj* was to confront the anarchist and violence-prone Indian nationalists with an alternative to violence, derived from Gandhi's earliest experiments with satyagraha. As Gandhi wrote, '*Hind Swaraj* [was] written in order to show that [his countrymen] are following a suicidal policy [of violence], and that, if they but revert to their own glorious civilization, either the English would adopt the latter and become Indianized or find their occupation in India gone'. Even the title of the book was most significant; he dealt with his version of swaraj that was relevant for India. This was the first and perhaps the most elaborate discussion of swaraj or freedom from Gandhi's point of view. This was also the most authentic text of Gandhian social and political ideas dealing with swaraj and satyagraha. Furthermore, Gandhi also drew on the dichotomies between the spiritual, moral fabric of Indian society, and the violent, politically corrupt nature of European state even more dramatically than any of his predecessors. While condemning 'the brute force' of Western powers, Gandhi distanced himself from the militant nationalists for their support to violence, which was suicidal as a strategy as it would provoke 'an organized violence' by the ruling authority. Violence was, therefore, counter-productive. *Hind Swaraj*, as evident, served two purposes: on the one hand, this was a detailed commentary on Western civilization that thrived on naked force; this also laid down, on the other hand, the fundamental pillars what later became basic precepts of Gandhi's social and political ideas. Although his satyagraha experiment in South Africa contributed immensely to *Hind Swaraj*, he was influenced by other sources as well.

Hind Swaraj is a foundational text for understanding

Gandhi and his ideology. A rather incendiary manifesto to galvanize the masses into action, the book was banned in 1910 by the government for fear of sedition. Whether it was a seditious tract is debatable; but it is certainly a significant text with refreshing ideas, i) critiquing the Western civilization, and also ii) seeking to build a vernacular model of action that the people of India understood.

Hind Swaraj provides a scathing critique of Western civilization. The three recurrent themes are: (i) colonial exploitation, (ii) industrial capitalism, and (iii) rationalist materialism. According to Gandhi, colonialism triumphed in India not because of its strength but because of our weaknesses that allowed 'this intimate enemy' to strike roots in India. He was probably the first to have attributed the British rule in India to 'moral decline' that affected the entire nation. For Gandhi, the aim of his project was therefore to recover the self under colonialism. Attributing colonialism in India to 'our weaknesses', Gandhi thus argued,

> The English have not taken India; we have given it to them. They are not in India because of their strength, but because we keep them. … Recall the Company Bahadur. Who made it Bahadur? They had not the slightest intention at the time of establishing a kingdom. Who assisted the Company's officers? Who was tempted at the sight of their silver? Who bought their goods? History testifies that we did all this. … When our Princes fought among themselves, they sought the assistance of Company Bahadur. That cooperation was versed alike in commerce and war. It was unhampered by questions of morality. … Is it not then useless to blame the English for what we did at the time? … it is truer to say that we gave India to the English than that India was lost.[10]

According to Gandhi, the British conquest of India was solely due to our moral failure. Imperialism struck roots in India in course of time because of the cooperation of the Indians with the British government. There was no restraint presumably because of a moral decadence of the race, known as Indians. There is another side of the argument. Gandhi was contemptuous of Western civilization that under the garb of civilizing the colonial 'subjects' pursued its 'selfish interests' and nothing else. Based on 'brute force', the Western civilization was thus both 'narrow' and 'perverted'. So, in Gandhi's perception, by providing legitimacy to colonialism, the so-called modern civilization subverted 'the natural evolution' of societies clinging to the so-called traditional ways of life. Drawn on the civilizational resources of a traditional society like India, Gandhi produced perhaps the most effective trans-cultural protest against the hyper-masculine worldview of colonialism

Hind Swaraj was the most creative response to the perversion of industrial capitalism. For Gandhi, industrialization remained the driving force behind Western civilization. 'Machinery is,' he characterized, 'the chief symbol of modern civilization; it represents sin. [Hence] if the machine craze grows in our country, it will become an unhappy land'. Condemning the role of machine in 'de-humanizing' the workers toiling in the factories for 'profit' in which they had no share, the Mahatma thus argued that 'it is necessary to realize that machinery is bad. We shall then be able to do away with it. ... If, instead of welcoming machinery as a boom', he further mentioned, 'we would look upon it as an evil, it would ultimately go'. According to Gandhi, 'a snake-bite is a lesser poison' than 'the mill industry' because while the former merely harmed the body, the latter 'destroys body, mind and soul'. Gandhi's critique of machine civilization was a creative response and thus most original. While the earlier nationalists attributed the Western conquest of India to 'a superior military strength', Gandhi actually probed into the processes that led to such a dramatic rise of the Western powers. Unlike his colleagues, Gandhi had no doubt that 'the source of modern imperialism lies specifically in the system of social production which the countries of the Western world have adopted'. It is the limitless desire for 'ever-increased production and ever-greater consumption and the spirit of ruthless competitiveness' that not only sustained the system but also impelled these countries to establish colonies that could be exploited for economic gains. Industrialization was an evil simply because the purpose of production was not to create an egalitarian but a capitalist society. For industrialism to survive and thrive, these Western industrial nations needed colonies to market their goods. Since colonialism and industrialism were complementary to each other, industrial capitalism was, as Gandhi saw, inherently harmful to human civilization.

According to Gandhi, there remained a tension between 'true civilization' and 'a civilization based on machine'. While the latter is based on brute rationalist materialism, the former draws its sustenance from *dharma*. In modern civilization, *artha* (money) and *kama* (desire) are totally divorced from *dharma* on the basis of the alleged superiority of 'rational materialism'. Critical of the unbridled march of 'reason', Gandhi never conceded to abdicate his 'faith' for reason. Instead, he would test his faith with his reason, but would not allow reason to destroy his faith. In other words, 'technological rationalism', defending 'crude materialism' lay at the root of destruction of true civilization where *dharma* was a device to ascertain morality. 'To observe morality', argued Gandhi, 'is to attain mastery over our mind and our passions'. Religion was the template for morality. He never compromised with the importance of religion in our social life though he opposed religious superstitions, which, according to him, were 'cruelties, practised in the name of religion'. But there was no end to this process and 'they will happen so long as there are to be found ignorant and credulous people'. Although there was no space for religious superstition, for obvious reasons, Gandhi was not 'irreligious' either, for he argued that 'we will certainly fight tooth and nail, but we can never do so by disregarding religion. We can only do so by appreciating and conserving the latter.' While criticizing rationalist materialism of the West, Gandhi appeared to have drawn heavily on the Hindu tradition in which *dharma* in the sense of morality and religion remained crucial. He therefore condemned the modern civilization because it

> takes note neither of morality nor of religion. Its votaries calmly state that their business is not to teach religion. Some even consider it to be a superstitious growth. Others put on the cloak of religion and prate about morality. ... Immorality is often taught in the name of morality. This civilization seeks to increase bodily comfort by pursuing crude [rationalist materialism], and it fails miserably even in doing so.[11]

Hind Swaraj is thus Gandhi's creative response to the theoretical basis of Western civilization. Drawn on the civilizational resources of Hindu religion and its tradition, he put forward a new theoretical framework to conceptualize both colonialism and industrial capitalism. He later expanded these foundational ideas of *Hind Swaraj* on various occasions.

Harijan holds a special place in Gandhi's effort at conceptualizing and/or reconceptualizing social and political ideas that were dear to him. As the following discussion shows, the Mahatma transcended the historical period in which he evolved by dwelling on issues, which are relevant even in the twenty-first century.

NATION, NATIONALISM AND NATIONAL IDENTITY

Gandhi's writings published in *Harijan* are very significant to discern Gandhi's views on nation, nationalism and national identity. He elaborated his views on these in two different ways: on occasions, he made statements explaining these concepts in India's context. He, however, preferred to deal with them while responding to the questions, addressed to him by the readers of *Harijan*. Unlike M.A. Jinnah, Gandhi conceptualized the Indian struggle for independence in a non-nationalist and non-national language. He rarely used the term 'nation' except when forced to do so under circumstances in which Jinnah defended the two-nation theory. In opposition to Jinnah, Gandhi argued that the language of nationalism was both incompatible to India and inherently absurd. India was not a nation but a civilization, which had over the centuries benefited from the contributions of different races and religions. Indians were, therefore, not 'a motley collection of groups but shared common aspirations and interests and a vague but nonetheless deeply felt commitment to the historical civilization.'

THE COMMUNAL QUESTION

Harijan was a forum where Gandhi dealt with the Hindu-Muslim question at some length by publishing his views at regular intervals. There seem to be two definite ways in which the Mahatma sought to conceptualize the inter-communal relationship. On the one hand, Gandhi was disturbed by the rapid deterioration of the relations between these communities primarily because without the Hindu-Muslim unity, there could be no swaraj. He thus argued, 'I must be impatient for Hindu-Muslim unity because I am impatient for swaraj. [And] the present bickering and petty recriminations between communities are an unnatural aberration.' Attributing the continuity of the British power in India to 'the Hindu-Muslim division', Gandhi, on the other hand, argued that 'the British established themselves by taking advantage of our mutual quarrels and have remained by keeping them alive'. What is striking and clear is that Gandhi appeared to have over-emphasized the divisive nature of the British rule and undermined the socio-economic dimension of the Hindu-Muslim schism largely due to catholicism of Hinduism. It seems that Gandhi strove to analyse the issue on the basis of a surface reading of the problem. This is reflected in his statements seeking to show the apparent unanimity between Hindus and Muslims despite clinging to different religious faiths. On one occasion, he, for instance, referred to Sir Ali Imam whose 'dress, manners, food were the same as the majority of the Hindus'. Even the name Jinnah, Gandhi argued, 'could be that of any Hindu'. He also mentioned 'Sir Mahommed Iqbal [who] used to speak with pride his brahminical descent. Iqbal and Kitchlew are names common to Hindus and Muslims.' Hence, Gandhi concluded, 'Hindus and Muslims of India are not two nations'.

CRITIQUE OF INDUSTRIALISM / WESTERN CIVILIZATION

Gandhi was an ardent critic of modern civilization as it emerged in the West and as it was imported to India in the wake of colonial rule. He attacked the very notions of modernity and progress, and challenged the central claim that modern civilization was a leveler in which the productive capacities of human labour rose exponentially creating increased wealth and prosperity for all and hence increased leisure, comfort, health and happiness. Far from attaining these objectives, modern civilization, Gandhi argued, contributed to unbridled competition among human beings and thereby the evils of poverty, disease, war and suffering. It is precisely because modern civilization 'looks at man (sic) as a limitless consumer and thus sets out to open the floodgates of industrial production that it also becomes the source of inequality, oppression and violence on a scale hitherto unknown to human history'. What the Mahatma argued in the *Hind Swaraj* regarding industrial civilization was further reiterated in *Harijan*. There are articles, comments and statements replete with his condemnation of industrialism and the articulation of an alternative to modern civilization.

For Gandhi, India's economic future lay in charkha and khadi. 'If India's villages are to live and prosper, the charkha must become universal.' Rural civilization, argued Gandhi 'is impossible without the charkha and all it implies, i.e. revival of village crafts'. Similarly, khadi 'is the only true economic proposition in terms of the millions of villagers until such time, if ever, when a better system of supplying work and adequate wages for every able-bodied person above the age of sixteen, male or female, is found for his field, cottage or even factory in every one villages of India.' Since mechanization was 'an evil when there are more hands than required for the work, as is the case in India, [he recommended] that the way to take work to the villagers is not through mechanization but it lied through revival of the industries they have hitherto followed.' His target was a particular type of mindset, seduced by the glitter of industrialism, defending at any cost industrialization of the country on a mass scale. His support for traditional crafts was based not on conservative reasoning, but on solid economic grounds in the sense that by way of critiquing the Western civilization, he had articulated an alternative model of economic development that was suited to the Indian reality. He was a reformist and not a revivalist and his vision of villages therefore represented an alternative society that was different from the industrial-West.

Corollary to his idea of village was the notion of participative democracy whereby he provided a structure of mass involvement in the day-to-day functioning of what he defined as 'village republics'. Critical of 'the pyramidic structure' of power, his preferred alternative was 'oceanic circle', the centre of which were individuals. This was Gandhi's 'panchayati raj' upholding the principle of devolution of power that he had urged in his ideal of swaraj. In today's India, the 73rd and 74th Amendments to the Constitution of

India once again affirm the influence of Gandhi in policy making.

NON-VIOLENCE, KHADI AND SATYAGRAHA

According to Gandhi, ahimsa or non-violence was a mode of constructive political and social action just as truth seeking was the active aspect of Satya (Truth). Taken together, truth and non-violence constituted the basis of an immutable soul-force, an essential component of Satyagraha. Radically different from the prevalent ideas of politics that drew on violence, ahimsa was also a novel experiment, based on Gandhi's own assessment of the socio-political situation in India. Satyagraha was not merely passive resistance, it denoted 'intense activity' involving large masses of people. Satyagraha is 'a science' of political struggle in the sense that a satyagrahi, endowed with highest moral values, is trained to fight the most ruthless state machinery in accordance with the canons of non-violence.

THE FUTURE STATE

Harijan is a tract in which Gandhi documented his views on the future state of India. Although Gandhi declined to comment on the nature of government in a society based deliberately on non-violence, he nonetheless mentioned that the structure of a state, 'constructed in accordance with the law of non-violence'. The federal structure, as conceived by the 1935 Government of India Act, was, according to Gandhi, 'an utter impossibility [since] it contemplates a partnership, however loose, among dissimilars'. Aware of the difficulties of bringing together disparate units under one central authority,

Gandhi suggested 'cooperative federalism' as probably the most appropriate scheme for a multi-cultural, multi-lingual and multi-religious state like India. Proposing a voluntary federation for India, Gandhi's suggestion regarding the proposed constituent assembly was therefore tuned to protect the multi-cultural character of the country. As the assembly would be elected on the widest possible franchise it would possibly be the most appropriate forum to sort out the majority-minority conundrum through discussion. With India's independence, the Mahatma was confident, it would not be difficult to defuse the fear of minorities of being submerged by the majority since '[n]o charter of freedom will be worth looking at which does not ensure the same measure of freedom for the minorities as for the majority'. He seemed to have applied the same logic while conceptualizing an alternative world order. Just like 'nation states' where the distinction between the majority and minority appears redundant, 'an International League of Nations [in which] all nations, big or small . . . are fully independent', Gandhi argued, 'the smallest nation will feel as tall as the tallest. The idea of superiority and inferiority will be wholly obliterated'.

While defining the future state Gandhi paid serious attention to education (*nai talim,* in his words) since it was one of the basic ingredients of a non-violent state. Critical of the British system of primary education since it was 'devised without any thought of the economic advancement of the country', Gandhi's alternative was based on sound economics, for all education will be through the 'medium of a craft'. It was not education plus training in a craft, 'but it is education', he underlined, 'by means of a craft'.

Gandhi's comments on the British police are illustrative of what he perceived as an ideal form of bureaucracy that was to emerge in the aftermath of colonialism. Drawn on and inspired by ahimsa, Gandhi perceived the police as conducive to radically different socio-economic and political order in which 'the spirit of violence will have all but vanished and internal disorder will have come under control'.

WHAT IS THIS BIOGRAPHY (NOT) ABOUT

There are innumerable biographies of Gandhi. In what respects, this biography is different? Given its focus on 'the civilizational Gandhi', the biography does not deal exclusively with 'the historical Gandhi', who fell to an assassin's bullet on 30 January 1948. The available biographies provide useful inputs towards understanding Gandhi as an activist-theoretician who launched and also guided major pan-Indian anti-imperial movements in which ideologies other than ahimsa were peripheral, if not absent. They all contribute to this historical biography by providing much of what is critical to a historical biography that goes beyond a mere description of historical personalities in a simple 'life and times' format. Since the aim of this historical biography is to bring important historical figures to life for students and general readers alike, the available literature, despite their quality, may not satisfactorily address the audience presumably because of the technicalities, usually associated with research-based historical works. This apart, this biography is different because it strives to graphically illustrate the evolution of the Mahatma, who was not merely a pan-Indian political leader, but also a social reformer challenging the inhuman social practices, justified in the name of Hinduism. In other words, Gandhi had a two-fold agenda: on the one hand, he was, for obvious reasons, opposed to imperial rule in India; by challenging social orthodoxy, he, on the other hand, also contributed to the articulation of various protest movements that went parallel to the pan-Indian anti-British campaign.

This historical biography is an interpretative treatise that seeks to contextualize Gandhi and his ideas. It tends at times to decentre its central figure, which will probably make this exercise a class by itself. Instead of focusing merely on Gandhi's personal life, the biography seeks to grasp and also conceptualize the evolution of ideas in the context of anti-colonial nationalism. The Gandhian response to nationalism is, however, unique and can never be understood within the Western-centric approaches to nationalism. Despite being Gandhi-centred, this biography is thus imbued with questions (and some times responses as well) which, though location-specific, are relevant to similar circumstances. Secondly, what separates the present biography from the available ones is also the attempt to understand the social and political ideas of the Mahatma not in isolation but in conjunction with other equally persuasive alternative ideological traditions that generally remained complementary to the nationalist struggle. Unlike the conventional biographies, the proposed study of Gandhi's life and times provides a historical account of the period when the nationalist response to anti-imperialism was also articulated in demands for partitioning the subcontinent in 1940. How did Gandhi reconcile to the division of the subcontinent in 1947 on the basis of religion? The literature is generally silent and the question is hardly addressed in conclusive terms. A critical response to this will perhaps illuminate 'the last couple of years' of the Mahatma when he was clearly peripheral in the Congress negotiation for power and became 'a mere appendage' to the Congress High Command who could not easily be dispensed with.

---

1 Gandhi wrote a partial autobiography, (*An Autobiography or The Story of My Experiments with Truth*), a political treatise (*Hind Swaraj*), a few pamphlets, a very large number of article in the two weeklies that he edited, *Indian Opinion* (South Africa) and *Young India* (India) and even a large number of letters to Viceroys, fellow politicians and disciples; besides, he delivered speeches at conferences, congresses and at his regular prayer meetings.

2 *The Collected Works of Mahatma Gandhi* (hereafter *CWMG*), Vol 48, p. 353.

3 *CWMG*, Vol. 58, p. 400.

4 *Hind Swaraj* is quoted from Anthony Parel (ed.), *Hind Swaraj and other Writings*, Cambridge University Press, Cambridge, 1997, unless otherwise stated. Parel (ed.), *Hind Swaraj*, pp. 40-41.

5 M.K. Gandhi, *An Autobiography or The Story of My Experiments with Truth,* (hereafter *My Experiments with Truth*), Navajivan Trust, Ahmedabad, 1995 (reprint), p. 4.

6 ibid., p. 26.

7 Uma Dhupelia Mesthrie, *Gandhi's Prisoner? The Life of Gandhi's Son*, Permanent Black, New Delhi, 2004.

8 Parel (ed.), *Hind Swaraj*, p. 6.

9 *CWMG*, Vol. 19, p. 277.

10 Parel (ed.), *Hind Swaraj*, pp. 39-41.

11 ibid.

1

~

ARTICULATION OF A NEW IDEOLOGY: GANDHI, SATYAGRAHA AND AHIMSA

GANDHI'S MOVE FROM INDIA TO SOUTH AFRICA WAS FOR survival. His South Africa sojourn not only gave him financial security, but also prepared him for a bigger role for human civilization. The lawyer Gandhi became a saviour for the local Indians, abused as 'coolies' or 'samis' by the Europeans. Gandhi gave them a voice of protest through a unique means of political action – a philosophy of non-violent resistance known as Satyagraha. His success in South Africa earned him a reputation of a leader who mobilized the religiously fractured Indians. By dint of his sincere efforts, Hindus, Muslims and Parsis came forward, and together fought against the racist government. It was an unprecedented achievement for an Indian who hardly knew the social characteristics of the local Indians. In the evolution of Gandhi, political struggle in South Africa had a significant role for two reasons: first, Indians who so far had remained the target of racism fought against its foundation under Gandhi's stewardship. And secondly, the protest was articulated in a unique fashion. Satyagraha was conceptualized and appeared in an embryonic form during the struggle against the racist South African regime.

Gandhi went to South Africa on a fixed assignment. But he spent there twenty-one years (1893-1914) and returned to

India when he had already made a mark as a leader and a representative of Indians who forced the government to concede his demands. There was no doubt that he was politically baptized in a society that saw some of the worst kind of racist torture by the white elites. Gandhi was persuaded to stay back in South Africa by the local Indians who found in him an able and articulate spokesman of their grievances. The Indians in South Africa were relatively better off since they controlled local trade and business. Yet, they were not treated at par with the whites. By joining hands with Gandhi, these local businessmen of Indian origin came together to challenge the government. Thus, Gandhi became a symbol of protest against humiliation to the Indians who were never socially recognized as equal outside the Indian fraternity. By challenging the authority, Gandhi spearheaded a campaign against racist South African government that thrived, obviously, on various devices of discrimination against the non-whites.

The aim of this chapter is two-fold. First, as evident, the South African experience provided foundation to the Gandhian political campaign that was to unfold in India soon. It was a fairly long period that Gandhi spent in South Africa. One cannot gloss over the importance of these two decades in assessing Gandhi as an individual and his social and political ideology. Given the significance of these years, it would not be inaccurate to suggest that they were a watershed in his life. A simple lawyer who had come for professional reasons became a catalyst for the movements started against social and racial discrimination. This was a role, which Gandhi gradually perfected when he confronted the colonial regime in India.

Hence the second aim of this chapter is to acquaint the readers with how Gandhi pursued his agenda on his return to India. His success in organizing the masses in South Africa on local issues convinced him of the importance of regional concerns in political mobilization. It was not therefore surprising that Gandhi organized the peasants of Champaran and Kheda and workers of Ahmedabad on their grievances against the landlords and industrialists respectively. By drawing upon local issues, Gandhi launched successful campaigns against vested interests; by involving the local organizers, the strategist Gandhi sustained the movement beyond comprehension. These movements were different from those Gandhi conducted in South Africa at least in one significant sense: these were grassroot movements seeking to redress the tribulations faced by the peasantry and workers that were to become major constituencies of nationalist politics. While these movements were region specific and organized against local vested interests, Gandhi's campaign against the 1919 Rowlatt Act was an all-India effort challenging the British government. The anti-Rowlatt agitation was the first movement that spanned beyond the familiar domain of nationalist politics. Gandhi was anointed as the leader who mobilized masses regardless of ethnic divisions. A new era of India's freedom struggle began and new idioms of politics were articulated.

By dwelling on these three very different phases of Gandhi's initial tryst with struggle against racism and colonialism, the chapter will set the tone for the three major pan-Indian anti-British movements under Gandhi's stewardship. These chapters of Gandhi's experiments may not be as significant as those he conducted later, they nonetheless identify major trends, though embryonic, of his politics that loomed large in the days to come. Hence, the purpose here is to elaborate the role of Gandhi in those specific contexts, both in South Africa and India, where he launched and guided movements against social and political authorities in accordance with his ideological priorities.

GANDHI IN SOUTH AFRICA (1893-1914)

When Gandhi reached Durban in May 1893 he was received by Abdulla, one of the wealthiest Indian merchants who had invited him to South Africa to settle a legal dispute. Gandhi was a natural choice given his training in the British jurisprudence in Middle Temple. It was a boon in disguise for him since he had not been able to make his mark as a lawyer in India. The experiences in South Africa would prove momentous in preparing him for a bigger role in India's freedom struggle. So far, he appeared to have accepted the colonial exploitation as a fait accompli. But now, he challenged the draconian laws and regulations that ill treated human beings in the name of fair play and justice.

Once in South Africa, Gandhi began confronting the racist government. Within a week of his arrival, while he was travelling from Durban to Pretoria he was thrown out of a first-class railway compartment despite having a valid ticket. It was a very cold night and he had to suffer terribly in a non-European waiting room at Maritzburg station. In his words, 'doubt took possession of my mind. Late at night, I came to the conclusion that to run back to India would be cowardly. I must accomplish what I had undertaken'.[1] He was bewildered at the outset, but was determined to fight. His experience at Charlestown, a rail terminus was not very different either. He took a stagecoach for Standerton. Here too, the white officials forced him to sit on the footboard, instead of on the seat for which he had paid. His refusal to move out of his seat evoked anger and resulted in physical assault on Gandhi. He had borne the beating, but did not concede the demand. On arrival in Standerton, he narrated his experience to his Indian friends, but was disappointed by their responses. According to them what had happened to him was not very unusual for the Indians in the Transvaal. He reported the incident to an agent of the coach company knowing fully well that no action would be taken against the assailants. Nevertheless, he continued his journey to Pretoria. At Johannesburg the stationmaster even barred him from buying a first-class ticket, but later consented only after Gandhi defended himself by reference to railway rules and regulations. An argumentative Gandhi won the battle and began his journey for Pretoria. Here too, he was confronted with racist white South Africans and was about to be pushed out of the compartment, but for the intercession of a fellow European passenger. This lone incident of kindness was significant in Gandhi's conceptualization of racism. It would be wrong to dismiss the entire white population as racist. One required putting moral pressure on the white leadership to recognize the legitimate needs and demands of the coloured population.

The five days journey from Durban to Pretoria seemed to Gandhi as one of the most 'creative experiences' of his life. He saw racism in action. He was appalled by the fate of the Indian merchants who had learnt to swallow humiliation without protest. He pondered over the situation and decided not to accept injustice as part of the natural or unnatural order of South Africa. He would challenge the atrocious policies of the government simply because they did not fit into the 'graceful' British Empire. Racism had no legitimate place in the British Empire. Racism was a policy, perfected by the rulers by taking full advantage of the ignorant Indians who were not aware of their rights and duties under the empire. Gandhi also realized that the plight of Indian settlers was largely due to illiteracy. Hence, he felt the need of basic English education among the Indians. Moreover, Indians lost on a number of counts also because they were not organized and thus failed to fight the government as a group. Once in Pretoria, he translated his ideas into practice and organized a meeting of the Indians 'to present to them a picture of their conditions in Transvaal'. It was a grand success. He broached the idea of an organization and volunteered to teach English to the Indian merchants.

Gandhi was preparing the Indians for a showdown with the government. The situation was not, however, favourable for two reasons: (a) Transvaal, ruled by the Dutch, was a Boer state and hence was outside the orbit of the British Empire; and (b) the Boer government had already chased a large contingent of Indian settlers out of the Orange Free State. Gandhi supported the British during the Boer war because this gesture, as he thought, would strengthen the case of the Indians in South Africa to demand a fair deal in return. Hence, despite his strong feelings against the racist South African government, Gandhi articulated his bitterness during the 1890s in a language which appeared mild in contrast to that of the Mahatma who effectively challenged the edifice of colonialism both as a system of thought and governance. Interestingly, the speeches and writings in which he justified his role as a colonial subject constitute what can be termed as a classic text of collaborationist nationalism. The following excerpts seem apt in this context:

> If an unflinching devotion to duty and extreme eagerness to serve our sovereign can make us of any use in the field of battle, we trust, we would not fail. . . .
>
> The motive underlying this humble offer is to endeavour to prove that, in common with other subjects of the Queen Empress in South Africa, the Indians too, are ready to do duty for their Sovereign on the battlefield. The offer is meant to be an earnest of the Indian loyalty.[2]
>
> … the English-speaking Indians came to the conclusion that they would offer their services unconditionally and absolutely without payment . . . in order to show the colonists that they were worthy subjects of the Queen.[3]

Besides defining self-subjection of the colonized, these excerpts, with phrases like, 'eagerness to serve' and the 'offer of their services without pay unconditionally' are both a description and measure of the social distance between the colonizer and the colonized. What is evident here is that Gandhi, who grew up in the tradition of loyalist discourse, defended his argument by reference to the duty of the subject race to the empire in crisis. Even as a subordinated nation, Gandhi championed unequivocally the demands for the rights of South African Indians because as British subjects, Indians were entitled to some basic rights. This was probably a watershed in Gandhi's political thinking, because he was no longer prepared to be unconditionally loyal to the British paramountcy. What can be argued here is that the South African experience appeared significant in identifying the limitations of a racist administration vis-a-vis the subject race. Here began the transformation of Gandhi from a loyalist whose loyalty to the empire drove him to the side of the British during the Boer war in the teeth of opposition from some of his countrymen to the most effective political leader challenging the continuity of the Raj in the subcontinent of India by organizing non-violent mass campaign in opposition to the mighty imperial power. By asserting the rights of the subject people, Gandhi therefore moved from loyalty to opposition to the British rule. Hence, what began as a stray reference became an important feature of Gandhian political thought that was to unfold later. Similarly, non-violence as a means of political action acquired new dimensions in the light of changes in Gandhi himself who asserted, though within the constraints of bargaining and pressure politics, subjects' right to rebel.

Gandhi was soon disillusioned with the South African government that hardly changed its attitude vis-à-vis Indians. Meanwhile, he had become successful as a lawyer. He earned his fees by identifying loopholes in the laws for his merchant clients who always held Gandhi in high esteem. His first major encounter with colonial government came a year after his arrival in Durban in 1894. Gandhi found out that the Natal government, on racial grounds, was pushing a legislation to deprive Indians of the right to vote. He prepared his brief by reference to well-established British conventions and other canons of British jurisprudence. Conceding that 'disenfranchisement' was possible on property qualification, Gandhi defended his argument as a loyal subject of the empire. He even suggested that the government might consider the scheme, adopted in Cape Colony where voting rights were granted to those possessing property worth £ 75 and an annual income of £ 50. Despite the strength of the argument, Gandhi failed to persuade the government that adopted the bill by simple majority in the Natal legislature. Never conceding defeat, Gandhi decided to send a petition to the colonial secretary in London. The petition had 10,000 signatures covering almost the entire Indian population. Several copies of the petition were sent to the prominent British politicians. Gandhi brought the event in the eyes of media both in Britain and Natal. The bill was finally blocked at Westminster and the Queen declined to give her consent. Thus, the goal for which Gandhi fought was achieved. Two unique developments took place simultaneously here. First, as mentioned earlier, Gandhi felt that lack of an organization for the Indians in South Africa was one of the major weaknesses. So, he launched the Natal Indian Congress in 1894. Despite being political in its agenda, this was an organization devoted to moral and social uplift of its members. Gradually Natal Congress became a lively forum for the Indian settlers and Gandhi was undoubtedly its galvanizing force. In fact, the reduction of annual poll tax imposed on the indentured Indian labourers from £ 25 to £ 3 was the first successful political agenda of the Natal Congress. Gandhi argued that the amount was enormous as it was not consummate with the average income of the labourers. The second development was indicative of

Gandhi's rise as a strategist. Until now Gandhi was not allowed to practice in the Supreme Court because of the opposition from the Bar Society of Natal. Since denial was based on racist prejudices, the chief justice of the Supreme Court admitted him but in keeping with the etiquette of practicing barristers, ordered him to remove his turban in the courtroom. A change in Gandhi's attitude was noticeable for he had preferred to walk out of the courtroom a year ago when he was subjected to the same condition. Justifying his action as most appropriate, Gandhi thus argued,

> I saw my limitations. The turban that I had insisted on wearing in the District Magistrate's Court I took off in obedience to the order of the Supreme Court. Not than if I had resisted the order the resistance could not have been justified. But I wanted to reserve my strength for fighting bigger battles. [4]

On his return to Durban in December 1896 after a brief visit to India, Gandhi experienced another racist attack against him and those with him in the ship that was to anchor in Durban. A crowd of more than 3000 whites had congregated to prevent him and fellow Indian passengers from landing in the port. The crowd resolved to 'burn Gandhi [since] he has vilified [white South Africans] in India and wants to flood Natal with Indians'. Gandhi was saved by the wife of R.C. Alexander, the 'old' and 'popular' superintendent of police of Durban. The scene was so inflammatory that Gandhi had 'almost given up the hope of reaching home alive'. Finally with the support of Mrs Alexander, he escaped in the disguise of a constable.

The more the racist attacks on Gandhi, the stronger he

became in his resolve to fight against the racist regime. When in 1906, the colonial government sought to impose the Transvaal Asiatic Law Amendment Ordinance, which required all Indians to register themselves again, Gandhi immediately resorted to action. This particular ordinance was a continuity of the 1885 Boer Legislation that set up a register of Asiatics. According to this legislation, Indians were legally bound to give 'thumb-print' to obtain the right of residence. The same restriction was sought to be re-imposed. This ordinance was also more severe than its earlier counterpart in the sense that it insisted on print of all ten fingers and also the failure to register would immediately lead to fine, jail or deportation. Not only was the proposed step most humiliating to the Indians, it also disillusioned Gandhi who had thought that his support to the British in the Boer war would at least change the government's attitude towards the Indians. In order to register their protest, Indians in Johannesburg gathered at the English Theatre on 11 September 1906. It was resolved that nobody would submit to this legislation. Gandhi was inspired and found resources for satyagraha. Interestingly, Gandhi still did not lose faith in the British jurisprudence, as he challenged the legislation on grounds of fair play to the subjects of the crown. His statements in the meeting, however, also revealed that Gandhi was also being graduated as a rebel against colonial rule. It was evident when Gandhi welcomed imprisonment for his protest against the Immigration Restriction Act of 1907. Once it was made a law – which came to be known as the Black Act – he launched a protest movement by refusing to register. After he was released, he went to London to persuade the government to allow at least the educated Indians to enter Transvaal. But the racist South African government would not relent. Gandhi was disillusioned, for the British Empire was now seen as offering slavery, not partnership.

The opposition to the Black Act contributed to Gandhi's conceptualization of the satyagraha. During the Transvaal civil rights campaign (1907-1913), he had an opportunity to test and refine his protest movement, known as satyagraha that had already gained momentum. Two issues figured prominently during this phase of satyagraha: (a) abolition of the Black Act, and (b) removal of restrictions on the entry of Indians into Transvaal. The colonial government reacted immediately by verbally assuring to review the Black Act provided Indians registered voluntarily. Trusting the government, Gandhi urged fellow Indians by saying that 'we must register voluntarily to show that we do not intend to bring a single Indian into the Transvaal scrumptiously or by fraud'.[5] But Gandhi was befooled. Indians registered but the Black Law was hardly outlawed. Gandhi's response to the government betrayal was the famous occasion on 16 August 1908 when, outside the Hamida Mosque in Johannesburg, thousands of registration certificates, old as well as new, were burned.

Another controversy arose over a judgement of the Cape Supreme Court that derecognized Indian marriages since they were not registered according to the laws in South Africa. There was no law for the registration of ordinary marriages in India and validity of these marriages was never questioned earlier. With Searle judgement, these marriages were made null and void since they were outside the preview of legal marriages in South Africa. The consequence of this judgement was disastrous as it 'nullified in South Africa', argued Gandhi, 'all marriages celebrated according to the Hindu, Mussalman and Zoroastrian rites'. The married Indian women thus 'ceased to rank as wives of their husbands and were degraded to the rank of concubines while their progeny were deprived of their right to inherit the parents' property'. Such an insinuating judgement was bound to provoke moral outrage. The lawyer Gandhi petitioned to the government for reconsideration. No respite was forthcoming. The rebel Gandhi preferred satyagraha against 'this unspeakable insult'. Women voluntarily joined the movement against the judgement. New Castle miners, especially indentured Indian labourers, went on a strike. Gandhi's satyagraha had a new constituency. On 6 November 1913, more than 2000 people began their journey from Charlestown and crossed the frontier into the Transvaal to reach Tolstoy Farm that housed the civil resisters arrested for defying the Black Act and the immigration ban. They were arrested in Transvaal and brought back to Durban for imprisonment. This was a grand success for Gandhi's satyagraha in which women took the leadership. So terrorized was the government that it 'could not now any longer leave the Transvaal sisters', argued Gandhi, 'free to pursue their activities. They too were sentenced to imprisonment for the same terms – three months – and were kept in the same prison as their male counterparts.' This was a revelation to Gandhi and his approach to gender equation underwent a radical change. By agreeing to involve the women in political movements as equal partners, the 'orthodox' Gandhi seemed to have appreciated their contribution in the wider struggle against the racist government. The transformation in his views is probably due to the influence of Western feminism given the fact that gender equality was not adequately addressed in the Indian tradition as strongly as in the West.

Gandhian satyagraha gave a jolt to the racist South African government. The Indian Relief Act of 1914 abolished the requirement for the Indians to register and carry passes. The tax of £ 3 was shelved. The system of indenture was discontinued and Indian marriages were recognized. Despite having conceded to some of the principal demands of the satyagrahis, the racist government still stuck to the policies of immigration – both between states and into South Africa. So South African experiments catapulted a 'brief less barrister' – as Gandhi was when he reached Durban – onto the centre stage of political movements involving those who were since muted for historical reasons.

What did Gandhi achieve in South Africa? There is no doubt that the South African experience made Gandhi confident and perhaps prepared him for a protracted struggle against the British rule in India. He might not have achieved what he strove, but he 'returned home with a new method of action and a long-mediated programme for India's regeneration'. Satyagraha was a new mode of protest that Gandhi had crafted and tested in his struggle against racism in South Africa. The strength of satyagraha lies in human suffering. As Gandhi himself elaborated, 'even before satyagraha was started, satyagrahis knew that they would have to suffer even unto death, and they were ready to undergo such suffering. Since the spirit of revenge being alien to a satyagrahi, it was best for a satyagrahi to hold his peace when he encountered extraordinary difficulties in proving the fact of his suffering. The second significant achievement was his success in mobilizing the disparate Indians in South Africa who were divided on various ethnic counts. The Indian Ambulance Corps that he founded during the 1899 Boer War was illustrative of his effort in bringing the deeply divided Indians together. Given its multi-cultural character, the corps was characterized as 'a microcosm of all classes and creeds. ... Hindus, Muslims, Christians and Sikhs, Madrasis and upcountrymen (sic), free Indians as well indentured labourers'. This tradition was firmly established in the Phoenix Settlement in Natal and later Tolstoy Farm in Johannesburg. However, Gandhi's focus on the Indian cause 'prevented him from involving the non-Indian Africans as potential political allies'. In defence, one can argue that Gandhi was concerned with the Indians who were subject to racist discrimination and hence he concentrated on them. Moreover, because he attributed racism to mere colour prejudice, he believed that this was something 'quite contrary to the British tradition and only temporary and local'; he perhaps missed out the serious structural implications of racism for South African society. Thirdly, the South African experience also helped Gandhi conceptualize the nature of Western industrial civilization. In his *Satyagraha in South Africa*, he developed his critique of Western civilization that he expanded in a sophisticated form in *Hind Swaraj*. He did not approve of the 'philosophical substance' of the arguments, made by 'highest character among the Europeans' in defence of the superiority of Western machine civilization. There were, however, two arguments that need attention: first, as the arguments in favour of Western civilization runs, it was neither vulgar racism nor brute trade jealousy that justified draconian governmental feat; what was at stake was the preservation of the distinctive character of the Western civilization that would be diluted if cross-cultural communication was allowed. Hence the aim was 'one of preserving one's own civilization, that is of enjoying the supreme right of self-preservation and discharging the corresponding duty'. Secondly, in order to gratify this desire, the Western nations had adopted various measures to avoid 'distortions' in Western civilization. Gandhi challenged the major arguments defending racist exploitation by the South African government. In his opinion, no civilization would ever lose its dynamics simply because of contact with others; in fact, cross-cultural borrowing would enrich its contents. He was critical of the idea that 'nations which do not increase their material wants are doomed to destruction'. This remained at the root of the Western nations' expansionist strategy. It was in pursuance of this strategy that 'Western nations have settled in South Africa and subdued the numerically overwhelmingly superior races of South Africa'. The opposition of the Indian indentured labourers caused consternation among the white settlers who felt threatened economically by the growing importance of the Indian businessmen in trade and commerce. There was no doubt that 'trade by Indians hits the British traders hard' and as a result, 'the dislike of the brown races had at present become part and parcel of the mentality of the Europeans'. Finally, South Africa offered a unique ambience in which Gandhi made several social and political experiments, which he probably could not have managed in India. For instance, the Phoenix Settlement that was established in Natal in 1904 translated Gandhi's vision of a society that was free from caste, clan and ethnic prejudices. This is where Indian women were really free from the patriarchic bondage; they were relatively 'free' than their counterparts in India. Phoenix thus became

> "a nursery for producing the right men [and women] and right Indians. ... whatever energy is put forth in Phoenix", as Gandhi wrote, "is not so much taken from India, but it is so much given to India. ... Phoenix is a more suitable place for making experiments and gaining proper training. Whereas in India there may be undesirable restraints, there are no such undesirable restraints in Phoenix. For instance, Indian ladies would never have come out so boldly as they are doing at Phoenix. The rest of the social customs would have been too much for them".[6]

Tolstoy Farm that came into being in 1910 continued with the same tradition. These establishments were testing grounds for Gandhi's ideas. So dear was the idea of community living to him that he founded Sabarmati Ashram (near Ahmedabad) after his return to India. In India's freedom struggle, the Sabarmati Ashram continued to remain an important centre of social and political activities seeking to translate Gandhi's ideas into practice.

GANDHI IN INDIA

Given his South African fame, Gandhi was already known in India even before his return in 1914. On the advice of his political mentor, Gopal Krishna Gokhale, he undertook an extensive tour of the length and breadth of the country. What was the political context in India then? The Indian National Congress that was founded in 1885 was divided between 'Moderates' and 'Extremists'. The former were constitutionalists and believed that the British rule could be improved only through constitutional means, while the latter were not hesitant to employ force to fulfil their political goals. Gandhi was not very sure of the moderate means; he however, detested the extremist methods because violence was inherently an evil. So, what was the alternative? Gandhi was confident that satyagraha that he developed and tested in South Africa was perhaps the best mode of political resistance to colonialism. As a pragmatic nationalist, he however, decided to conduct satyagraha in a piecemeal manner in three different locations against local vested interests. While in Chamapran in Bihar and Kheda in Gujarat, he addressed the peasant grievances; in Ahmedabad he mobilized the textile workers for their legitimate demands. Although these movements were organized around completely different issues, they were nonetheless formatted in the satyagraha mould. This is where Gandhi succeeded and satyagraha emerged as the best mode of political mobilization for the disparate masses and also against the most barbaric ruler.

At Champaran, peasants raised their voice against the European planters for forcing them to produce indigo under the *tinkathia* system (that imposed the production of indigo in three-twentieth part of their land). The movement that began in the 1860s gained momentum even before the arrival of Gandhi on the scene. Led by the local middle-and-rich peasant leaders, the pre-Gandhian efforts, however, had failed to involve the actual cultivators. This is where Gandhi's intervention was most effective. A unique political movement, the 1917 Champaran Satyagraha was first of its kind in India which Gandhi led in accordance with his plan and ideology. Gandhi's presence in Champaran represented hope for the raiyats of the plantations. His act of civil disobedience and determination to endure prison convinced the peasants that the Mahatma was their saviour. His extreme simplicity had brought him closer to them than all the erstwhile leaders. Even Rajendra Prasad who accompanied him during the Champaran movement expressed that 'it is a matter of mystery to me how these people seemed to develop the confidence that their deliverer had come'.[7] Not only his co-workers, his arrival in Bettiah in the Champaran region also caught the British sub-divisional officer by surprise as evident in his following report:

> We may look on Mr Gandhi as an idealist, a fanatic or a revolutionary according to our particular opinions. But to the raiyats, he is their liberator, and they credit him with extraordinary powers. He moves about in the villages, asking them to lay their grievance before him, and he is daily transfiguring the imagination of masses of ignorant men with visions of an early millennium.[8]

To the masses, Gandhi represented a resurrection of hope. His non-violent resistance provided a viable alternative in the struggle against colonialism where force had become both illegitimate and ineffective. The Champaran Satyagraha forced the government to adopt the 1918 Champaran Agricultural Act whereby, those compelled to let their land for indigo cultivation were given some relief. What Gandhi left was carried forward by local peasants and Champaran became a strong base for non-violent political mobilization though the Congress leadership never allowed them to organize protests against the indigenous landlords. Despite the failure of the peasants to lead movements against the vested interests, the Champaran Satyagraha articulated the neglected voice of protesters. Gandhi emerged as the supreme leader and non-violence gained salience. This was not a subaltern protest, but one in which the subalterns were inducted into the process of political mobilization. In other words, the Champaran Satyagraha represented 'a battle in which many different levels of consciousness coexisted [presumably because of] the complex perspective of the participants'.[9] Apart from projecting Gandhi as a perfect mobilizer, this satyagraha also contributed to a unique multi-class political platform combining the clearly antagonistic classes. Not only did Gandhi succeed in containing the class wrath within a specific limit, he also created a situation in which the struggle against the exploiters coincided with the challenge against colonialism. So, Gandhian non-violence, as the Champaran Satyagraha demonstrates, provided a potent means for a legitimate and effective resistance within the new political dispensation in which the Congress was gaining importance. The Champaran movement was significant in Gandhi's political life not only in terms of conceptualizing satyagraha as a device but also in terms of its application to build a political platform regardless of class or other differences.

Quite similar to the Champaran experiment, the 1918 Kheda Satyagraha was a Gandhi-led no-revenue campaign.

Hard-hit by economic adversity due to destruction of crops by rains, rise in agricultural wages, high rate of inflation and the outbreak of bubonic plague, the Patidar peasants organized a movement against the government's decision to not waive the land revenue. Launched by Mohanlal Pandya and Shankarlal Parikh of a small town of Kathlal in the district of Kheda, the movement gained momentum as the Gujarat Sabha, an organization under the aegis of the Congress extended its support. Once approached by the Gujarat Sabha, Gandhi arrived in Kheda in March 1918 to launch a satyagraha against the government's decision to confiscate properties of the defaulters. The campaign lasted for four months and in June, the Government of Bombay decided not to implement the order and peasants who failed to pay the revenue were reprieved. Like the movement in Champaran, this movement, spearheaded by the local Congress activists, continued with local support. Gandhi's presence was more symbolic than anything else. Even his lieutenants, Vallabhbhai and Vitthalbhai Patel remained insignificant in the entire movement in which the local leaders became most important. As a cementing factor, Gandhi brought the satyagrahis together for the movement that had an agenda set by the local leaders in their own terms. In other words, Gandhi was important in the Kheda satyagraha so long as he agreed to support the demands of local leaders. This was evident when the villagers refused when Gandhi urged them to join the British Army during the First World War.

During the Kheda Satyagraha, Gandhi also participated in Ahmedabad textile mill strike of February-March 1918. This was a different kind of experiment involving the workers.

The successful campaign in Champaran had catapulted Gandhi to the centre stage of nationalist politics. When the workers in Ahmedabad became restive, Anusuyya Sarabhai, a social worker who was the sister of Ambalal Sarabhai, the president of the Ahmedabad Mill Owner's Association, invited Gandhi to intervene and resolve the crisis. What triggered off the strike was the withdrawal of 'plague-bonus' to the workers, equivalent in some cases to 80 per cent of the wages that was paid to dissuade them from fleeing the plague-ravaged towns. Once the epidemic was over, the mill owners decided to discontinue the monetary benefit. For the workers, this decision hit them adversely simply because of the spiralling price-rise due to the outbreak of the War.

Drawn on his belief that there was no major contradiction between capital and labour, Gandhi sought to defuse the crisis through dialogues with the mill owners. The mill owners appeared to be adamant and characterized Gandhi's intervention as 'unwarranted'. On 22 February 1918, the mill owners locked out the labourers despite Gandhi's repeated requests. With the closure, Gandhi decided to champion the workers' cause though he asked them to tone down their earlier demand of 50 per cent wage hike to 35 per cent. Although the workers agreed to his suggestion, the mill owners did not relent and workers seemed to have lost morale. It was at this juncture that Gandhi began the 'first' of his seventeen 'fasts unto death' on 15 March 1918. This fast that lasted for three days appeared to have forced the mill owners who deeply respected Gandhi to come to an agreement with the striking workers. As per the agreement suggested by the arbitration board, the workers' demand was partially fulfilled because they got 27.5 per cent wage hike instead of their original demand. So, the compromise formula looked like a face-saving formula and a tactical defeat for Gandhi though he forced the mill owners to accept the principle of arbitration in which workers' representatives along with their employers had a say.

A unique event in Gandhi's political life, the Ahmedabad strike added a new chapter to Indian nationalist movement. Though critical of Gandhi's 'obsession' with 'passive resistance', the *Bombay Chronicle* appreciated the principle of arbitration as 'a turning point in labour-employer relations in Ahmedabad' in particular and a novel system of 'resolving industrial disputes' in general. Similarly, the *Times* criticized Gandhi for 'blackmailing' the mill owners who happened to be his 'admirers' by his 'fast unto death' though it hailed his role in articulating 'arbitration' as 'an effective device' to break the *impasse* between the workers and industrialists.

These three movements projected Gandhi as an emerging leader with different kinds of mobilizing tactics. What was common in all these movements was the fact that, a) they were organized around local issues; and b) in mobilizing the people for the movements the importance of the local leaders cannot be underestimated. There is no doubt that Gandhi's appearance on the scene gave a fillip to these movements. Yet, if we carefully chart the movements, we will discover that Gandhi was invited to lead when the local organizers had adequately garnered support for the cause. By his involvement with these movements at a stage when they struck roots in the concerned localities, Gandhi projected a specific kind of leadership: he was not a primary but a secondary organizer. There is no doubt that the movements gained momentum with his intervention. The masses interpreted Gandhi's message in their own terms and rumours surrounding the powers of this messianic leader served to break the barriers of fear involved in confronting formidable enemies. As evident in Champaran and Kheda, Gandhian intervention in elite-nationalist politics established for the first time that an authentic nationalist movement could be built upon the organized support of the peasantry though its political object was not what Gandhi endorsed. The peasants were meant to become 'willing participants in a struggle wholly conceived and directed by others'. Gandhi provided 'a national framework of politics in which peasants are mobilized but do not participate' in its formulation. This was also true of the Ahmedabad strike where Gandhi accommodated the interests of the mill owners even at the cost of the workers since their demand was partially conceded. Based on his belief that capital and labour were not contradictory to each other, Gandhi agreed to the negotiated settlements as probably the best solution under the circumstances. Workers failed to get what they had asked for. Yet Gandhi's role was most significant in articulating a form of political mobilization in which the workers were also decisive. Just like the Champaran and Kheda satyagrahas that extended the constituencies of nationalist politics by incorporating the peasantry, the Ahmedabad textile strike was a turning point, for it accorded a legitimate space to the workers in what was conceptualized as nationalism.

These three movements constitute a milestone in what

Gandhi articulated as nationalist politics. A leader emerged to radically alter the complexion of India's struggle for freedom. With his involvement in mass movements Gandhi forged a new language of protest for India by both building on older forms of resistance while at the same time accepting the colonial censure of all forms of violent protest. Two complementary processes seemed to have worked: at one level, local issues had obviously a significant role in organizing masses for protest movements in the localities; at another, the presence of Gandhi at a critical juncture helped sustain these movements that perhaps lost momentum due to the growing frustration of the local organizers. So, Gandhi became a missing link that not only galvanized the masses into action but also contributed immensely to the successful conclusion of these protest movements involving completely different constituencies of nationalist politics, namely, peasantry and labour. These movements appeared to have set the tone and tenor of the future movements, which Gandhi was to lead. He emerged as a mass leader who felt the pulse of the people perhaps most accurately than anybody else. And the consequence was obvious because it was Gandhi who transformed the struggle for freedom to a wider nationalist campaign involving various categories of people including those who had remained detached. As Jawaharlal Nehru most eloquently put,

> [Gandhiji] attracted people. They did not agree with his philosophy of life, or even with many of his ideals. Often they did not understand him, but the action that he proposed was something tangible which could be understood and appreciated intellectually. Any action would have been welcome after the

> long tradition of inaction, which our spineless politics had nurtured; brave and effective action with an ethical halo about it had an irresistible appeal, both to the intellect and emotions. Step by step he convinced us of the rightness of the action, and we went with him, although we did not accept his philosophy. … Gandhiji, being essentially a man of action and very sensitive to changing conditions … the road he was following was the right one thus far, and if the future meant a parting it would be folly to anticipate it.
>
> All this shows that we were by no means clear or certain in our minds. Always we had the feeling that while we might be more logical, Gandhiji knew India far better than we did, and a man who could command such tremendous devotion and loyalty must have something in him that corresponded to the needs and aspirations of the masses.[10]

GANDHI ON THE ALL-INDIA SCENE

The Rowlatt Satyagraha translated the Gandhian deeds into action at the pan-Indian level. Drawing on his faith on the spontaneous resistance of the masses to injustice, Gandhi was confident of the success of the campaign against the Rowlatt Act. Designed to crush the revolutionary movements in Bengal, Maharashtra and Punjab, the 1919 Rowlatt Act authorized the British government to act sternly against those, identified as terrorist groups. The Act recommended, (a) amendment of the Indian Penal Code in a manner to enable the government to 'check activities prejudicial to the security of the state', and also (b) to invest the ruler with the authority to short-circuit 'the processes of law in dealing with revolutionary crime'. Despite opposition by the Indian members in legislative council, the Bill was adopted on 18

March 1919. Gandhi was against the enactment of such an oppressive law and decided to challenge the government. In his letter to V.S. Srinivasa Shastri, he thus wrote,

> I consider the Bills to be an open challenge to us. If we succumb we are done for. If we prove our word that the government will see an agitation that they have never witnessed before, we shall have proved our capacity for resistance to arbitrary or tyrannical rule. ... for myself if the Bills were to be proceeded with, I feel that I can no longer render peaceful obedience to the laws of a power that is capable of such a devilish legislation as these two bills, and I would not hesitate to incite those who think with me to join me in the struggle.[11]

How did Gandhi launch the movement that catapulted him on the centre stage of the nationalist struggle? As a constitutionalist, he first wrote a pledge refusing to obey the Act that allowed the government to act arbitrarily. He sent a telegram to the Viceroy, Lord Chelmsford explaining the reasons for his decision to start a satyagraha against the Rowlatt Act. Finally, he addressed an open letter to 'the People of India' urging them to join the satyagraha.

Launched on 6 April 1919, this satyagraha was a defining moment in formulating Gandhi's political ideas for two specific reasons: (a) Gandhi now realized the potential of the growing mass discontent in the anti-British struggle; and (b) this satyagraha was also a litmus test for the Mahatma who now was confident of satyagraha as a technique for political mobilization. For Gandhi, '[t]his retention of Rowlatt legislation in the teeth of universal opposition is an affront to the nation. Its repeal is necessary to appease national honour.' Hence he urged,

> whether you are satyagrahis or not, so long as you disapprove of the Rowlatt legislation, all can join and [he was confident] that there will be such a response throughout the length and breadth of India as would convince the Government that we are alive to what is going on in our midst.[12]

When the Rowlatt satyagraha was about to be launched Gandhi was not sure whether it would click as a political struggle against the British. Gandhi's uncertainty was short-lived and the movement dramatically altered the political complexion of the freedom struggle that was hardly national so far. As 'the first country-wide' agitation against the British it not only 'transformed nationalism in India from a movement representing the classes to a movement of the masses', it also paved the way for Gandhi's emergence as a dominant figure in Indian politics.

The movement officially began with the nation-wide *hartal* (strike) on 6 April 1919. It was a peaceful *hartal* and no untoward incidents were reported. The movement, however, lapsed into violence once Gandhi was arrested on 9 April. The arrest of Gandhi was a preemptive measure, which provoked unprecedented mass violence. For the government, it was a testing time for it had never confronted a movement of this nature before. To contain the agitation, it therefore unleashed a reign of terror. The worst incident was the massacre of innocent people on 13 April in Jallianwalla Bagh in Amritsar. In order to terrorize the people participating in the movement, martial law was imposed on towns in Punjab. On this fateful day, a peaceful unarmed crowd of mainly villagers who had come for a fair and did not know of the ban on meetings, were brutally gunned down by Michael O'Dyer. The killings provoked mass consternation. But Dyer's only regret before the Hunter Commission was that he ran out of bullets and the narrow lanes prevented him from bringing an armoured car, for 'it was no longer a question of merely dispersing the crowd, but one of producing a moral effect not only on those present but more specifically throughout the Punjab'.[13] The unprecedented scale of the British repression seems to have quelled the situation and movement had shown signs of dissipation. No major protest rally was organized. Rabindranath Tagore abdicated Knighthood in protest against Dyer's brutal act. Gandhi was convinced that without adequate organizational preparation, satyagraha could be suicidal. Yet, the movement caused concern to the British authority for two reasons: first, it put the British authority, for the first time, on the defensive. Secondly, the movement did not seem to have run out of steam even after the arrest of Gandhi. Defending the spontaneous outburst against the brutal authority as 'natural', a pamphlet was being circulated especially in the cities in which people were exhorted to participate in the movement against the Black Bill. Urging the people not to sit 'idle' because

> the Black Bill has been set in motion [and] the leader of the Satyagraha and a great man of action – Mahatma Gandhi – has been arrested. ... Now is the time to show how much inherent power the Indians possess. When man has got power to avert his own calamity, then what difficulty can there be in abrogating the Black Bill. ... [S]o long as the Rowlatt Bill is not repealed, every Indian should take the vow of satyagraha ... and be ready to sacrifice for the cause.[14]

The movement was stronger in cities and larger towns than in rural areas. The strike on 6 April was observed most enthusiastically in almost all the Indian provinces. But the places where the movement really took off was Amritsar, Gujranwala, and a number of other smaller towns in Punjab; Ahmedabad, Viramgam and Nadiad in Gujarat, Delhi, Bombay, and to a lesser extent Calcutta. What surprised the government most was the relative tranquility in Calcutta, which had always been the epicentre of the nationalist assault on the British. In a communication to the secretary to the Government of India, the chief secretary of Bengal, J.H. Kerr thus wrote,

> the main features of the recent disturbances have been the insignificant part played by the Bengali element, the intervention of the Marwaris, and the fraternalization of Muhammadans and Hindus, of which the most striking illustration in Calcutta was the attendance of Hindus at the meeting in the Nakhoda Mosque. [The evolution] of the Movement point[s] to the existence of some general organization ... but the indications seem to be that the disturbances were organized from outside Bengal, and the attempts to rouse the mass of people against Government have certainly been less successful here than elsewhere.[15]

How did Gandhi mobilize people? It is true that Gandhi gave the Indian masses a new mantra – the mantra of satyagraha. While challenging the British during the Rowlatt satyagraha, he was supported by the Home Rule League, founded by Annie Besant and Bal Gangadhar Tilak and their followers. He also drew upon the support, extended by his Muslim friends. Nevertheless, before embarking on action,

Gandhi had set up his own organization. Satyagraha Sabha was constituted with its head office in Bombay. The sabha was vested with the responsibility of conducting the campaign against the Black Bill. Yet, the success of the Rowlatt Satyagraha in those selective areas was largely attributed to the enthusiastic participation of the local leaders. In Bihar, Bengal and Delhi, prominent local leaders were involved from the very beginning. Without Hasan Imam's participation in Bihar, the movement would not have gained momentum; similarly, the role of C.R. Das and Byomkesh Chakrabarti in Bengal was most significant in sustaining the momentum of the satyagraha. In Delhi, Swami Shraddhananda played a crucial role in political mobilization during the campaign. Apart from these lieutenants who had organic links with the localities, Gandhi's success is attributed to an indigenous model of political action that influenced common people in a manner as never before. It is true that one of the reasons for Gandhi's success in galvanizing the masses for action despite adverse consequences was his skilful exploitation of popular religious symbols. But this will not conclusively explain the growing popularity of Gandhi, for even before him Bal Gangadhar Tilak in Maharashtra, and Sri Aurobindo in Bengal had resorted to using religious symbols for political mileage, but with limited success. What was distinctive about Gandhi was his intelligent application of symbols, religious and otherwise, which were meaningful to a cross-section of the Indian population, located at various levels of social hierarchy. Instead of endorsing the much-hyped 'composite culture', Gandhi always believed that Muslims were a distinct social community. Since religion was the dominant loyalty among the Indians, he believed that it would be politically inappropriate to dismiss religion as 'divisive'. This is what explains the increasing participation of the Muslim leaders and their followers in the Rowlatt Satyagraha and other Gandhi-led pan-Indian movements that followed soon. Muslims joined the movements spontaneously in Bengal, Bihar and Punjab largely because the local Muslim leaders urged them to do so. As evident, Gandhi emerged as an effective strategist who articulated the first fruitful national campaign against the British rule. The Rowlatt Satyagraha not only had organic roots in the localities, it was also illustrative of Gandhi's capacity to draw masses irrespective of caste, community and religion.

Gandhi was now ready for a pan-Indian political movement against the ruler, and the Rowlatt Satyagraha provided the impetus. Although Gandhi underlined the importance of ahimsa in satyagraha, he did not appear to emphasize its importance as strongly as he later did. For him, what was crucial was an organized attack on the British interest through satyagraha campaign. As he argued,

> popular imagination has pictured satyagraha as purely and simply civil disobedience, if not in some cases, criminal disobedience. ... As satyagraha is being brought into play on a large scale on the political field for the first time, it is in an experimental stage. I am therefore ever making new discoveries. And my error in trying to let civil disobedience take the people by storm appears to me to be Himalayan because of the discovery, I have made, namely, that he only is able and attains the right to offer civil disobedience who has known how to offer voluntary and deliberate obedience to the laws of the State in which he is living. [16]

Thus, Gandhi capitalized on the obvious mass discontent, which, he translated into satyagraha. Now, what are the organizational principles? In his scheme of things, a satyagrahi should know these principles before embarking on a campaign. As he mentioned, before they got involved in any political campaign against the ruling authority, 'they should thoroughly understand its deeper implications. That being so, before restarting civil disobedience on a mass scale, it would be necessary to create a band of well-tried, pure-hearted volunteers who thoroughly understood the strict conditions of satyagraha.' Thus was conceptualized the notion of satyagraha as a mobilizing principle governing the behaviour of those involved in the Gandhi-led nationalist campaign. And the more Gandhi concerned himself with the organizational norms within which a national movement had to be conducted, the more he began to elaborate upon the concept of ahimsa. A leader was responsible to direct the mass discontent into a course of action. Masses were not trained and their behaviour even in resistance was always that of a mob. The leadership was crucial in transforming the mob into an organized mass with meaningful action to undertake. As Gandhi himself confessed, 'nothing is so easy to train the mobs, for the simple reason that they have no mind, no pre-meditation. They act in frenzy. They repent quickly.' He was not hesitant to characterize demonstrations during the first phase of the Non-Cooperation Movement as 'a mob without a mind'. Hence he concluded that such demonstrations

> cannot ... procure swaraj for India unless disciplined and harnessed for national goal. The great task before the nation today [urged Gandhi] is to discipline its demonstrations if they

> are to serve any useful purpose. ... The nation must be disciplined to handle mass movements in a sober and methodical manner. ... We can do no effective work [he further added] unless we can pass instructions to the crowd and expect implicit obedience.[17]

So, to involve the masses in meaningful political campaigns, one had to articulate satyagraha into specific courses of action, especially its 'modalities of resistance'. This is where ahimsa assumes tremendous significance. Ahimsa was that specific organizational principle that governed the behaviour of a satyagrahi. In other words, ahimsa was critical to the entire exercise of satyagraha, without which the very act of resistance would appear to be futile. Ahimsa was a foundational principle as well. Not only did it articulate the nature of the campaign, it would also structure the form of resistance by guiding those involved in it. This was indeed 'the science of non-violence' in the sense that it provided a grammar of Gandhian political mobilization in which 'civil resisters represent the non-violent army of the nation. And just as every citizen cannot be a soldier on the active list, every citizen cannot be a civil resister on the active list'.[18] Interestingly, the onus of strictly adhering to the science of non-violence rested with the leadership and not with the masses. Just like a soldier of an army 'who does not know the whole of the military science; so also does a satyagrahi not know the whole of satyagraha. It is enough if he trusts his commander and honestly follows his instructions and is ready to suffer unto death without bearing malice against the so-called enemy. ... [The satyagrahis] must render heart discipline to their commander. There should be no mental reservation'.[19] Here Gandhi was referring to mass civil disobedience where the role of the leader was immensely important in guiding the masses whereas in individual civil resistance 'everyone was a complete independent unit [and] every resister is his own leader'.[20]

As evident, despite its significance in earlier satyagrahas in Champaran, Kheda and Ahmedabad, ahimsa was not clearly articulated by the Mahatma till the 1919 Rowlatt Satyagraha when its importance was duly recognized both in mobilizing people and also defining the goal of the campaign. Ahimsa came to the surface, as it were, and its political importance in Gandhian resistance was upheld beyond doubt. Satyagraha was thus based on the principles of *satya* (truth), ahimsa (non-violence) and *tapas* (self-suffering). No definition was clearer than Gandhi's own oral submission before the Hunter Committee on 9 January 1920. Admitting that he was 'the author of the Satyagraha Movement', Gandhi defined satyagraha by stating that

> it is a movement intended to replace method of violence and movement entirely upon Truth. It is, as I have conceived it, an extension of the domestic law on the political field and my experience has led me to the conclusion that that movement and that alone can rid India of the possibility of violence spreading throughout the length and breadth of the land, for the redress of grievance.[21]

By activating peasants in Kheda against the enhancement of land revenue, the South Africa rebel gave a new twist to the nationalist movement, which soon expanded its constituency by upholding the Ahmedabad Cotton Mill workers' demand. Despite failure in Kheda, his success in Champaran and

Ahmedabad highlighted the effectiveness of non-violent campaign in the face of large-scale atrocities.

Non-violence attained all-India publicity in the wake of Gandhi's campaign against the Rowlatt Bills. He offered non-violent civil disobedience in the form of satyagraha and sought the cooperation of moderates on the ground that 'the growing generation will not be satisfied with petition, etc. We must give them something effective. Satyagraha is the only way, it seems to me, to stop terrorism. From this point of view, I am justified in seeking your help.'[22] The Rowlatt Satyagraha was a failure because the objective of repealing the Rowlatt Bills was not realized. Gandhi withdrew the movement as it ceased to be non-violent in Gujarat and Punjab. That Gandhi was a true apostle of non-violence was evident with the revocation of the movement once it erupted into violence. Notwithstanding Gandhi's disappointment, the Rowlatt campaign was a breakthrough for him who was so far a stranger to Indian politics. Besides Gandhi's role in nationalist politics, Rowlatt Satyagraha also projected the extent to which ahimsa as a means of political action could be effective. So, Gandhi led a movement reverberations of which were felt throughout the subcontinent – from Northwest Frontier to Madras, and from Sind to Bengal. The success that he attained was partly due to local discontents which found a focus and a means of expression in Gandhi's call for *hartal* and partly due to anti-British sentiments of the people that gained salience with the adoption of the Rowlatt Act.

What began in the 1919 Rowlatt Satyagraha seems to have set the tone of the anti-British campaign. Between 1920 and 1942, not only did Gandhi consolidate his position in the

Congress, non-violence also appeared invincible both as an ideology and as a method of political struggle. The 1919-1922 non-cooperation was Gandhi's answer to those who clung to violence and the Western style of politics. Non-violence was not merely a novel form of direct political action but also an effective alternative to the prevalent Western mode of politics, which appeared stagnant and powerless against the iron rule of British administration. Although Gandhi's overzealous call to attain *Swaraj* within a year did not materialize, the form of politics with non-violence as an instrument for mobilization threatened the very foundation of the empire.

CONCLUSION

Gandhi arrived in South Africa in 1893. By the time he left South Africa for India, he had already risen to prominence as a leader who successfully fought the racist government on behalf of the Indian settlers there. In the making of Gandhi, the South African experience was therefore most critical for a number of reasons: first, his personal experience of brutal racism made him firm in his resolve to combat the discrimination. Not only did he learn to challenge the authority by peaceful means, he also imbibed the spirit of uniting the South African Indians irrespective of their ethnic divisions. South Africa was, for him, both a laboratory for germination of ideas and also their testing ground. Secondly, it was in South Africa where Gandhi articulated his novel form of protest. Drawn on a marriage between Indian and Western philosophical traditions, satyagraha was a unique blend. It was not passive resistance, but a form of resistance in which the participants absorbed suffering without nurturing any ill feelings for the perpetrators. Thirdly, despite serious opposition to the ruler, Gandhi still remained 'a loyalist' in South Africa. His support to the South African government in the Boer War is exemplary. As a constitutionalist who had great respect for the British constitution and British jurisprudence, Gandhi believed that 'the British rule was on the whole beneficial to the ruled' and that it was 'on the whole acceptable'. He had faith in 'the British sense of justice and fair play' that, however, gradually got eroded when he found that the British government remained non-committal despite strong evidence of 'foul' play by the racist South African regime.

The South African experience was remarkable in transforming Gandhi from a loyalist to a rebel. Once he returned to India, his strategy was different. In Champaran and Kheda, he championed the peasant causes. Supported by the local leaders, Gandhi organized the affected peasants against revenue remission. Similarly, in Kheda, he supported the movement of those peasants affected by the decision of the Bombay government to confiscate their property for their failure to pay tax. The Ahmedabad textile strike provided Gandhi with an opportunity to deal with the workers who were struggling for 'plague bonus'. Here the adversaries were the Gujarati mill owners who happened to be close to him. He was in a dilemma for obvious reason. The strategist Gandhi persuaded the workers to slash down their demand for increase of bonus and convinced the mill owners to accept the increase. The strike came to an end and Gandhi gained tremendous nation-wide popularity.

By the time the Rowlatt Satyagraha was launched, Gandhi was totally transformed. He had certainly become a rebel. He challenged the British government not because of the draconian nature of the Act, but because it would deprive Indians of seeking legal aid against governmental atrocities in the name of 'fair play and justice'. His loyalty to satyagraha also set a severe constraint on the extant of his opposition. He withdrew the movement as soon as it became violent. This appears to be a pattern in Gandhian form of protest as we see in the following chapters. Suffice it to say here that Gandhi pursued the ideology of non-violence so consistently that he never allowed a slightest deviation from what he believed to be its kernel. Nonetheless, the Rowlatt Satyagraha was historically most significant in Gandhi's political career in at least two fundamental ways: first, he was catapulted on to the centre stage of Indian nationalist movement that no longer remained confined to the major cities during the campaign against the Black Bill. It was truly a pan-Indian movement that caused severe consternation to the British government. With Gandhi's arrival on the political scene, the nationalist struggle against the British acquired a national character at least in terms of a unity among the provincial Congress leaders who so far had remained divided into 'Moderate' and 'Extremist' camps. Secondly, the Rowlatt Satyagraha brought in disparate Indians on one political platform. There is no doubt that this shows Gandhi's remarkable ability to cement a bond among individuals who were divided ethnically for a cause. He truly built a multi-class platform in which opposition to the British government seemed to have prevailed over other considerations. Satyagraha also became organic to his ideology of non-violence. A new era began in which Gandhi would not only write the script for the national freedom struggle, but would also remain its sole guide, if not arbiter in the movements that followed the 1919 Rowlatt Satyagraha.

---

1 *Satyagraha in South Africa, CWMG,* Vol. 29, p. 38. This discussion is drawn on this tract unless otherwise stated.

2 *CWMG,* Vol. 3, pp. 113-14 and 119-20.

3 ibid., p. 129.

4 Quoted in Krishna Kripalani, *Gandhi: A life*, National Book Trust, New Delhi, 2000, p. 32.

5 ibid., p.71.

6 *CWMG*, Vol. 9, p. 382.

7 Rajendra Prasad, *At the Feet of Mahatma Gandhi*, Bombay, 1961, p. 7.

8 A report of the Sub Divisional Officer, Bettiah on 23 September, 1917 – quoted in Jacques Pouchepadass, *Champaran and Gandhi: Planters, Peasants and Gandhian Politics*, Oxford University Press, New Delhi, 1999, pp. 217-18.

9 ibid., p. 234.

10 Jawaharlal Nehru, *An Autobiography*, John Lane, The Bodley Head, London, 1941, pp. 254-55.

11 Gandhi to V.S. Srinivasa Shastri, 9 February, 1919, *CWMG*, Vol. 15, pp. 87-88.

12 Gandhi's speech on Satyagraha Movement, Trichinoploy, 25 March, 1919, *CWMG*, Vol. 15, p. 155.

13 Sumit Sarkar, *Modern India: 1885-1947*, Macmillan, New Delhi, p.19.

14 An Appeal to the Public: Mahatma Gandhi Arrested – Friends Wake Up – quoted in Ravinder Kumar (ed.), *Essays on Gandhian politics: The Rowlatt Satyagraha of 1919*, Clarendon Press, Oxford, 1971, pp. 337-38.

15 J.H. Kerr to the Secretary of State, Government of India, 14 April, 1919 – quoted in Ravinder Kumar (ed.), *Essays on Gandhian Politics: The Rowlatt Satyagraha of 1919*, Clarendon Press, Oxford, 1971, p. 328.

16 M.K. Gandhi, 'The duty of satyagrahis', *CWMG*, Vol. 15, p. 436.

17 M.K. Gandhi, 'Democracy versus mobocracy', *Young India*, 8 September, 1920, *CWMG*, Vol. 18, pp 240-44.

18 Gandhi's press statement, 26 July, 1933, *CWMG*, Vol. 55, p. 299.

19 M.K. Gandhi, 'What are basic assumptions? , *CWMG*, Vol. 67, pp. 436-37.

20 Gandhi to Jawaharlal Nehru, 14 September, 1933, *CWMG*, Vol. 55, p. 428.

21 For Gandhi's evidence before the Hunter Committee, M.K. Gandhi, *Satyagraha*, Navjivan Publishing House, Ahmedabad, 1958, pp.19-34; D.G. Tendulkar, *Mahatma: Life of Mohandas Karamchand Gandhi*, Imprint, New Delhi, 1960, Vol. 1, 1960, pp. 280-83.

22 Gandhi to P. Desai, 9 February 1919, *CWMG*, Vol. 15, p. 88.

2

THE RISE OF GANDHI AS A PAN-INDIAN LEADER: THE NON-COOPERATION AND CIVIL DISOBEDIENCE MOVEMENTS

BY 1919, GANDHI HAD EMERGED AS A NATIONAL LEADER commanding the movements against the British. In contrast with the moderate and revolutionary terrorist methods of anti-colonial struggle, he introduced satyagraha, first in South Africa and later in Champaran, Kheda and Ahmedabad. In the campaign against the Rowlatt Act, satyagraha became a nationalist response. This was truly a pan-India movement affecting areas that had remained untouched on earlier occasions, and also the groups of people who had remained peripheral in the pre-Gandhian nationalist campaign. Undoubtedly a unique event, the Rowlatt Satyagraha proved that an all-India movement was possible, despite the social and ethnic divisions, internal to the people. This suggests two important dimensions of the Gandhi-led nationalist offensive: first, Gandhi's success in mobilizing people regardless of internal schisms, is an indicator of the importance of the political agenda that he articulated; and secondly, this underlines the role of the organization in sustaining a movement especially in adverse circumstances. The fact that Gandhi had a firm grip over those challenging the Black Act was quite evident when he called off the movement when it turned violent, though he later characterized his decision as 'a Himalayan blunder'. Despite its failure to repeal the act, the Rowlatt Satyagraha was a watershed in Indian politics for two important reasons: first, a new era began in the anti-British struggle in India where Gandhi set the agenda of the movement and remained its supreme commander. It was possible perhaps due to his capability in preparing a second-line of leaders who were young, and zealously endorsed his plan of action. The strong organization that the Congress built was largely illustrative of the efforts of these young leaders who were politically baptized by Gandhi and had undertaken both social and political activities in the localities by involving the people. It was therefore not surprising that one of the reasons for the success of the Rowlatt Satyagraha was certainly the local grievance, which the leaders utilized tactfully to rouse mass enthusiasm for the campaign. Secondly, the Rowlatt Satyagraha appeared to have outlined the contour of Indian freedom struggle under Gandhi's stewardship. The immediate withdrawal of the movement due to deviation from non-violence suggests that Gandhi was not ready to compromise on the means of the political struggle. To Gandhi, non-violence was not just a creed; it was also a faith that could never be diluted. Despite critiques that satyagraha brought in the disparate Indians under the Gandhi-led Congress, clearly suggests its relative merit vis-à-vis the competitive political ideologies searching for constituencies. There is no doubt that as far as freedom struggle was concerned Gandhi remained the basic reference point either in critiquing or re-tuning his approach to anti-colonialism.

Gandhi inaugurated a new era in India's freedom struggle

involving various social strata. He was also instrumental in transforming the Indian National Congress from an urban-based loose organization dominated by lawyers mainly from the metropolitan cities of Calcutta and Bombay into a political party with its organizational network even in remote and far-flung villages. The structural core of Gandhi's democratization of the Congress lay 'in the proliferation of units capable of attracting and channelling a mass membership base'. The Congress that was just a platform for ventilation of grievances became a mass organization to challenge the British government. There is no doubt that it was only at the aegis of Gandhi that the Congress metamorphosed into a giant organization with its tentacles all over the country. As Jawaharlal Nehru most forcefully put,

> the whole look of the Congress changed; European clothes vanished and soon only *khadi* was to be seen; a new class of delegates, chiefly drawn from the lower-middle classes became the type of Congressmen; the language used became increasingly Hindustani, or sometimes the language of the province where the session was held, as many of the delegates did not understand English, and there was also a growing prejudice against using a foreign language in national work; and a new life and enthusiasm and earnestness became evident in Congress gatherings.[1]

As a result, freedom struggle acquired a mass base that was missing in the past. Furthermore, despite internal ideological divisions within the Congress, its nationalist goal was never compromised. In order to fulfil the aim, Gandhi baptized the Indian masses in the language of ahimsa. Satyagraha was certainly its driving force.

The aim of this chapter is to locate Gandhi within the national context by dwelling on the pan-India movements, namely 1919-22 Non-Cooperation and 1930-32 Civil Disobedience. And since the aim is to 'de-centre' Gandhi, the chapter also focuses on the gradual unfolding of the movements that, on occasions, became 'autonomous' and deviated from the Gandhian path of non-violence. This probably is indicative of the peculiar characters of these major political interventions involving the masses that seldom remained confined to the well-defined parameters of Gandhian nationalism. The movements were justified and sustained in the name of Gandhi and non-violence despite the fact that there were occasions when the participants became violent while protesting.

THE NON-COOPERATION MOVEMENT (1919-22)

Mass arousal during the Rowlatt Satyagraha was unprecedented and convinced Gandhi of the growing discontent against the British rule. It was not therefore surprising that he launched another anti-government campaign in 1920. Known as the Non-Cooperation Movement, it was inspired by a brilliantly simple yet politically dangerous idea that the colonial state in India owed its sustenance to the cooperation of Indians, and it would disintegrate if they withdrew it and set up alternative institutions to replace the existing ones. Following his usual style, Gandhi began the non-cooperation with an advance notice to the viceroy. The movement drew on non-cooperation with the government and its various agencies. Beginning with resignation from government services, non-cooperation was also articulated as refusal to use the institutions of government and schools, and at a later stage, noncompliance towards taxes and refusal to serve the armed forces, and the burning of foreign clothes. Gandhi was forced to adopt such stern measures as a last resort. 'I can retain,' thus argued Gandhi, 'neither respect nor affection for a Government which has been moving from wrong to wrong to defend its immorality.' Gandhi electrified the circumstances. Thousands of people, whether formally associated with the Congress or not, plunged into action against the 'satanic' government. Gandhi was hailed as 'a saviour' even by Rabindranath Tagore who, despite critiquing Gandhi's strategy of bonfire of foreign clothes, admired 'the Mahatma', the title which he coined for Gandhi, by saying that 'it is fortunate that this movement is headed by a man like Gandhi whose saintly life has made him adored all over India. As long as he is at the helm I am not afraid of the ship, or doubtful of its safe arrival at the post of destination.'[2]

Gandhi promised *swaraj* (independence) within a year if non-cooperation was total and widespread. Was Gandhi unrealistic in making such a promise, many apprehended. It was a hollow statement if we interpret it literally. To expect independence within a year of non-cooperation was utopian, since the British state was firm and strong in every respect as evident from the preparedness of the government during the agitation against the Black Act. What was the message then? With this slogan, Gandhi sought to articulate his dream of a strong India that was capable of attaining independence. For him non-cooperation was: (i) a way of demonstrating the hollowness of the colonial state without the cooperation of the average Indians, and also (ii) to show that Indians are capable of managing their business with ease and comfort. In this sense, non-cooperation was a political ideal underlining the Gandhian dream of 'a new order', free from exploitation and anger. There was another dimension as well. His assurance for *swaraj* within a year also inspired the masses to participate in the anti-British movement despite the adverse consequences. He injected in the masses 'freedom from fear'. What was initiated in the Rowlatt Satyagraha was translated in a bigger way in the Non-Cooperation Movement. A new zeal amongst the masses was evident. Not cowed down by the brutalities of the British government, the masses ventured into a 'world of imagined communities' for an aspired goal of independence. 'The essence of his teaching was,' thus argued Jawaharlal Nehru, 'fearlessness and truth, and action allied to these, always keeping the welfare of the masses in view. ... It was a psychological change, almost as if some expert in psycho-analytical methods had probed deep into the patient's past, found out the origins of his complexes, exposed them to his view, and thus rid him of that burden.'[3]

The Allahabad conference of the Central Khilafat Committee held on 1-2 June 1920 articulated the non-cooperation agenda by deciding to launch a four-stage movement that included boycott of titles, withdrawal from schools, colleges, civil services and also from army, and finally non-payment of taxes. The first step was a *hartal* on 1 August, which was total as it coincided with the death of Bal Gangadhar Tilak. The Congress had, by then, a well laid-out organizational network in the country. Muslims had also emerged as a separate block in Indian politics. It was, therefore, a masterstroke on the part of Gandhi to ally with the

Muslim leaders and strengthen the nationalist platform. Hence, the three issues that he adopted were: Punjab wrong, Khilafat wrong and attainment of *swaraj* in one year. Punjab became an emotive issue especially after the killing of innocent people in the Jallianwalla Bagh; Khilafat also gained momentum because of the decision of the British government to dismantle the Ottoman Empire and to undermine the spiritual and temporal authority of the Ottoman sultan as Caliph of Islam. Finally, *swaraj*, though ill defined, created hopes among those fighting the British in response to Gandhi's call. These issues were formally endorsed by the Congress at its special session in Calcutta in September 1920.

The Non-Cooperation-Khilafat merger was a testimony of Gandhi's ability to temper rivalries and to secure cooperation among the Hindu-Muslim political leadership. As he himself explained,

> I hope by my "alliance" with the Mohamedans (sic) to achieve a threefold end – to obtain justice in the face of odds with the method of Satyagraha and to show its efficacy over all other methods, to secure Mohamedans friendship for the Hindus and thereby internal peace also, and last but not least to transform ill-will into affection for the British and their constitution which in spite of its imperfections has weathered many a storm.[4]

This statement clearly suggests the growing importance of at least elite Muslims as an important constituency of nationalist politics. As a true liberal, he expressed his unflinching faith in the British constitution and peaceful methods of satyagraha. He also realized that Hindu-Muslim unity was a pre-requisite for India's future as a nation. Muslims joined hand with Gandhi to gain political mileage. Once they were recognized as a critical minority in India, neither the British nor the Congress could afford to ignore them in any negotiation for future India. Realizing the politics of 'presence', Muslims also agreed to extend support to the Congress agenda that included satyagraha against the British government for 'Punjab wrongs'. So, for both Gandhi and Ali brothers (Maulana Muhammad Ali and Shaukat Ali), the brain behind the merger, the Non-Cooperation Movement was a master strategy for uniting Hindus and Muslims for a nationalist cause. The unity was, however, short-lived because the nucleus of politics shifted with the growing mass participation in movements against the British.

The Rowlatt Satyagraha made Gandhi realize his efficacy as a leader who could easily sway the masses. Now, he would set the nationalist agenda. Justifying his involvement in nationalist politics by saying that 'I take part in politics … because politics encircle us like the coil of a snake from which one cannot get out, no matter how much one tries. I wish, therefore, to wrestle with the snake.' So confident was Gandhi in the 1920 special session of the Congress that he defied the resistance of his colleagues who were sceptical of the Muslim support for the non-cooperation cause. Since non-cooperation was 'a matter of conscience' for him, he was willing to go ahead even without the Congress approval. While defending his decision in favour of non-cooperation, Gandhi thus argued,

> the Congress is after all the mouth-piece of the nation. And when has a policy or a programme which one would like to see adopted, but on which one wants to cultivate public opinion. But when one has an unshakable faith in a particular policy or action, it would be folly to wait for the Congress pronouncements. On

> the contrary one must act and demonstrate its efficacy so as to command acceptance by the nation.[5]

This statement is most significant both for understanding Gandhi's rise to power in Indian politics and also the growing dependence of the Congress on his leadership. He became the supreme commander who could afford to ignore the institutional Congress platform that had so far remained central to the nationalist decisions. His popularity as a leader, especially in the aftermath of the Rowlatt Satyagraha, was unmatched and hence the Congress leaders found it difficult to counter the Gandhian arguments justifying non-cooperation. Furthermore, the growing participation of the Muslims in the movement primarily because of the Khilafat cause had also strengthened Gandhian leadership that was equally capable of mobilizing Hindus and Muslims against a common cause.

It is not very clear whether Indian Muslims were really disturbed by an attack on Caliph, as contemporary researches have shown. This was nonetheless an issue that united the *ulemas* (the religious leaders) with the westernized educated Muslims and was thus helpful in mobilizing Muslims in general. As Gail Minault argues, 'a pan-Islamic symbol opened the way to pan-Indian Islamic political mobilization'.[6] Furthermore, this issue acquired different connotation in India because of the prevalence of the British rule. The nationalist Muslims easily gained political mileage because 'religious faith and anti-British political zeal' reinforced each other. For Gandhi, it was a grand opportunity to convince the Muslims of the necessity of a united political platform to combat the British harming the interests of both the Hindus and Muslims. The Non-Cooperation-Khilafat merger thus gave dividends to Gandhi in the form of Hindu-Muslim unity. He thus stated,

> if I had not joined the Khilafat movement, I think, I would have lost everything. In joining it I have followed what I especially regard as my dharma. I am trying through this movement to show the real nature of non-violence. I am uniting Hindus and Muslims. I am coming to know one and all and, if non-cooperation goes well, a great power based on brute force will have to submit to a simple-looking thing.[7]

As evident, the anti-British dimension of the Khilafat cause inspired Gandhi to associate the leading Muslims with the mainstream nationalist movement. It was a quid-pro-quo for the Muslim leadership. With Gandhi's support, the Muslim campaign for Khilafat acquired a national character and those who emerged as Muslim representatives in the course of the movement became perforce the spokesmen of the Muslims in India. However, the grand alliance between the Congress and the Khilafat organizations 'did not mature into a permanent Hindu-Muslim accord'. Gandhi hoped that if Hindus supported the Khilafat cause 'unconditionally' this would lead to an everlasting bond. But this didn't happen. Gandhi was 'blamed' for 'exploiting a religious grievance of the Muslim community for a political cause'.

While association with the Khilafat movement was strategic, Gandhi's arguments against the Punjab 'wrongs' were emotionally charged. Hurt by the brutalities in Punjab at the behest of Michael O'Dyer, he was pushed towards non-cooperation as possibly the most appropriate means to challenge the government. He was appalled by the rapid deterioration of the British rule that epitomized fair play and justice. In 1919, he 'pleaded … for cooperation with the Government' because he

> honestly believed that new era was about to begin, and that the old spirit of fear, distrust and consequent terrorism was about to give place to the new spirit of respect, trust and goodwill. [He sincerely] believed that the officers that had misbehaved during the martial law regime in the Punjab would be at least dismissed and the people would be otherwise made to feel that a Government that had always been found quick (and rightly) to punish popular excesses would not fail to punish its agents' misdeeds.[8]

He minced no words while condemning the ruling authority that smacked of basic human values. Defending his decision to go ahead with the non-cooperation agenda even without the support of his colleagues, he thus argued,

> Government be an insufferable wrong, if the report of Lord Hunter's Committee and the two dispatches be a greater wrong by reason of their grievous condonation (sic) of these acts, it is clear that we must refuse to submit to this official violence. Appeal to the Parliament by all means if necessary, but if the Parliament fails us and if we are worthy to call ourselves a nation, we must refuse to uphold the Government by withdrawing cooperation from it.[9]

On another occasion, he expressed his disillusionment with the government that had lost moral authority to rule due to 'wrongs' in Punjab. He was unambiguous in his condemnation of the British government when he stated,

> but to my amazement and dismay, I have discovered that the present representatives of the Empire have become dishonest and unscrupulous. They have no real regard for the wishes of the people of India and they count Indian honour as of little consequence. I can [thus] no longer retain affection for a Government so evilly manned as it is now-a-days.[10]

Gandhi was thus persuaded to believe that the British government in India was brutal and had 'no intention of enacting the ideals of [the British] constitution'.[11] Hence he was justified in resorting to non-cooperation with the rulers. It is now clear that the twin wrongs – Punjab and Khilafat – enabled Gandhi to articulate his attitude towards the British Raj. There is also a break with the past if we look at his anti-British strategy. He was constitutionalist only in a limited sense: he made a representation to the government before he embarked on the campaign. In this sense, there was continuity with his style, adopted in South Africa and its aftermath in India in the context of the Rowlatt Satyagraha. But the comparison ends there. The Non-cooperation-Khilafat merger, however, projected a different Gandhi who was not at all ambiguous in his assessment of the colonial rule – it was brutal, inhuman and dishonest. Hence, non-cooperation with the administration was Gandhi's response, unlike in the past, when he opposed the government for having denied the constitutionally-guranteed rights to the subjects. Atrocities in Punjab in the name of 'fair play and justice' and failure to placate the genuine Muslim sentiments over Caliph made him a crusader of the 'the cruel and selfish' colonial rule in India. The aim of the movement was thus to harm the British socially, economically and politically. Gandhi had reasons to be confident because of the following factors: first, Indian masses had supported him in his campaign against the Black Act. Despite his failure to repeal the Act, Gandhi emerged as an undisputed leader who involved the masses in the movement against the ruler. Secondly, although it was a strange coincidence, Gandhi drew political capital out of the Muslim grievances against the British for demeaning the Caliph. By appreciating the Khilafat cause, the Mahatma created conditions for Hindu-Muslim amity at least for a political goal. There is no doubt that the Khilafat campaign gained significance presumably because of its merger with the Non-Cooperation Movement and also by Gandhian endorsement of the Khilafat cause. Thirdly, by the time the movement was to be launched Gandhi had already become a nationalist leader with considerable followings across the country. The earlier satyagraha experiments also drew to Gandhi a group of local leaders who were inspired by and committed to his political ideology. Not only did they provide Gandhi with adequate organizational support, they also created conditions for Gandhian values to strike roots even in areas Gandhi had hardly visited. Fourthly, by revitalizing the Congress, he also prepared a strong organizational network to pursue the nationalist goal. From a mere political platform, active only on the occasion of the annual sessions, the Congress became a movement organized around well-defined principles and strategies. It would not be wrong to suggest that by the time the non-cooperation was launched, the Congress had become Gandhian in the sense that other competitive ideologies were either peripheral or extinct for all practical purposes. It is true that the Congress translated the nationalist vision into practice by undertaking various programmes in which the role of the masses was significant; but Gandhi always remained its steward.

NON-COOPERATION MOVEMENT AND ITS IMPACT

The Non-Cooperation Movement was certainly a break with the past. Gandhi's arrival on the political scene introduced various new dimensions to the nationalist politics. India's freedom struggle was no longer confined to the educated elites only, but was expanded to incorporate peripheral social groups. Concomitant to the extension of constituencies of nationalist politics was the adoption of new slogans that radicalized the Congress to a large extent. Not content with the so-called mendicant politics, the Gandhi-led Congress undertook several measures, which created new constituencies of support. Gandhi rose to prominence at a time when both, the moderate as well as revolutionary terrorist methods were proved futile given the incessant attempts of the people at the grassroots to challenge the colonial state which allowed vested interests to grow and thrive. Thus, the involvement of new social groups in the freedom struggle helped crystallize their search for a new socio-political order. Not always significant, these forces undoubtedly articulated new socio-economic and political issues, which had never figured in the pre-1921 Congress agenda presumably because of its narrow social basis. So, a complex interplay of factors involving the colonial state, the Congress and mass drive for changing the prevalent socio-economic and political order led to the Non-Cooperation Movement, which though essentially an anti-British offensive, laid the foundation of an altogether new movements challenging both the vested interests and the alien state.

Organizationally, the Congress, no longer confined merely to the elites, soon developed into a national movement with agricultural links extending far into the country and its support coming from wide sections of the population. An important reason as to why the Congress became a mass organization probably lay in an effective merger of the non-cooperation and Khilafat causes. Recognizing the Muslims as a separate political group in the 1916 Lucknow Pact,[12] the Congress adopted perhaps the most meaningful strategy to build a mass movement by projecting Hindu-Muslim unity. It is, however, debatable whether only the Khilafat cause which was not at all directly related to India's struggle for independence, cemented the bond between the Muslims and Hindus in the wake of the Non-Cooperation Movement though the disintegration of the Caliph was too remote to have an impact on the ordinary Muslims in India. Whatever the factors that contributed to the expansion of the Congress, the rise of its membership was spectacular, as the following table demonstrates:-

Year	*Total Number of Delegates*	*Muslims*	*% of Muslims*
1918	4868	205	4%
1919	8,126	314	4.5%
1920	14,582	1050	7.2%
1921	4,729	—	—
1922	3,248	111	3.6%

Source: Gopal Krishna, 'The development of the National Congress as a mass organization', *Journal of Asian Studies*, Vol. 25 (3), 1966, p. 421.

Although the figures are by no means exhaustive, it draws our attention to the gradual increase and decline of the Congress delegates during and after the non-cooperation campaign. One is thus inclined to underline the importance primarily of the religious content of the Khilafat in political mobilization in the Non-Cooperation Movement given the sudden increase of the Muslim delegates and their indifferences later. Notwithstanding the adverse consequences of articulating the Muslim demands as separate from those of the Indian National Congress in later days, Gandhi's decision to champion the Khilafat cause broadened the social basis of the nationalist movement. Attributing exploitation at different levels to the alien state, the Congress leadership succeeded in infusing popular misery with a political content. It is therefore not surprising that different kinds of political movements were organized during the non-cooperation days which though drew upon anti-British feelings, were basically attacks on the well-entrenched vested interests. There is thus a point when one argues that the call for non-cooperation let loose hitherto unknown socio-economic and political forces that decisively shaped and thus consequently made the nature of the nationalist intervention more complex than ever.

Apart from including boycott of schools, colleges and law courts, the non-cooperation campaign adopted a more militant stance concentrating on boycott of foreign clothes (including public bonfire) and boycott of the visit of the Prince of Wales in November 1921. Since the 1920 special session of the Congress in Calcutta, delegates were reported to have insisted on non-payment of taxes; the administration expressed concern because such an issue was likely to gain an easy acceptance especially in Bengal since it was championed by those 'ex-detenus and intelligentsia which … have at their disposal many thousands of men who are available for propaganda amongst the masses of the most unscrupulous, reckless and dangerous character'.[13] Despite Gandhi's reluctance, boycott was included in the Congress agenda in Bombay AICC meeting of 28-30 July primarily to accommodate the radical elements within the Congress. It has been shown that the economic boycott though complementary to economic swadeshi, actually enhanced the profit of Indian textile magnates. Before the war, Indian mill owners, for instance, controlled only 25 per cent of the textile market which expanded to 42 per cent by the end of 1921; the prices also rose by three times.

As regards boycott of schools and colleges, the non-cooperation campaign probably attained a dramatic success. Gandhi was convinced that the English education was futile and urged the students to leave the government-controlled educational institutions; the appeal had significant results in the context of the opening of a large number of national schools and colleges throughout the country. As the table below shows, though their popularity was not the same, the national schools and colleges attracted a large number of students:

Province	*Institutions*	*Scholars*
Madras	92	5072
Bombay	189	17,100
Bengal	190	14,819

United provinces (UP)	137	8,476
Punjab	69	8,046
Bihar and Orissa	442	17,330
Central Provinces	86	6,338
Assam	38	1,908
NWFP	04	120

Source: P.C. Bamford, Histories of Non-Cooperation and Khilafat Movements, *Government of India, Delhi, 1925, p. 104.*

Though it is true that the number of students in these schools and colleges was not large enough to cause any anxiety, what alarmed the administration was the impact of the boycott slogan on the government institutions as a whole. Almost 80 per cent of them were seriously affected between 1919 and 1921. While explaining this phenomenon, an official report thus admitted,

> There was something in the movement that appealed to most diverse types of minds. ... Imagination has been fired and a spiritual uplift initiated. Something that had been wanting in our college life had been supplied. ... the situation presented possibilities of romance and adventure that irradiated [otherwise sterile] student life. Picketing and procession were [therefore] as irresistible to such minds as a bump supper and a "rag" to Oxford undergraduates. [Students] became for the first time conscious that they were wasting time over a kind of education not suited to their needs and leading them to an office stool.[14]

National schools and colleges failed to provide an effective alternative to the prevalent academic institution and by 1923, except in Bengal, the lack of interest in such an experiment was clearly evident. The official explanation is also significant in having brought out the limitations of existing system of education which was at its best tuned to the creation of merely a pool of clerks.

Whatever the reasons, the educational boycott was more effective in contrast with other agendas for non-cooperation. For instance, the initial appeal for self-sacrifice was hardly successful: only 24 titles were surrendered out of 5186, and the number of lawyers giving up practice was 180 in 1921. Polling was low in many places in the 1920 Council elections, falling to 8 per cent in Bombay city, and 5 per cent in Lahore; candidates contested in all but 6 out of 637 seats and council functioning could not be disrupted. Compared with the erstwhile Congress campaign, the Non-Cooperation Movement demonstrated that the old closed shop of limited politics had been thrown wide open. Far greater numbers than before from all parts of the country were participating in an overt political campaign, using a far wider range of techniques than earlier politicians had ever used simultaneously. The political nation was thus expanded to accommodate various kinds of interests, manifested in the type of the movements, organized with a view to redressing local grievances, which on various occasions, were attributed to colonialism. As a consequence, the nation had to confront with various new constituents, which were either peripheral or too insignificant to deserve attention in political mobilization.

An important dimension of the nationalist politics unfolded with the recognition of the working classes as an important constituency of the nationalist struggle. In 1921, there were 396 strikes involving 6,00,351 workers and a loss of 6,994,426 working days. What provoked strikes was the recession in the post-war period, which forced the factory owners to cut production with a four-day week. The Bengal jute mill workers were hard-hit by this new schedule of production, which largely accounted for an epidemic of strikes in 1921: a total of 137 strikes affecting 1,86,479 workers. The leadership was vested in the newly emerged section of 'the Hindu right as well as a number of left groups dedicated to the creation of a socialist movement focused on the grievances of the workers and peasants'. Organizing the workers in trade unions, these labour activists caused alarm to the British administration, which by highlighting their *bhadralok* background strove assiduously to create a fissure between the workers and the leadership. Apart from Jute Mill towns, the participants in the non-cooperation campaign tried to organize a strike in Raniganj-Jharia coalmines. Although both the leaders, Swami Viswanand and Swami Darsanananda were involved in the movement against the mine owners essentially to ameliorate the conditions of the mine workers, the strike was reported to have been instigated by the Marwari businessmen who wanted to get into coal business, so far monopolized by the Europeans.

The Chandpur incident of 1921 is probably the most publicized event during the non-cooperation days showing the appeal of Gandhi as a leader who was acceptable to the Assam tea-garden workers regardless of religion, caste and region. Inspired by Gandhi's call for swaraj for the people which meant an end to exploitation, the tea-garden workers in Chandpur, mostly from the UP and Bihar, started a long trek without seeking their manager's permission for leave which brought them to Chandpur in Tippera district on 15 May 1921. Despite adverse consequences, the workers undertook such drastic steps probably in response to the prevalent rumour that 'Gandhi raj has been established and hence the exploiters garden owners are on the run'. In order to prevent the workers from boarding a steamer for their journey, the local administration employed Gurkha military police who resorted to indiscriminate firing. Such 'an inhuman act' provoked mass resentment, which was translated into steamer and rail strikes in east Bengal. The C.R. Das-led Bengal Congress immediately took up the cause of the workers to sharpen its attack on the colonial state. The chain of strikes in Bengal that followed the Chandpur firing was partly attributable to the involvement of the leading Congressmen like C.R. Das and J.M. Sengupta, and partly due to a spontaneous rising of the entire population especially the lower classes who expressed through the strikes their acute sense of economic exploitation and racial abasement under white rule. A disturbed Ronaldshay who appeared panic-stricken in view of the widespread nature of the strike thus wrote,

> The most disquieting feature is the extent of the hold which events have shown they have already acquired over large classes of people. They have been able to call strikes in the inland steamer lines and the Assam-Bengal Railway, and they have been able to call *hartals* in a number of east Bengal towns simultaneously.[15]

The 'strike fever', as it was characterized in the official discourse was endemic and affected primarily the industries of eastern India. Part of the reason lay in the fact that the leadership succeeded in attributing workers' misery principally to the Europeans! American ownership that with its association with the colonial state, was naturally insensitive to the grievances of the Indians. Besides, the role of the local Congress leadership appeared crucial in organizing the disparate workers for a cause by providing an ideological direction as well as material help. For leaders, like C.R. Das and J.M. Sengupta, labour was increasingly becoming an important constituency of the nationalist politics, recognized later in the 1922 Gaya Congress session; and thus by championing the workers' cause, they initiated a process which though signalled and articulated through various contradictions in the Gandhi-led movement, widened the social base of the freedom struggle. Because strike 'do not fall within the plan of non-violent non-cooperation' Gandhi while condemning the strike fever thus argued,

> In India we want no political strikes. ... we must gain control over the unruly and disturbing elements. ... we seek not to destroy capital or capitalists, but to regulate the relations between capital and labour. We want to harness capital to our side. *It would be folly to encourage sympathetic strikes.* (emphasis added).[16]

By according priority to village reconstruction through self-help, Gandhi articulated his plan for an economic revival 'through spinning wheel and hand-woven cloth (charkha and khadi), panchayats or arbitration courts, national schools and campaign for Hindu-Muslim unity, and against the evils of liquor and untouchability'. Although these programmes may not have been uniformly effective as strategies for political mobilization, they nonetheless unfolded a new process by involving the hitherto neglected section of society in a struggle, which despite its pronounced political content, was equally a battle against the well-entrenched vested interests in the localities. It was therefore not surprising that peasants of Kanika in Orissa challenged the local zamindars for having demanded an extra rent. Drawing upon Gandhi, the militant section of the Orissa Congress leaders organized 'the peasants for the establishment of Gandhi raj when no one would have to pay rent'; so convinced were the peasants that they 'boycotted and intimidated,' on occasions, 'those who were inclined to pay rents to the zamindars'. The movement though led by the Orissa Congress, did not receive Gandhi's approval, and was later unconditionally revoked. Gandhi was, however, inclined to encourage a no-revenue campaign in a *rayatwari* settlement area, like Bardoil and not in any zamindari region where it would inevitably involve 'no rent'. By trying to contain 'no rent' campaigns, Gandhi projected a specific type of leadership, which mobilized peasants exclusively in its terms and conditions. Peasants were organized and mobilized on the so-called unifying issues, which transcend even the well-defined boundaries among the antagonistic classes. So, it was logical when Gandhi 'deprecated all attempts to create a discord between landlords and tenants and advised the tenants to suffer rather than fight for they had to join all forces for fighting the most powerful zamindar, namely the Government.'

Gandhi's political agenda sharpened the division within the nationalist leadership which saw the peasant cause as integral to the anti-imperial struggle. For the Kisan Sabhas, 'no rent' was a logical demand in a vertically-divided society, though it adversely affected the landlords who were Indians; so, the struggle of the peasantry took a different turn in areas where they were predominant. In the Congress-dominated areas, the contradiction that reigned supreme was between imperialism and nationalism and the local leadership therefore succeeded in integrating the movements in the localities with its pan-Indian counterpart on the basis of an anti-imperial logic. Despite surplus extraction, the contradiction between landlords and peasants never became sharp enough to cause a fissure in the multi-class platform, which the leadership so carefully nurtured. Midnapur in Bengal is a glaring example showing the extent to which the Congress leaders effectively tuned the peasant movement to identify imperialism as singularly responsible for severe dislocation in society. Such a correlation gained ground in the peasant mind probably due, *inter alia,* a peculiar socio-economic and political configuration in district.

THE CIVIL DISOBEDIENCE MOVEMENT, 1930-32:

The Non-Cooperation Movement confirmed the popularity of the Congress and Gandhi's rise as its undisputed leader. The movement was abruptly suspended on 11 February 1922 following the eruption of violence in Chauri Chaura in Gorakhpur on 4 February. The violence of Chauri Chaura that drew national attention was retaliation against the police who resorted to firing once the situation went beyond its control. What had culminated in violence began with villagers leading a procession to the local police station. It was this procession of volunteers that clashed with the police on the afternoon of this fateful day. After having failed to dissuade the crowd, the police fired killing three volunteers and injuring several others, which naturally infuriated the mob. When the mob started pelting stones, the policemen retreated and took shelter in the police station. The crowd locked them in and set the building afire by 'sprinkling kerosene oil seized from the nearby market'. Twenty-three policemen, including two sub-inspectors of police, nineteen constables and two *chaukidars* were battered and burnt to death. The mob fury did not stop there, as it was reported officially that

> [t]he death of the policemen was not the end of this riot. Police property was systematically destroyed, rifles were smashed, and the bits of brass with which police *lathis* were capped (to make them deadly weapons) were taken off. Over three dozens *chaukidars* managed to escape by throwing away their conspicuous red turbans and milling into the crowd. The police turbans (*pagris*) of these rural policemen were torn to shreds.[17]

When Gandhi saw violence threatening to overtake his campaign, he called it to a halt. By suspending the movement following the Chauri Chaura incident, the Congress Working Committee at Gandhi's behest instructed the local Congress committees to direct the farmers to 'pay the land revenue and other taxes due to the Government . . . and also resolves to withdraw from every other preparatory activity of an offensive nature'. Yet in seven years, the Congress changed its stance radically and demanded *Purna Swaraj* in the 1929 Lahore session of the Congress. And with its adoption began the preparation for another civil disobedience. The Chauri Chaura, however, remained a matter of concern for the Mahatma. As early as January 1930, he expressed his uncertainty about another anti-British campaign by stating that

> I must confess that I do not see the atmosphere for it today. I want to discover a formula whereby sufficient provision can be made for avoiding suspension by reason of Chauri Chaura. A time must come when there may be a fight to the finish with one's back to the wall. With the present temper of many Congressmen, with our internal dissensions, with the communal tension, it is difficult to discover an effective and innocent formula. It may be impossible to offer civil disobedience at this stage in the name of the Congress.[18]

According to Gandhi, civil disobedience was the only means of challenging both the British rule which appeared to him 'a perfect personification of violence' and the growing hatred towards the agents of this rule which took the form of causal assassination'. 'The call of 1920,' he further wrote, 'was a call for preparation. The call in 1930 is for engaging in the final conflict.'[19] Gandhi launched the Civil Disobedience Movement by sending a charter of demands to the viceroy on 2 March 1930 which were as follows:

> (1) total prohibition; (2) reduction of the rupee ration to 1:4 (3) reduction of land revenue by at least 50 per cent and making it subject to legislative control; (4) abolition of the salt tax; (5) reduction of the military expenditure by at least 50 per cent; (6) reduction of the salaries of the highest grade service to one half or less so as to suit the reduced revenue; (7) imposition of protective tariff on foreign cloth; (8) passage of the Coastal Tariff Reservation Bill; (9) discharge of all political prisoners save those condemned for murder, withdrawal of all political prosecutions and abrogation of Section 124-A, Regulation III of 1818 and the like and permission of all Indian exiles to return; (10) abolition of the CID or its popular control; and (11) issue of licences to use firearms for self-defence, subject to popular control.

Gandhi's eleven point ultimatum to the viceroy, however, disappointed many leading Congressmen including Nehru since it contained no demand for any change in the political structure, not even the dominion status. 'Bewildered' at Gandhi's charter of demands, which ultimately boiled down to a campaign for salt preparation, Nehru thought that it was a sad climb down from the *Purna Swaraj* resolution. As Nehru argued, '[s]alt suddenly became a mysterious word, a word of power. The Salt Tax was to be attacked, the salt laws were to be broken. We were bewildered and could not quite fit in a national struggle.'[20] Irwin, the viceroy was not perturbed at all. In a letter to the Secretary of State, Wedgewood Benn, he thus wrote, 'at present the prospect of a salt campaign does not keep me awake at night'. Although the eleven-points demand appeared an anti-climax to many Congressmen, the CWC welcomed Mahatma Gandhi's proposal and authorized him and other volunteers to start civil disobedience. Endorsing the campaign for a mass civil disobedience, the working committee thus emphatically declared,

> in the event of a mass movement taking place, all those who are rendering voluntary cooperation to the government such as lawyers, and those who are receiving so-called benefits from it, such as students, will withdraw their cooperation or renounce benefits as the case may be, and throw themselves into the final struggle for the freedom.[21]

Gandhi's eleven points incorporated demands of almost every section of Indian society. By choosing salt as the central issue, he strove to organize an anti-British campaign in which the participation of a majority of the people was ensured since salt was essential for everyday survival. The boycott of foreign cloth was also included as a strategy because of its effectiveness in the earlier Congress campaigns. Hence, the Civil Disobedience Movement revolved primarily around the attacks on government's salt monopoly and the boycott of foreign cloth.

On 12 March 1930, the Salt Satyagraha began with a carefully organized a month-long march covering 240 miles, which Gandhi undertook from Sabarmati Ashram in Ahmedabad to Dandi on the west coast of Gujarat. There were seventy-eight chosen volunteers who accompanied Gandhi in the Dandi March (12 March to 5 April) which inaugurated the Salt Satyagraha. For the government, by deciding to breach the Salt Act, Gandhi became 'a laughing stock involved in kindergarten stage of political revolution'. Salt could never become, as the government was emphatic, 'an issue of concern'. The most that could happen was that small quantities of inferior salt would be sporadically produced in some coastal areas and consumed locally – which would neither threaten the government nor would affect the price of salt adversely. Nevertheless, the movement gained momentum. As Subhas Chandra Bose commented, 'at every step the Mahatma received an unexpectedly warm welcome and that made the Government realize that the coming campaign would be a much more serious affair than they had thought at first'. Gandhi reached Dandi on 5 April. With 'the consummate showmanship of a great political artist', he picked up a palmful of salt in open defiance of the government and signalled his opposition to the unlawful Salt Act. In order 'to cope with the emergency', the government finally arrested Gandhi on 5 May under the archaic Bombay Regulation act xxv of 1827 that legalized detention without trial. Instead of dampening the enthusiasm of the participants, the arrest of Mahatma seemed to have stimulated the resistance against the government. The CWC was left with the local leadership to decide the course of action once the Mahatma was interned. In order to sustain the spirit of civil disobedience, the *Young India* thus exhorted,

> Each town, each village may have ... to become its own battlefield. The strategy of the battle must then come to be determined by local circumstances and change with them from day to day. The sooner the workers prepare for this state of things, the earlier shall we reach the goal. They should need little guidance from outside. They know that there must be no deviation from the principles of civil disobedience as laid down by Mahatma Gandhi or from the main programme of action as fixed by the Congress.[22]

Hence, it is argued that there was no 'all India blueprint for civil disobedience in 1930-31' as there had been in 1919-22 Non-Cooperation-Khilafat campaign, and as a result, the movement in practice became 'a series of loosely coordinated local conflicts'. There is no doubt that the success of the civil disobedience campaign was largely due to the importance of salt as an emotive issue. Once the scope of the movement was extended to the breach of forest laws, the non-payment of taxes to *ryotwari* areas, and the boycott of foreign clothes, banks, shipping and insurance companies, it took the form of a well-orchestrated campaign against the British rule. No part of British India escaped it though the intensity differed widely in proportion to which the campaign addressed the local grievances. That the movement caught the imagination of the people is evident from the number of those, incarcerated for their participation in campaign:

Province	*Hindus*	*Muslims*	*Others*	*Total*
Madras	2,930	31	05	2966
Bombay	3,986	110	18	4,114
Bengal	4,684	106	—	4,790
UP	4,740	108	—	4,848
Punjab	1,094	226	523	1,843
Bihar & Orissa	6,285	37	01	6,323
Central Provinces	2,536	27	—	2,563
Assam	411	04	—	415
NWFP	42	434	—	476
Delhi	646	69	01	716
Total	*27354*	*1,152*	*548*	*29,054*

Source: Home-Poll 23/26, 1931 – borrowed from Judith N Brown, *Gandhi and Civil Disobedience: The Mahatma in Indian politics, 1928-34*, Cambridge University Press, Cambridge, 1977, p. 124.

The raid of the salt depot at Dharsana by the Congress volunteers was illustrative of their determination to challenge the government forces non-violently despite severe provocation, as the following report by Webb Miller of the New Freeman shows. 'In eighteen years of reporting in twenty-two countries … I have never witnessed such harrowing scenes as at Dharsana. The Western mind can grasp violence returned by violence, can understand a fight, but it is, I find, perplexed and baffled by the sight of men advancing coldly and deliberately and submitting to beatings without defence. Sometimes the scenes were so painful that I had to turn away momentarily. One surprising feature was the discipline of volunteers. It seemed they were thoroughly imbued with Gandhi's non-violent creed.'

As evident from the above table, the number of Muslims who were jailed was insignificant. In fact, here lies the greatest failure of the Mahatma who did not succeed in popularizing the civil disobedience cause to the Muslims to the extent he did in the context of the earlier campaign of non-cooperation in 1919-22. There is no doubt that the Khilafat cause had made his task easier but Civil Disobedience Movement had no such agenda. This seriously weakened the movement especially in Muslim dominated areas of Bengal, Punjab and Sind. And the Congress' claim that its appeal and support base was national received a severe jolt from which it hardly recovered.

Although the Civil Disobedience Movement began with the breach of salt laws, civil resistance spread to other fields. Simultaneously with Mahatma's march in villages, an intense propaganda was carried on by those involved in the campaign asking the people to give up service under the British government and to prepare for non-payment of tax as well. It was not therefore surprising that violation of Salt Act soon became just one activity and resistance to the government took various forms. Jawaharlal Nehru attributed this to

> the promulgation of various ordinances by the Viceroy prohibiting a number of activities. As these ordinances and prohibitions grew, the opportunities for breaking them also grew and civil resistance took the form of doing the very thing that the ordinance was intended to stop.[23]

At every village where Gandhi stopped he spoke briefly. On one occasion, while reiterating the famous eleven points, he attacked the Salt Act by saying that 'Who can help liking this poor man's battle? The cruel tax is not respecter of persons. It is therefore as much the interest of the Mussalmans as of the Hindu to secure its abolition. This is a fight undertaken in the name of God and for the sake of millions of paupers of this country'.[24] Besides highlighting the inhuman nature of the British government, Gandhi in his speeches always couched his argument with issues relevant to the village life, on khadi, cow-protection, hygiene and untouchability. He also appealed to those serving the government. By the time the Dandi March came to an end, about one third of 760 village headmen had resigned. This might not have seriously affected the alien administration though it was symbolically significant when the governmental authority did not seem to be weak.

The Salt Satyagraha affected virtually every province though in some areas, the campaign assumed massive proportions due to its physical proximity with sea. Thus, Bombay presidency bore the brunt of the salt campaign. Apart from damaging the British economic interests, the salt campaign contributed immensely to political mobilization by generating an atmosphere of contempt for the government, which deprived people of a basic necessity of life, viz., salt. By publicizing the government retaliation against the non-violent salt campaign in the press, the Congress sustained the tempo of the movement to such an extent that the governor general, not perturbed at all when the movement was launched, appeared panic-stricken and admitted that Gandhi planned a fine strategy round the issue of salt [because] salt had value for a broad mass appeal and emotive publicity.

Similarly, the boycott of foreign cloth was an effective nation-wide campaign, organized by the Congress volunteers who perfected this method since the 1905 Swadeshi movement. Its impact was devastating on the British commercial interests and there was a sharp decline of British cloth imports, from £ 26 million in 1929 to £13.7 million in 1930, and quantity wise, from 1248 million yards in 1929-30 to only 523 million yards in 1930-31. It is true that the Great Depression was responsible for a large-scale dislocation in international trade and commerce, yet economic swadeshi helped the Indian milliners significantly. Thus, in his presidential address to the Bombay Milliners Association, Homi Modi underlined the Congress contribution by admitting that the Swadeshi movement undoubtedly helped the Indian industry during a period of grave difficulty and now the future may be regarded as full of hope. Apart from sustaining the traditional constituencies, the civil disobedience campaign is remarkable in having extended the Congress influence to women and children. A Home Department report shows that of the 2954 prisoners on 15 November 1930, no less than 2050 were below 17 while 359 were women.

As a strategist, Gandhi succeeded in infusing popular misery with a political content by attributing it to the oppressive nature of the Raj. Astonished by the immense popularity of the civil disobedience campaign, the moderate Tejbahadur Sapru thus candidly admitted,

> The Congress has undoubtedly acquired a great hold on popular imaginations. On the roadside stations where until a few months ago I could hardly have suspected that people had any politics. I

> have seen with my eyes demonstrations and heard with my ears the usual Congress slogans. The popular feeling is one of excitement. It is fed from day to day by continuous and persistent propaganda on the part of the Congressmen – by lectures, delivered by their volunteers in running trains and similar activities . . . there is no doubt whatever in my mind that *there is the most intense distrust of the Government and its professions.* Indeed I have little doubt in my mind that racial feeling has been fanned to a very dangerous extent . . . it seems to me that the Congress is really fighting for its own supremacy in the country. (emphasis added).[25]

With a gradual expansion of its organizational network, the Congress certainly became stronger than before. For Gandhi, the violation of salt law was the 'last throw of a gambler', insisting that even 'the risk of violence was worth it'. The movement appeared inevitable given the government intransigence to concede the most humane demand which was unfortunate, as Gandhi himself articulated, because 'on bended knees I asked for bread and received stones instead'. Hence, he repudiated the salt law and regarded it as his 'sacred duty to break the mournful mandatory of compulsory peace that is choking the heart of the Nation for want of free vent'.

The civil disobedience campaign had galvanized the rural masses into action. Areas like Bardoli and Kheda in Gujarat, Bankura and Arambagh in Bengal, Bihpur in Bihar came to prominence in the first phase of the movement. By resorting to rural constructive work through local ashrams, Gandhians sustained the nationalist spirit which had manifested itself in the form of salt satyagraha during the civil disobedience campaign. Salt provided the initial catalyst in the struggle for *Purna Swaraj*. With the onset of monsoon and also the geographic constraint of its effectiveness as a strategy, illegal manufacture of salt gradually lost its significance. Hence, the Congress volunteers adopted other techniques to continue with its anti-British campaign. In Midnapur, for instance, despite enormous physical coercion and sale of property the refusal to pay the *chowkidari* tax instantaneously mobilized the peasants against the state demonstrating the extent to which the local grievances gave the leverage in the civil disobedience movement. Moreover, as the Bengal Congress was organizationally weak due, *inter alia,* to factional rivalry among its leaders, the province experienced during the civil disobedience days a considerable diversity of forms of popular initiative at the grassroots clinging to both Gandhian and revolutionary terrorist tactics.

The Civil Disobedience Movement, unlike the earlier campaign of non-cooperation remained largely non-violent except perhaps the stray incident of the Chittagong armoury raid when a revolutionary terrorist group raided the arsenal to seize arms. Apart from being non-violent, the civil disobedience campaign also demonstrated Gandhi's capacity in integrating different levels of political awareness and activity. Not only did he extend the constituencies of nationalist politics, he also united different generations 'in a common campaign – an outcome he had intended in order to heal divisions' in Congress and divert into constructive work 'the frustrations which bred violence'.[26]

The first phase of the civil disobedience campaign came to an end with the Gandhi-Irwin pact of 5 March 1931 and Congress agreed to participate in the Second Round Table Conference to discuss the future constitution of India.

Gandhi's Congress colleagues were unhappy. Subhas Chandra Bose, for instance, characterized the pact as 'a curse [because it] contained nothing of value'. Similarly, the die-hards in England and in India took it as 'a defeat or a humiliation for the all-powerful British Government'. The Round Table conference failed to provide a conclusive solution especially to the demands of various minorities for separate electorates. So, negotiations with the government over India's future failed and Gandhi returned empty-handed from London. He was left with no option but to resume the battle especially when the government unleashed repression and in a preemptive strike banned the Congress on 4 January 1932. Apart from 'the non possumus attitude of the Viceroy', Subhas Chandra Bose attributed Gandhi's decision to begin civil disobedience campaign to two factors: first, the general temper of the public, and secondly, the influence of the Left wing. As for the first, people got disillusioned since the government continued to be repressive even after the truce between the Congress and the government. And, they seemed to have been cheated as the Round Table Conference also ended with no favourable results. Furthermore, the steady propaganda carried on by 'the Left Wing Congressmen, youth leaguers and Left Wing Labourites' had also left an impact on Gandhi. The movement began with vigour, but gradually lost the momentum for a variety of complex reasons. Apart from Muslims, who largely remained aloof in the first phase of the campaign, the harijans also did not participate as enthusiastically as in the past presumably because of Gandhi's opposition to their demand for separate electorates. The well-off peasants remained less enthusiastic because they felt betrayed by the sudden withdrawal of the first phase of the civil disobedience campaign. Therefore, the Congress was weakened organizationally though its image as a powerful opponent to the British rule was further consolidated due largely to its sustained campaign against the Raj. However, what is striking of this period is the growth of parallel leaderships representing various social constituencies within the national movement that certainly undermined Mahatma's claim as a national leader. At least two important power blocs – one led by M.A. Jinnah and other by B.R. Ambedkar – began playing crucial roles in the nationalist articulation of freedom struggle. Indian political scene thus became far more complex because of (a) the distance between the two communities; and (b) the growing separation between the dalits and caste Hindus. The Gandhian nationalist democratic ideology was naturally hardhit. Mahatma no longer remained 'the undisputed nationalist leader'. Hindu-Muslim chasm appeared to have been consolidated in the wake of the Civil Disobedience Movement. With the introduction of separate electorates for the Muslims in areas where they were demographically preponderant, differences between the communities further widened. Gandhi's opposition to extend separate electorates to the dalits caused, for obvious reasons, a further division among the Hindus. So, Gandhi's rise to power during the non-cooperation days was seriously eclipsed with his failure to consolidate the Muslim support for the Salt Satyagraha despite the association of the eminent Muslim leaders in the campaign. The pattern seems to have continued and finally led to the 1947 partition of the subcontinent. Yet, it would be wrong to argue that Gandhi was a spent-force in the aftermath of the Civil Disobedience Movement because of three significant reasons: first, he continued to be the rallying point for the Congress that remained perhaps the most effective anti-British platform with a pan-Indian organization. Secondly, given his capacity to unite people irrespective of class, caste and creed, his appeal was universal in tone and content unlike Jinnah and Ambedkar who drew on ideologically-restricted and politically-divisive agenda. Thirdly, despite the rising significance of the Muslims as a constituency, Gandhi was still a major player in the nationalist negotiation for power. And, Mahatma's 'magical power' in mobilization against the British remained intact, as evident in the Quit India Movement or 'the open rebellion' of 1942.

CONCLUSION

The Rowlatt Satyagraha began a new experiment in Indian nationalism by drawing upon the Gandhian technique of satyagraha. The Non-Cooperation and Civil Disobedience movements confirmed the growing popularity of the technique and also the acceptability of its author, Gandhi. So far confined to the educated middle class, the freedom struggle percolated down to the villages and Gandhi remained its supreme leader. As it was admitted by the viceroy in his official communication, the Non-Cooperation Movement, whatever be its other achievements, has spread political ideas. I may say revolutionary ideas, among the masses of the people and their placid contentment has been disturbed far beyond our anticipation.

In the evolution of Gandhi, the period, 1920-32, is most significant for a variety of obvious reasons. He became the

Mahatma who rose to prominence not merely as a nationalist leader, but also as 'a great soul' of India. Drawn on civilizational resources, his ideology of ahimsa infused fresh life into the nationalist movement that was fractured due to ideological rivalries among those participating in the anti-colonial struggle. So, the emergence of Gandhi as the undisputed leader of the Congress marked a radical break with the past. Almost all the pre-Gandhian nationalist leaders were sceptical of Gandhi. By involving the masses in the anti-British campaign, Gandhi articulated a qualitatively different ideology, which translated the popular grievances into action against the alien state. A new era dawned in Indian politics and N.C. Chaudhuri thus commented,

> [t]he victory of Gandhism which was the victory of a new kind of nationalism over all previous forms of rational nationalism, preached and practiced in modern India, forces the men of all schools not only into silence but into incomprehension.[27]

Given the economic crisis following the First World War, one is inclined to attribute Gandhi's success during the Non-Cooperation Movement merely to the adverse consequences of the overall deterioration of the economy. In the official report, it was thus confidently argued,

> the success which attended the Non-Cooperation and Khilafat Movements ... is undoubtedly attributed to the Great War, for neither the agitation could have attained the dimension which it did for the economic pressure to which people were subjected to in consequence of prolonged and widespread hostilities. This pressure aggravated and magnified local grievances and spread of unrest thus making, for a time, the work of the agitators easy.[28]

Since the masses bore the brunt of the war, the logic drawing on the adverse consequences of war appears plausible. What is, however, unique is Gandhi's success in infusing a political content with mass suffering by attributing to the British rule. So, the campaign, he launched, did not merely aim at the redressal of economic grievances but was also an attack on the alien state, which was held responsible for the general decadence of the country. Moreover, the Non-Cooperation Movement succeeded in mobilizing Hindus and Muslims together largely because of an effective merger between the Non-Cooperation and Khilafat causes. Although this was a rare occasion when both the Hindus and Muslims fought the British together the Congress by recognizing the Muslims as separate from the rest strengthened, at least indirectly, a process that culminated in the articulation of the Two Nation theory in the 1940 Lahore resolution.

The Non-Cooperation Movement was significant in another sense: Gandhi emerged as an effective mediator between the Hindus and Muslims who failed to form a joint front against the British. It is true that there were Muslims in the Congress. But their lukewarm participation in the Congress-led movements caused concern to the existing nationalist leadership. Furthermore, the nationalist flirtations with typical Hindu symbols especially during the Revolutionary Terrorist phase of the freedom struggle alienated not only the Muslims but also the socially peripheral sections. By endorsing the Khilafat cause, the Mahatma brought about radical changes in the Muslim perception of the nationalist struggle. They were drawn into the nationalist mainstream. Gandhi thus held together both the Hindu and

Muslim politicians, mediating between their diverse ideologies and aims. The outcome was evident in the Congress sessions at Nagpur and Calcutta when the merger of the non-cooperation with the Khilafat agitation was officially adopted by a majority of delegates. It was Gandhi's victory. His strength lay in the support of sections of the Muslim community, roused to activity in the Khilafat Movement, in the support of the representative from regions that so far remained peripheral in nationalist politics – Bihar, UP, Punjab, Gujarat and the Hindi-speaking parts of Central Province – and in the support of merchant groups who were earlier loyal to the Raj. His success in mediating among the groups with conflicting aims and goals 'made him the most dangerous opponent and the most powerful potential ally in the political situation of 1920'. Apart from bringing the Hindus and Muslims together in the wake of the non-cooperation and Khilafat merger, Gandhi was also a mediator between the educated, high caste groups who participated in the nationalist politics since the formation of the Indian National Congress in 1885, and the wider social groups that also became part of the nationalist intervention in the freedom struggle especially after 1920. It was not therefore surprising that even Tilak who held ideas contrary to ahimsa urged his Congress colleagues to regard Gandhi as 'a political power' who should not be thwarted or opposed by the Nationalists lest they should find themselves in a minority and lose their lead in politics.

Through the salt campaign in 1930 in the wake of the Civil Disobedience Movement, Gandhi involved various new social groups, hitherto peripheral, in the nationalist campaign. By selecting salt as the principal issue of the agitation, he proved how effective he was as a strategist in opposition to a ruthless state. In the popular perception, the state was easily identified as the target of attack since salt was the basic item in daily existence. Neither was government's salt monopoly seriously threatened by the Salt Satyagraha, nor did the Civil Disobedience Movement shook the foundation of the Raj. It also failed to unite Hindus and Muslims under a joint platform. Yet, it performed 'an important preparatory function in the civil disobedience campaign by generating widespread demonstrations of contempt for laws considered oppressive and for British administration. The Salt Satyagraha had different kinds of manifestation at the grassroots. Yet, the campaign unleashed a political process whereby the Congress activists at various levels were linked together for a common cause. Despite the expansion of the constituency of nationalist politics, the civil disobedience campaign was constrained from the outset as the Muslims generally stayed away from the campaign. Although the Muslim League did not support the Congress, there are instances showing that Muslims appreciated the salt campaign, which, if succeeded, would reduce their burden too. Whatever the impact of such stray instances on Hindu-Muslim relations, the schism between the two communities institutionalized first by the 1916 Lucknow Pact was further consolidated in the wake of the Civil Disobedience Movement which despite its success otherwise, remained, to the Muslims at least, merely a Congress campaign.

---

1 *Jawaharlal Nehru: An Autobiography*, John Lane the Bodley Head, London, 1941, pp. 65-66.

2 *Amrita Bazaar Patrika*, 21 Nov., 1920.

3 Jawaharlal Nehru, *The Discovery of India,* Oxford University Press, Delhi, 1989, pp. 358-59.

4 *Young India*, 28 April, 1920.

5 *Hindustan Standard*, 19 August, 1920.

6 Gail Minault, *The Khilafat Movement: Religious symbolism and political mobilization in India*, Oxford University Press, Delhi, 1999, p. 11.

7 Gandhi to Maganlal Gandhi, 4 May, 1920, *CWMG*, Vol. 17, pp. 386-87.

8 *Young India*, 28 July, 1920, *CWMG*, Vol. 18. p. 89.

9 *Young India*, 9 June, 1920, *CWMG,* Vol. 17, p. 483.

10 *Young India*, 28 July, 1920, *CWMG,* Vol. 18. p. 89.

11 Judith Brown, *Gandhi's Rise to Power*, Cambridge University Press, Cambridge, 1972, p. 246.

12 For details, Hugh Owen, 'Negotiating the Lucknow Pact', *Journal of Asian Studies*, Vol. 31 (3), 1972, pp. 561-87.

13 National Archives of India, New Delhi (NAI hereafter), Home-Poll 3/1921 and KW, a note by SP O'Donnell, the secretary to the Government of India, 14 January, 1921.

14 P.C. Bamford, *Histories of the Non-Cooperation and Khilafat Movements*, Government of India, Delhi, 1925, pp. 102-03.

15 IOR, Mss. Eur. D 609(2) Zetland Collection, Ronaldshay to Monatague, 15 June, 1921.

16 Gandhi, 'The lesson of Assam', *Young India*, 15 June, 1921. Gandhi reiterated his argument in a meeting in Calcutta on 11 September, 1921 by condemning the strike fever which tended to disrupt unnecessarily the amicable relationship between the industrialists and the workers. *The Statesman*. 22 September, 1921.

17 Chauri Chaura Records, Gorokhpur, (trial) nos. 44-45, 1922 – Quoted in Shahid Amin; *Event, Metaphor, Memory: Chauri Chaura, 1922-1972*, Oxford University Press, Delhi, 1995, p. 16.

18 *Young India*, 9 January, 1930, *CWMG*, Vol. 42, pp. 376-77.

19 *Young India*, 11 March, 1930 *CWMG*, Vol. 43, p. 117.

20 Jawaharlal Nehru, *An Autobiography*, John Lane and Bodley Head, London, 1941, p. 210.

21 NMML, AICC, G-86/1930, the Congress working committee resolution adopted at Sabarmati Ashram meeting, held between 14 and 16 February, 1930.

22 *Young India*, 17 July, 1930, *CWMG*, Vol. 43, p. 358.

23 Jawaharlal Nehru, *An Autobiography*, John Lane and Bodley Head, London, 1941, p. 215.

24 Gandhi's speech at Broach, 26 March, 1930, *Young India*, 4 April, 1930, CWMG, Vol. 23, p.127.

25 IOR, Halifax Papers, Mss. Eur, C152(25), Tejbahadur Sapru to Irwin, 19 September, 1930.

26 Judith N. Brown, *Gandhi and Civil Desobedience: The Mahatma in Indian Politics, 1928-34*, Cambridge University Press, Cambridge, 1977, p.147.

27 N.C. Chaudhari, *The Autobiography of an Unknown Indian*, University of California Press, Berkeley and Los Angeles, 1968, p.400.

28 P.C. Bamford, *Histories of the Non-Cooperation and Khilafat Movements*, Govt. of India Press, 1925, p.xiii.

3

~

DO OR DIE: GANDHI'S ARTICULATION OF FREEDOM

THE ADOPTION OF A RESOLUTION ON 8 AUGUST 1942, AT GOWALIA Tank Maidan in Bombay, led to a mass movement which turned into a revolt. This call for freedom became famous as the Quit India Movement. Unlike the earlier non-cooperation and civil disobedience movements, which were basically non-violent campaigns against the British rule, the Quit India Movement was an ultimatum to the British for the final withdrawal. It was a Gandhi-led un-Gandhian way of struggle since the Mahatma exhorted to take-up arms in self-defence and resort to armed resistance against a stronger and well-equipped aggressor.

THE QUIT INDIA: A DIFFERENT POLITICAL CAMPAIGN

The Quit India Movement involved those who remained peripheral in the other past Gandhi-led movements. In a relative sense, the 1942 Quit India Movement was expansive at least in terms of participants. Politics here denotes collective action performed with a power perspective in which an attempt is constantly made to gain authority and influence over certain areas of human activity. The role of ideas is also important for they play a crucial role in political mobilization in adverse circumstances. Politics, thus defined, will be of help in capturing the mass zeal, evident during the August revolution for analytical purposes. Although it is the culmination of the Gandhi-led nationalist campaign, which began with the Non-Cooperation Movement, the Quit India resolution launched a political campaign, which was different from the earlier-ones in a number of ways. The Quit India Movement was not merely another instance of the civil disobedience campaign; it was also 'an open rebellion'. All the past satyagraha movements, writes the *Harijan,* were protests against 'the unwanted or unapproved acts' of the Raj, the authority of which was, however, conceded. Hence, the Congress 'registered protests by breaking the salt laws, forest regulations, the enforcement of section 144 Indian Penal Code, curfew orders, executive bans on meetings, etc., and [we] bowed our heads to lathis of the police who represented the collective self of the people – the government, or underwent sentences of imprisonment as model prisoners etc'. The situation, however, changed as soon as 'even the tacit recognition of the government by the people is consciously withdrawn, a government ceases to have any sanction and persons who attempt to exercise governmental authority are usurpers and no obedience is due to them and any punishment meted out having no sanction became the acts of ruffian.' The AICC resolution of 8 August, demanding, as Gandhi articulated 'that the British authority should end completely irrespective of the wishes or demands of various parties' is certainly a significant departure from the earlier practices when the authority of the government had 'political sanctions to carry out the laws such as they are, and hence was legitimate'. With the onset of the Quit India Movement, the political equation between the Government and Congress had undergone a radical change in the context of the Raj being identified as 'an usurper of authority and power'.

In such a situation, the Congress became more militant than ever. Insisting on the immediate British withdrawal, the party therefore exhorted the people,

> to refuse to recognise government officials and ... owe no obedience to them. When a policeman appears with a *lathi* or a revolver, he, having no licence to use such powers, has to be disarmed. We should not bow our heads to receiving the strokes as formerly but pull away their sticks and render them powerless. They have no authority to arrest us. Therefore the present day arrest and detention is on par with kidnapping. All our leaders have [therefore] been kidnapped?[1] .

To the Congress, the British therefore had no right whatsoever to rule India and it was a 'sacred duty' of the Congress nationalists to strengthen the anti-imperial campaign by means other than non-violence, if the situation so demanded. In order to contain 'a satanic government' the Congress nationalists were urged to attack the system of communication because 'they use[d] telegraphs and telephones for issuing their illegal fiats, railway to rush troops and armed police, [and] the trunk roads for mechanized forces'. Identifying the government officials as 'mercenaries' aiding and abetting 'a foreign interloper', the Congress appealed to the people for withdrawing any kind of social collaboration with them. As the British government degenerated into a 'fifth columnist government', the resistance to it, as the appeal went, was but 'a sacred duty' of Indians irrespective of religion, class and caste. Thus, the struggle, noted F.O. Bell, an ICS officer who served Bengal between 1930 and 1947,

> has been animated by violence and terrorism. There should be no surprise to those who preached it as an open rebellion who knew the sorry [sic] history of Mr. Gandhi's previous experiments with ahimsa who set the countryside alight with the slogan "do or die" who pledged on the emotions of callous students who commanded that when the law took its course and Congress committees ceased to function, every individual must be his own guide in the conflict and who sheltered within the party the revolutionaries and hooligans who are always ready to profit by anarchy.[2]

A cursory glance at the movement shows that the Quit India campaign was a popular nationalist upsurge that started in the name of Gandhi but went substantially beyond any confines that Gandhi may have envisaged. Ideologically, the August revolution drew upon non-violence and its concomitant value system. In its actual unfolding, however, the movement developed its own dynamics. What it reveals is the tension, prevalent between Gandhi and the participants in the context of the final assault on the imperial power. Although such a tension was there in earlier Gandhi-led movements, in the 1942 campaign it was probably more evident than ever. Hence, it is not counter-factual to argue that Gandhi was the undisputed leader of the movement over which he had little command.

THE QUIT INDIA RESOLUTION AND ITS AFTERMATH

The Quit India Resolution provoked mass arrest and the alien state which was stronger than ever due to her military preparedness in the context of the war, left no stone unturned to assert its authority. Not only was there an organized army at its disposal, the all-pervasive imperial state was also getting ready to launch a pre-emptive strike against the Congress. In fact since 1940, the Government of India had warned the provincial government of a possible political campaign challenging the British power in India. The reason was simple: in the context of the war crisis, the state in India was vulnerable and hence it was a golden opportunity for 'the Congress to strike it down when it is the weakest'. Strategically, the situation was ripe for a full-scale political movement, and therefore an immediate state action was warranted to nip the campaign in the bud. Although Lord Louis Linlithgow wanted to crush the Congress if it threw down a gauntlet to the government during the war, there was significant opposition from his colleagues who did not think it prudent on the part of the government. Challenging Linlithgow's assessment of the situation as 'flawed and short-sighted', Edward Benthall, an important member of the viceroy's council, asked the government not to provoke a political campaign by unleashing repression since 'the Congress leaders do not want to embark upon civil disobedience for the following reasons:

> (a) it might lead to communal trouble; (b) the masses are not prepared for such action now and indeed the present economic prosperity of the cultivators and others is not conducive to civil disobedience; (c) the businessmen who have influence in the Congress are doing well out of the war; (d) there is a general desire for a settlement [with the British] as opposed to civil

> disobedience which, if launched, would postpone any possibility of a settlement; and (e) civil disobedience would lead to violence which would discredit Gandhi in the eyes of the world.[3]

Although the situation was not alarming per se, the Executive Council urged the viceroy to streamline the administration in view of the probable mass-discontent due to the imminent economic crisis in the context of the war. Benthall's advice was most appropriate given the simmering of tension in the provinces due to the fact that 'India's participation in the war was purely a British act imposed on the Indian people without the consent of their representatives'. In such a volatile situation, the Congress leaders, he apprehended, 'may find themselves pushed into civil disobedience against their will and every resolution or pronouncement they make, to some degree makes it more difficult for them to remain inactive'.

Benthall's apprehension was not entirely unfounded because there was constant Left pressure for action. Moreover, Gandhi realized that without another anti-British campaign, it would be difficult to manage the youth members of the Congress who started looking towards communism. The 1940 Ramgarh session of Congress resolved to undertake a civil disobedience as soon as the party considered it fit enough for the same, and left entirely with Gandhi the form and timing of the movement. Gandhi agreed on the condition that he would select individuals participating in the first phase of the campaign, as he wanted people he could trust. Thus started probably the most limited and largely ineffective satyagraha in the history of India's freedom struggle. For Gandhi, however, the movement though restrained, was significant because the anti-war pronouncement of the satyagrahis registered hostility to a war waged without consulting the Indians; and since it was non-violent, the campaign would not provoke a major British crackdown on the nationalists. The 1940-41 satyagraha, despite its tremendous symbolical significance hardly evoked interests among the people. In its four different phases (between October 1940 and October 1941) the movement reached its peak in April 1941 when 20,000 satyagrahis courted arrests. In relation to the total membership of the Congress, the number was insignificant and hence some Congressmen identified the movement as a failure. In a statement published in *The Hindu,* a pro-Congress daily, the leading Congressmen from UP, Tamil Nadu, Bengal and Bihar, urged Gandhi to call-off the campaign. The Mahatma was, however, unmoved and declared that 'satyagraha must neither be withdrawn nor expanded into a mass movement, as some desired, since mass action would *embarrass the government* (emphasis added), and at this stage without communal unity is an invitation to civil war.'

The individual satyagraha petered out gradually and by the end of 1941, it was virtually over. Though India joined the war by being part of the British Empire, it had brought, on the balance, gains rather than losses for a substantial section of the population. The rise in agricultural prices was yet not very sharp and the peasantry had therefore no reason to feel aggrieved. Indian industrial development received a major boost due to the war demand, reducing imports significantly and forced reliance on indigenous products. Employment in Indian industries rose by 31 per cent between 1939 and 1942. Labour unrest was kept in check 'by substantial dearness allowances and supply of essential goods at subsidized rates'. For Indian businessmen and traders in general, war meant an opportunity for quick profits, particularly so long as it remained distant and did not involve the threat of destruction of property through aerial bombardment or evacuation.

The political situation in the country, however, changed dramatically with the Japanese conquest of Singapore in February and Rangoon in March 1942. With the rapid Japanese advance in the winter of 1941-42, it was widely believed that 'India's safeguard in the war ... was lost. After the fall of Singapore, the Bay of Bengal lay open. When Rangoon fell ..., it seemed as if the tide of Japanese conquest, which had flowed so swiftly and irresistibly over Malaya and then Burma – only yesterday a province of the Indian empire – would soon be sweeping into Bengal and Madras'.[4] Although there was less immediate alarm in Delhi and Bombay due to sheer distance from the Eastern war front, it seemed rather possible, as a note from the Eastern Command apprehended, 'that Japanese army might be able to penetrate as deeply and quickly into India as they had into Malaya and Burma'. The British administration was visibly alarmed. A panic-stricken central intelligence officer at Madras thus recorded,

> The grave news from Malaya and the Far East has entirely eclipsed the reports of Allied successes in Russia and Libya and public confidence in the might of Great Britain and the USA has, I think, deteriorated considerably. ... There has been much loose talk regarding war developments and many wild rumours have been current. One of the most recent of these is that some Indian Regiments in Malaya have mutinied and gone over to the enemy after shooting their British officers. A considerable

> number of people, mostly Indian women and children have left Madras during the fortnight and in many families, arrangements have been made to vacate the city should the present situation deteriorate.[5]

Not only was there preparation for evacuation of the British, the Government of India issued an order to the effect that 'in the event of Bengal being overrun by the Japanese, all officers of district rank and below in all departments were to remain at their posts to administer the district for the good of the people under the control of the enemy.' Furthermore, the government took ample care to suppress the news of the Japanese victory in the war. Simultaneously, with the increasing military preparedness in view of an impending Japanese attack, the India Office felt obliged to make some gestures to win over Indian public opinion. The viceroy was, however, opposed to the idea of devising a formula to ensure the cooperation of the Indian political parties, Congress in particular. In his view, the Congress was a party of 'ruthless politicians', and hence he did not believe that any new move from their part would change India's involvement in the war. He also felt that further transfer of power to Indians would encourage, what he called 'quisling activities' which he substantiated by reference to a note from military authorities in eastern India reporting that 'there is large and dangerous potential fifth column' in Bengal, Assam, Bihar and Orissa and that indeed potential of pro-enemy sympathy and activity in eastern India is enormous.

Apart from this there was international pressure too. The US President Theodore Roosevelt, raised the question of Indian political reform during his talk with Winston Churchill in December 1941; in February 1942, Chiang-Kai-Shek during his trip to India publicly expressed sympathy for 'India's aspiration for freedom'. For L.S. Amery, the secretary of state for India, the decision to send the Cripps Mission was 'to answer the charge that our policy in India is inconsistent with our general profession about fighting for freedom as well as the even more humiliating charge that if we are prepared to make concession to India now, it is simply the result of a decadent imperialism realizing that the game is up'. The announcement of the Cripps Mission was essentially a politically expedient device in so far as the Raj was concerned. However, the draft declaration was certainly a positive drive towards resolving the constitutional deadlock by promising post-war dominion status with the right of secession, a constitution making body, elected by provincial legislatures, with individual provinces being given the right not to join it and with states being invited to appoint representatives. Linlithgow threatened to resign because he was unhappy with the draft declaration, which was, he thought, unnecessary during the war crisis. Churchill while drawing his attention to its effect on the world opinion, especially the Americans, explained that 'it would be impossible owing to unfortunate rumours and publicity, and the general American outlook, to stand on a purely negative attitude and the Cripps Mission is indispensable to prove our honesty of purpose. ... If it is rejected by the Indian parties ... our sincerity will be proved to the world'.[6] The Cripps Mission was finally withdrawn for not adequately consulting Linlithgow and the Commander-in-Chief Wavell who expressed concern that Cripps was conceding far too real power to the Congress. That the appointment of the Cripps

Mission was essentially a strategy to win the British allies was evident when Churchill congratulated Strafford Cripps on his success in proving how great the British desire to reach a settlement was. The effect throughout and in the United States has been wholly beneficial.

Whatever the reasons, the failure of the Cripps Mission reveals the attitude of the British towards the Congress and future political movement under Gandhi's leadership. During the Non-Cooperation and Civil Disobedience Movements, the British authority was manifestly keen to negotiate with Gandhi at least before the onset of the campaign. In 1942, their attitude had changed dramatically and under no circumstances, the viceroy and his executive council were inclined to open a dialogue with the Congress leadership. The authority became more stern with the Congress threat to start a mass struggle on non-violent lines on the widest possible scale unless the demand of 'the immediate withdrawal of the British power from India' was met. Gandhi persuaded himself, as Tottenham, the home secretary, Government of India, reminiscensed, 'that the situation gave him an unrivalled opportunity to obtain full independence for India in view of the British difficulty in the war following the Japanese success in the eastern front'. Moreover, there were indications that 'dangerous preparations being pushed by the Congress in the provinces for immediate action, for cutting of telegraph wires, interference with railway services, the organizing of strikes, the tampering with the loyalty of government servants, the picketing of troops and a wide variety of similar unlawful and nefarious activities'. Hence it was agreed upon as an immediate crackdown on the Congress leadership because any delay would present to the Congress an opportunity to perfect its plans before striking openly. In its emergency meeting of 8 August 1942, the Executive Council thus decided that, (i) Gandhi and the members of the working committee should be arrested immediately in Bombay and interned; (ii) the agreed orders for the imposition of control on the press should be issued immediately; (iii) provincial and All India Congress committees to be declared unlawful; offices and funds seized and all potential organizers arrested; and (iv) if these measures fail to stultify civil disobedience, Congress as a whole will be declared unlawful association and emergency power to be promulgated giving fullest powers for dealing with all forms of Congress activity. The action taken, it was officially announced, was not punitive but preventive and was directed against those involved in a movement, which if successful, must cripple India's war effort and gravely prejudice the cause of the United Nations.

Within hours of the passage of the Quit India Resolution, the British government arrested all the Congress leaders. The arrests were made not only at the all India, but provincial and district levels too, and clamped down on the organization to disable it from functioning. Questions were raised in American and British ruling circles about the appropriateness of these measures and Amery, who was a war cabinet member as well, however, was obliged to explain in public why such penal measures were necessary. In a BBC broadcast from London, he defended the Government of India's decision for a crackdown on the Congress because:

> in the face of such a challenge, and of such a menace, there

> could be only one answer. That was for the Government of India to take firm and above all, swift action to deal with its authors before their preparedness were further advanced or before the campaign could gain momentum. ... by their prompt and resolute action, the Government of India saved India and the Allied cause from a grave disaster.[7]

He also justified the arrest of the Congress leaders since

> . . . the success of the proposed campaign would paralyse not only the ordinary civil administration of India but the whole war effort. It would stop the output of munitions, the construction of aerodromes and above all, shatters against air attack; it would put an end to recruiting; it would immobilize the forces.
>
> The war preparation would have suffered tremendously without incarcerating the leading Congressmen who were reported to have been "fomenting" strikes not only in industry and commerce, but in the administration, law courts, schools and colleges, the interruption of traffic and public utility services, the cutting of telegraph and telephone wires, the picketing of troops and recruiting stations.[8]

Though these kinds of activities were never authorized by the Congress in advance of 8 August, Amery 'inadvertently lent them credibility as Congress policy' by charting it out as clearly as possible. With a wide publicity of the broadcast in the Indian newspapers, the confusion and uncertainty felt by the ordinary Congressmen and their sympathizers was suddenly ended. Amery became 'the chief instrument in broadcasting the supposed Congress programme; what he said was avidly believed by the people. As a result, what Amery said had been the Congress plan 'was accepted as the Congress plan by indignant demonstrators groping for direction. Many wanted to take extreme measures; Amery's charge gave them an excuse for taking them in the name of the Congress. ... what Amery claimed to have prevented, he instead helped to bring about.'[9]

Despite his meticulous plan for press censorship, Amery's speech was widely hailed as that radicalizing text which galvanized the disparate masses into action. Hence, it is not a strange coincidence that the mass unrest hit the nation after the publication of the broadcast in the press on 10 August 1942. In his zeal to convince the allies by providing an inventory of the proposed plan of sabotaging the war effort, Amery unknowingly provided the nationalists with a radicalizing text which probably unleashed the whole process of moving a mass of strangers to united political action under circumstances, favourable to the Congress call. In this respect, this particular speech of the secretary of state appeared decisive in the absence of the Congress instruction regarding the way, the movement was to be organized; and thus made easy for the Congress leaders to exonerate their responsibility towards 'the disturbances'. The chief irony of 1942 was therefore, as Greenough aptly puts, 'that the awesome power of the press to inspire united action was unleashed by the British government; the radicalizing text was the composition of Leopold Amery, not Mahatma Gandhi'.[10]

THE CONGRESS PREPAREDNESS

The Congress became militant and hence the wave of insurrection activity. Deviating from non-violence, the Congress volunteers resorted to violence indiscriminately on various occasions. The state was equally repressive in view, *inter alia,* of its ready access to an organized army, and yet 'the open rebellion' assumed massive proportions in areas where the state appeared to have been seriously undermined. In the beginning, the movement was widespread, affecting almost every corner of the country; its organization was so well-entrenched that the British left no stone unturned to contain the upsurge which, in a way, caught the administration by surprise. So alarmed and panic-stricken was the administration especially in the context of a probable Japanese attack that the viceroy demanded a military solution.

Despite the fear of a severe military clampdown on the participants, the movement acquired the characteristics of a rebellion with a strong organizational backing. What it reveals is that though the Congress was outlawed and its organization was in disarray in the provinces, due to, among other reasons, factional squabbles, the call for an open rebellion organized the masses largely with a single aim of overthrowing the British rule in India. How big was the Congress organization in terms of membership on the eve of the August revolution? It is true that the drive for membership was not as effective as it was in the case of the earlier nation-wide campaigns, notably, the non-cooperation and civil disobedience, though the AICC endeavoured constantly to enlist 'four anna' members. In circulars to the Provincial Congress Committes (PCC), in April 1940, the Congress High Command underlined the need of expanding the organizational network at the grassroots 'to conduct propaganda on Congress policies and the programme of satyagraha'. The effort paid off and by May, there was considerable enthusiasm for satyagraha, but the Congress was not in a satisfactory condition. What caused consternation to the Congress President, Maulana Azad, was the lukewarm response to the Gandhian call of individual satyagraha. Except United Provinces (UP) PCC, none of the provincial wings of the Congress succeeded in enrolling the allotted number of satyagrahis. In fact, there was a sharp decline in membership. The dramatic decrease in membership from 4.5 million in 1938-39 to as low as 1.4 million is probably enough to prove that Congress became terribly unpopular in course of time.[11] Therefore, the Quit India declaration, as a commentator argues, was 'a cry of despair' or a cry 'of a party in panic'. The interpretation seems plausible given the decline in membership. What is not explained in the gradual decrease of membership is why such a weak organization became formidable with the declaration of the Quit India demand. Warning that the administration should not feel complacent in view of the membership decline, the Intelligence Bureau made a necessary distinction between 'Congress membership figures' and 'Congress influence'. While attributing the membership decline to (i) failure to renew membership; (ii) the defection of the leftist from the Congress; and (iii) success in containing the bogus membership, the official report cautioned that 'it would be unsafe to assume that Congress has become unpopular or noticeably lost its influence over the masses in provinces where it previously held undisputed sway'. Moreover, the anti-Congress activities of the Muslim League, the Hindu Mahasabha and other political parties increased appreciably during the past year and were to some extent responsible for detaching 'waverers' from active association with the Congress. Although the decline of membership was never accepted as a right yardstick to judge the party's strength, to the British administration, the information was useful to propagate the idea that Congress popularity as a nationalist anti-British party was on the decline and hence, the Congress had no moral right to speak for India as a whole.

THE QUIT INDIA RESOLUTION

The apparent decline in membership meant nothing serious in so far as the movement that followed after the adoption of the resolution was concerned. What became famous as the August movement was the culmination of a process that began with the 1940 Ramgarh session of the AICC. Though there was a noticeable lack of enthusiasm of the Congress volunteers in conducting the individual satyagraha, the Ramgarh resolution was a significant step towards the adoption of the Quit India Resolution. By insisting on an immediate British withdrawal, Gandhi and his associates were reported to have sent signals for the ultimate countdown. The governor general thus asked the secretary of state to issue an order to the effect that 'civil disobedience in time of war will not be permitted and/or a formal warning to them that they will not be permitted to proceed with preparations for civil disobedience'. Justifying a preventive measure because 'there is, however, no sign of any modification in stiffness of Gandhi's attitude or excessive nature of Congress claims as embodied in Ramgarh resolution with which there is no reason to doubt that he identifies himself,' the governor general further felt the need to extend the section proclamation to India as a whole. He saw a silver lining in the opposition of 'the moderate right wingers such as Birla & Co.' who expressed dissatisfaction with the Congress militancy, which appeared temporary, given the intimate association between the

Congress and the big-business especially in the context of the August movement.

What became Allahabad resolution (1 May 1942) was principally a reiteration of the 1940 list of Congress demands. The intercepted resolution, drafted by Gandhi, which was discussed by the AICC at its Allahabad session (27 April, 1942) (i) demanded 'an immediate British withdrawal'; (ii) declared that 'no foreign assistance needed for the freedom of this country'; and (iii) announced 'if Japan invaded India it shall meet with non-violent resistance'. During the discussion, there occurred an apparent rift among the CWC members regarding the attitude towards the Japanese. Jawaharlal Nehru opposing the fascist aggression, wanted the AICC to condemn the Japanese in categorical terms because 'we do not embarrass the British war effort because that in itself would mean an aid to the invader'. What caused alarm to Nehru was Gandhi's feeling that Japan and Germany will win, a feeling expressed clearly in Bapu's statement that if India were freed, her first step will probably be to negotiate with Japan, and India bears no enmity with Japan. Distancing himself from what appeared to be Gandhi's position, Nehru thus emphatically argued that 'if Bapu's approach is accepted we become passive partners of the Axis powers'. This would equally be damaging for India's freedom struggle since 'the Allied countries will have a feeling that we are their enemies'; so the sympathy with the Japanese, in whatever form, was suicidal. As Nehru further elaborated, 'Japan is an imperialist country [and] conquest of India is in their plan.'[12] Vallabhbhai Patel and Maulana Azad saw Nehru's points but found, however, unnecessary to dissociate from Gandhi's approach.

Moreover, the Allies did not play the expected role in so far as India's freedom struggle was concerned; instead, they declined to accord importance to India's freedom given the war crisis. Although the Cripps Mission was publicized as a significant step towards the British withdrawal, in reality, it was an attempt to solicit the Congress cooperation in the British war effort by demanding cessation of political activities and consequently a complete Congress surrender to the British authority in India. Thus, Patel was not inclined to negotiate with the British at all especially after what he called 'the repeated insults heaped upon us'. Conceding Patel's argument, Rajendra Prasad too expressed his support for 'Bapu's position' as the only practicable means to attain the British withdrawal from India; hence, he urged the Congressmen 'to strengthen Bapu's hands' forgetting the division among them. Azad did not seem perturbed about the possibility of a Japanese aggression because nationalism was strong enough to contain any imperialist design, however powerful physically.

The proposed resolution sought to cover the points contained in Gandhi's draft, but the approach was different. The discussion showed that the division of opinion revealed in the earlier deliberations still persisted. Nehru was therefore asked to prepare a draft of his own, and Rajendra Prasad, the Congress president, prepared another following Bapu's instruction *in toto*. The CWC was divided when the two drafts were put to vote. Given the fact that independence was a greater cause than anything else, the Congress president urged his colleagues to remain united in the context probably of 'the last battle for freedom'; his call yielded result since the resolution which was approved unanimously by the AICC on

1 May 1942 underlined Nehru's concern for equivocal condemnation for the Axis design, if there was any, to conquer India. Instead of mentioning the name of a particular country, the 1 May resolution

> repudiates the idea that freedom can come to India through interference or invasion by any foreign nation. . . . In case, an invasion takes place, it must be resisted . . . [through] non-violent non-cooperation . . . [Moreover], the All India Congress Committee is convinced that India will attain her freedom through her own strength, and will retain it likewise.[13]

Notwithstanding the differences among the Congressmen, the Allahabad resolution articulated in clear terms the Congress attitude towards the Japanese and possible steps in case of another imperialist aggression. Nehru was happy for having successfully persuaded his colleagues to adopt a resolution condemning Fascism which, he thought, was most apt given the Japanese help in organizing the Indian National Army (INA) under the stewardship of Subhas Chandra Bose as an alternative front in India's freedom struggle. So, it was not surprising that the Wardha resolution adopted on 14 July 1942, linked the defeat of Fascism to India's freedom; it, thus, declared,

> British rule in India must end immediately, not merely because foreign domination even at its best is an evil in itself and a continuing injury to the subject people, but because India in bondage can play no effective part in defending herself and in affecting the fortunes of the war that is desolating humanity. The freedom of India is thus necessary not only in the interest of India but also for the safety of the world and for the ending of Nazism, Fascism, militarism and other forms of imperialism and the aggression of one nation over another.

> The Congress would be pleased with the British power if it accepts the very reasonable and just proposal herein made; . . . [otherwise], the Congress will then be reluctantly compelled to utilise the non-violent strength it might have gathered since 1920 when it adopted non-violence as part of its policy for the vindication of the political rights and liberty.[14]

By far the most militant, the Wardha resolution caused alarm to the authority, which already began charting out measures to preempt the Congress strike. It was clear, as Benthall suggested, that the Congress was aiming at probably 'the most devastating strike' the British had ever experienced. The Congress leadership was more militant than ever. While interpreting the nature of the forthcoming movement, as enunciated by the Wardha resolution, Nehru was reported to have said,

> The Mahatma's new movement would impose no restrictions as has been the case in the previous movements of 1920 and 1930. Everyone would be free to use his own weapons according to his own choice. Revolutionaries could do as they pleased and also kisans and labour leaders. The Mahatma was not prepared to call off the movement on account of the acts of such people. ... If the people took over government buildings, courts, police stations and other places under risk of repression, this too would be our method of assisting in the movement. Mahatma Gandhi was no longer prepared to look upon such acts as "Himalayan blunders" as he had done in the past.[15]

The proposed Congress confrontation with the British appeared disastrous to the Raj primarily because of the British difficulty in containing the domestic agitation in the context of the war crisis. Hence Linlithgow, sought the Executive

Council's permission to undertake steps in advance, so that the movement could be destroyed before it took off. Defending the viceroy, the Executive Council asked him to publicize 'the views and intentions of Gandhi and the Congress High Command' in order precisely to prove that the more recent utterances of the Congress leaders interpreting the intention of the Wardha resolution, were seditious enough to warrant immediate action against them. India Office gave the viceroy a free hand in tackling 'the domestic disturbances' and thus Amery wrote, 'the only answer to my mind in such a situation is to act at once, take up the challenge to our authority and arrest the working committee and many more as you think necessary to show that in India we mean business.' Without such drastic measures as 'immediate arrest and prosecution and very drastic punishment', the movement, Amery apprehended, would assume devastating magnitudes since its object was 'to create a general atmosphere of defiance of government and of ill-feeling in the course of which the government will be driven to a series of action which will be increasingly misrepresented in order to fan the flame of resistance and to create the kind of situation in which the American and some of our people will begin to say that there is already a civil war in India and that things cannot be worse if we give Congress what they demanded'. That the secretary of state left no stone unturned in combating the Congress assault in all seriousness was made clear through his order to take prompt measures with the press to prevent the circulation of resolutions or of information about Congress generally. This may necessitate putting an end to the gentleman's agreement, but that cannot be helped.

The final countdown began because the Congress leadership, including Gandhi, appealed to the PCCs to remain united in the context of the last battle for freedom. In its circular to the PCCs on the eve of the Quit India call, the AICC urged their volunteers to stick to non-violence while conducting the campaign. J.B. Kripalani, the Congress secretary, however, expressed anxiety if an organizationally weak Congress was equipped to carry on the struggle to a successful conclusion. A majority of the Congress members were however, inclined to believe that the masses were ready for the final battle and 'the Congress influence' was at its peak despite the sudden dwindling of Congress membership. The situation was alarming as anti-war sentiments had a firm grip over the masses and the Government of India's Home Department appeared panic-stricken since the government was identified as treacherously dishonest and deceitful, and hence nobody should pay subscription for war, nobody should enlist in the government forces, nobody should pay rent and canal dues. Nehru, after his trip to the United Provinces was convinced that the forthcoming campaign was likely to attain the goal in view of the emotional attachment of the people with the cause of 'independence' and the role of Gandhi in galvanizing the masses into action. In his words,

> the mood of the country had changed, and from a sullen passivity it rose to a pitch of excitement and expectation. Events were not waiting for a Congress decision or resolution; they had been pushed forward by Gandhiji's utterances and now they were moving onwards with their momentum. It was clear that, whether Gandhiji was right or wrong, he had crystallized the prevailing mood of the people. There was a desperateness in it,

> and emotional urge which gave second place to logic and reason and a calm consideration of the consequences of action.[16]

On 8 August 1942, the AICC met in Bombay and approved what became famous as the Quit India Resolution. Harping on the formula on the familiar theme of the final British withdrawal from India, the resolution runs thus,

> The perils of today . . . necessitates the independence of India and the ending of British domination. No future promises or grievances can affect the present situation or meet that peril. They cannot produce the needed psychological effect on the mind of the masses. Only the glow of freedom now can release that energy and enthusiasm of millions of people, which will immediately transform the nature of the war.
>
> The AICC therefore repeats with all emphasis the demand for the withdrawal of the British power from India. . . . The Committee appeals to the people of India to face the dangers and hardships that will fall to their lot with courage and endurance and to hold them together under the leadership of Gandhi and carry out his instructions as disciplined soldiers of Indian freedom. They must remember that non-violence is the basis of this movement.[17]

The first few paragraphs of the resolution reiterate the spirit of both Allahabad and Wardha resolutions. For the Congress, India's independence was contingent on the British withdrawal and hence the resolution was passed accordingly. What however, was different was the Congress instruction to the effect of asking the participants to act independently in the forthcoming struggle in case of the arrests of the leaders. Gandhi appealed to the people to follow the *mantra,* Do or Die:

> we shall either free India or die in the attempt; we shall not live to see the perpetuation of our slavery. Every true Congressmen or [Congress] women will join the struggle with an inflexible determination not to remain alive to see the country in bondage and slavery. [18]

In a message to the nation just before his arrest, Gandhi spelt the task more precisely. Reiterating his faith in non-violence, he thus elaborated,

> everyone is free to go the fullest length under ahimsa; complete deadlock by strikes and other non-violent means; satyagrahis must go out to die not to live; they must seek and face death; it is only when individuals go out to die that the nation will survive. Karenge Ya Marenge [We will do or die].[19]

Neither the AICC resolution nor Gandhi's last message was allowed to be reported by the press. So, there was less trouble especially immediately after the incarceration of the entire Congress leadership including Gandhi. The government strategy seemed to have worked in snatching the wind away from the Congress sail, as Tottenham misconstrued by preventing the Congress message getting across to the people. Although there were protest marches in Bombay, Gujarat and Bengal, they did not pose a serious threat to the British administration. In other words, the decision to gag the press paid off at least initially and a confident viceroy sought the secretary of state's permission to deport Gandhi, in particular, to save India from further crisis. The idea of deporting Gandhi was in his agenda since the adoption of the Wardha resolution on 14 July 1942. When Linlithgow put it before the Executive Council for discussion, they unanimously and vigorously opposed it as this would cause bad reactions in India and would result in Gandhi staging a fast abroad, with a consequent crop of speculation, rumours about his ill-treatment etc. Not convinced in view of the strong opposition of the majority of the Executive Council members, Amery did not press the issue. There were also differences of opinion at the highest level of British administration as to whether Gandhi should be released if he undertook a fast unto death. The viceroy held the view that Gandhi should not be set free 'even if he fasted to death'. All the governors except that of Sind opposed the viceroy vehemently. R. Lumley, the governor of Bombay, for instance, was convinced that to allow Gandhi to die in detention would be the 'gravest blunder'. The governor of the Central Provinces was 'emphatically of the opinion that local reactions would be most unfavourable. . . . We would be left with no friends in India and even some of the Indian members of the Superior Services will turn against us.' And hence, he urged the viceroy 'that Gandhi should be released and restricted to Sevagram if he embarks on a fast'.[20] Apprehending the disastrous consequences of Gandhi's death during the imprisonment, Churchill's war cabinet appeared inclined to shift Gandhi to his ashram in case of fast, provided 'he could still be isolated from the outside world at Sevagram'. As there was no categorical support for his view at the highest level of the Raj, Linlithgow had no alternative but to accept that 'we must be prepared in the event of a fast to set Gandhi at liberty (leaving it to himself to decide where he wants to go or whether he prefers to remain in Aga Khan's house at Poona) once fast begins to endanger his life and I feel, in the circumstances, this is the best alternative', one could think.

With the arrest of the Congress leaders, the movement, Linlithgow felt, would fizzle out soon. In his letter to Amery, he thus conveyed 'we may congratulate ourselves upon our having struck at Congress before their preparations are completed'. He further added, 'we have far more important reason to be thankful: that we have brought on this business at a time when the war position is not such as to offer any immediate threat to India whether from the West or from the East.' He was emphatic that without such pre-emptive arrests, the situation could have been worse because 'Gandhi's plan was to wait for bad war news before raising the standard of revolt'.[21]

To stop the publication of news regarding arrests and the development of the movement, the Government of India imposed press censorship. Defending the decision, Reginald Maxwell, the Home Member, argued that two objective considerations governed the government's decision in this regard. Firstly, disorder of this character 'are infectious and news of what has occurred in one place may lead to its repetition in a number of other places which might otherwise have remained quiet'. And, secondly, 'much that has occurred would, if it were known to the enemy, be of great value to his plans for an invasion of this country'. In view of the war crisis, the plan for censorship was probably apt, but it would be a mistake, as Tottenham warned, 'to attempt any such general pre-censorship order on the press in India as a whole. It would annoy the Press intensely – even the pro-British Press – and would probably result in our losing quite an appreciable amount of useful spontaneous criticism of the Congress plan.' Challenging the government policy, fourteen of the Calcutta newspapers, excluding the loyalist *The Statesman* and *The Star of India,* ceased publication indefinitely. Although the viceroy seemed happy because the press, to him, was 'a great nuisance', some of the Executive Council members were inclined to withdraw the restriction in phases precisely to dispel the popular fear that it would contribute to the emergence of a state, 'not different from a fascist one'. There was, in fact, a serious argument, as M.O. Carter, the secretary to the governor of Bengal, put forward in favour of a gradual withdrawal of restriction. 'The stopping of publication for one week was', as Carter elaborated, 'intended to give full force to the campaign of leafleting, i.e. to force the public to read the leaflets.' There were reasons to be alarmed because the printing and distribution of leaflets was arranged with support of the nationalist press. By drawing attention to the disastrous consequences of such a campaign aiming at 'spreading alarm and panic by means of false rumours and exaggerated statements', Carter also underlined the importance of streamlining the overall intelligence network in the country. The suggestion did not appear feasible because it was felt that any kind of concession to the press would mean the weakening of government's determination.

Not only was the press generally sympathetic to the Congress cause, the Indian big-business too was ready to support the movement. In fact, with the beginning of individual satyagraha following the 1940 Ramgarh resolution, Indian business magnates were reported to have appreciated the Congress demand for 'swadeshi', and naturally the Indian mill owners actively supported a movement so advantageous to their interests. For any movement to succeed what is required most is financial backing and thus 'the Congress has relied and still relies on', the viceroy had no doubt, 'the large Indian financial and commercial interests for support, both political and financial'. The Congress needed that support to maintain its position and influence 'and is only too glad to receive it notwithstanding its professed democratic if not socialistic creed'. Big industry, on the other hand, 'is only too willing to furnish that support in ample measure so as to have the advantage of the Congress organization and machine on its side and as a valuable insurance for the future.' Hence, the viceroy concluded, 'it suits both sides equally well to work up an insistent agitation for the liquidation of British business and commercial interests in India'. What thus governed the intimate association between the big-business houses and Congress was conditioned largely, if not exclusively, by the possibility of mutual advantage: on the part of the Congress, money was 'a necessary expedient to provide the sinews of war'. The Congress had no difficulty to raise money from the Congress sympathizers among the trading community as and when the need arose. Just on the eve of the Quit India declaration, the Congress was reported to have collected thirty lakh rupees (three million) from renowned mill owners like Birla, Tata, Dalmia, Singhania and others including mill owners of Ahmedabad. Similarly, in Bombay, the mill owners, particularly from the Marwari and Gujarati community, contributed significantly to the funds that were collected by Vallabhbhai Patel before the movement started. Not only did the intelligence bureau fail to ascertain where this money was deposited, there was also no trace of these transactions. In fact, the big-business support to the open rebellion despite its adverse effect on production per se was attributed to the possible Japanese victory. The UP central intelligence officer thus wrote 'that the degree of financial backing for Congress has been in direct proportion to the morale of the Hindus and their belief in the invasion of India by the Japanese and the breakdown of the British government.'

There were two ways in which the big business tried to help the open rebellion: on the one hand, they were reported to have encouraged strikes despite the loss involved, to (a) champion the non-violent struggle; and (b) embarrass the British administration which was held responsible for such a breakdown. In fact, the Ahmedabad mill owners who, as an intelligence bureau report suggests, had decided to encourage strikes in their mills and pay salary for two months to the workers. On the other hand, there were evidences to show that the industrialists provided the Congress with funds. The Indian Chamber of Commerce (ICC), controlled by Birla brothers found the movement inevitable given the British intransigence in undertaking a fruitful dialogue with the Congress. In a resolution, adopted on 10 August 1942, at its meeting in Calcutta, the ICC expressed affinity with Gandhi and the movement, and agreed to sanction money to the Marwari Relief Committee,[22] which was, as the bureau report demonstrates, nothing but a garb to extend monetary help to the movement and its organization. Apart from its contribution, the ICC asked its constituents to financially help the movement as and when needed. Thus Karan Chand Thaper of the Thaper Brothers Ltd, an important Calcutta-based Punjabi business house, 'gave Rs. 10,000 to Jai Prakash Narain' who was assured of more financial help from the same source. S.J. Desai, the secretary of the ICC, was authorized to draw money any time for the Congress activity in view of its urgency. Likewise, the Bengal National Chamber of Commerce (BNCC) though declined considerably with the consolidation of the Marwari business interests through the ICC, deplored that 'the Government of India should not have precipitated in a crisis by not giving an opportunity to Mahatma Gandhi to come in contact' with the viceroy and explore the possibilities of a solution of the 'political deadlock'. Holding the British government responsible for the serious disruption in trade and commerce in several industrial centres of India, the BNCC urged the administration to initiate a dialogue with the Congress leadership as the only way to defuse this grave crisis. Generally sympathetic to the Congress, the BNCC too was identified as another source for funding. In his daily report, the deputy commissioner of police, Calcutta, advised the government to freeze the BNCC capital for alleged financial support to the rebellion.

The Congress leadership governed by the logic of national democracy, was generally found to support the Indian industrialists even at the cost of damaging its prospect among the workers. In order to secure India's economic future, the Congress was inclined to gamble in favour of the industrialists; while the business houses invested in Congress presumably to ascertain its future in the days to come when the Congress was likely to rule the state. There was an immediate benefit too, for Gandhi was alleged to have been instrumental at least on more than four or five big occasions for the personal benefit of certain Hindu millionaires in Calcutta and Bombay. So, the apparent intimacy between the Congress and the business establishments was largely conditioned by the prospect of mutual benefit to both the actors who strove to defend their respective interests out of such an association.

OPPOSITION TO THE QUIT INDIA RESOLUTION

Although the 1947 transfer of power is the culmination of various movements launched by the Indian National Congress, the 1942 August revolution is perhaps the greatest mass mobilization, based on nationalism. Notwithstanding the fact that Gandhi reigned supreme during the movement, the Quit India Resolution provoked opposition to the decision from among his colleagues within the Congress and other major political parties. In a way, the adoption of this resolution is a watershed in India's nationalist movement for a variety of reasons. First, the Quit India call was an ultimatum to the British which itself is significant given that in neither the non-cooperation nor civil disobedience campaign, the Congress insisted on a complete British withdrawal from India. Moreover, the campaign began when the apprehension of a Japanese invasion gripped the Raj following especially the downfall of Malaya and Singapore. This downfall had disastrous implications on the British Indian Army, stationed in the Rangoon front and elsewhere, and more particularly on the public opinion in India, underlining the probable Congress victory against the British which lost its credibility completely. The second consequence of the August resolution is more important because it brought out, in clear terms, the schism within the political parties involved in the nationalist struggle. Not only does the event highlight the ideological differences between the Congress and other contending parties, it also draws our attention to the division within the Congress over fundamental issues relating to the Hindu-Muslim question.

The 8 August resolution was adopted when the Congress was already divided following the acceptance of the 14 July Wardha resolution. Four prominent Congress activists, headed by C. Rajagopalachari, criticized the resolution on the ground that British withdrawal without a Hindu-Muslim settlement would lead to anarchy. They, thus, argued, 'it is essential that before a demand for withdrawal can be reasonably made, the major political organizations of this country namely, the Indian National Congress and the Muslim League, should evolve a joint plan with regard to the provisional government which can take over power and preserve the continuity of the state'.

The Hindu Mahasabha upheld its decision to cooperate with the British during the war despite the so-called governmental policy of Muslim-appeasement. Accordingly, it was decided to challenge the open rebellion, launched by the Congress, which would undoubtedly cripple the British war effort. In an appeal to the people, B.S. Moonjee, the president defended the need to abstain from the movement damaging 'the possibility of the rise of an agreed-constitutional system by undertaking such an undemocratic campaign'. The Hindu Mahasabha's decision to withdraw participation was conditioned largely by consideration that opposition to the war efforts was tantamount to supporting the Axis powers, particularly the Japanese; the Communist Party of India (CPI) defended its arguments condemning the open rebellion by drawing upon the ideological implications of joining the fascist camp. In other words, for the CPI, the challenge to the state power through a mass mobilization was unwarranted at a time when the fascist aggression was imminent.

> The war is India's great opportunity to fight for national liberation, no more in isolation, no more single-handed but as part of the battle for world liberation. It is the war of the Soviet peoples whom we pledged to support against an imperialist attack. It is the war of the heroic Chinese people whose five years of lone struggle we have admired with veneration. It is war of the British people with whom we have preached friendliness and cooperation despite the British imperial domination over us. It is the war of the enslaved peoples of Europe for whom our hearts bleed. It is an All-Peoples' war against Fascism and for freedom.[23]

The CPI opposition to the August revolution followed the grand strategy of helping those including the British, combating the fascist forces. The Muslim League abstained from the Congress-led Quit India campaign for reasons connected with the call for Pakistan. Hence, the League deplored the decision to launch an open rebellion 'in pursuance of the objective of establishing Congress-Hindu domination in India'. Condemning the movement, it was resolved at a hurriedly called meeting,

> this movement is directed not only to coerce the British Government into handing over power to a Hindu oligarchy, but also to force Mussalmans to submit and surrender to Congress terms and dictation.
>
> [The Muslim League is] firmly convinced that the present Congress movement is not directed for securing the independence of all the constituent elements in the life of the

country but for the establishment of Hindu Raj and to deal a death blow to the Muslim goal of Pakistan.

> ... if the Congress demand is accepted it would bring the 100 million of Muslims under the yoke of a Hindu Raj which must inevitably result either in anarchy and chaos or complete strangulation and annihilation of Muslim India and all that Islam stands for.
>
> In these circumstances, the working committee of the All India Muslim League . . . call upon the Muslims to abstain from any participation in the movement initiated by the Congress and to continue to pursue their normal peaceful life.[24]

The carefully worded resolution has three important dimensions reflecting the extent to which the Muslim leadership realized the importance of helping the British during the war crisis probably as the most significant guarantee for a Muslim homeland. First, by attributing the Quit India Movement to the Congress motive of establishing Hindu domination/Hindu Raj, the League successfully projected itself as a dependable ally of the Raj; secondly, by floating the idea that the success of the Congress movement meant an abject submission and surrender of the Muslims to the Hindus, the League employed an effective strategy drawing on the age-old Hindu-Muslim fissure to dissociate the Muslims from the campaign. The strategy paid off for a variety of complex reasons at a time when the distinctiveness of the community was championed consistently at the cost of the nation and the freedom struggle. Finally, the resolution also underlines the Congress failure to take the Muslims into confidence in such a gigantic effort like the Quit India Movement, which thus remained weak from the outset. By their withdrawal and opposition to the movement, the Muslims consolidated their claims as a separate community, which was crucial in the context of the British endeavour to resolve the constitutional deadlock through negotiation.

Similarly, B.R. Ambedkar representing the minority interests felt that the Quit India Resolution was an attempt 'to do away with the intervention of the British government in the discussion of the Minority Question and thereby securing for the Congress a free hand to settle it on its own lights'.[25] Upset with the Congress attitude towards the minority question at a crucial point of India's history, Ambedkar characterized the Quit India campaign as 'a mad venture', which was 'in effect, if not in intention, an attempt to win independence by bypassing the Muslims and other minorities'. Declaring in rather strong terms that Gandhi's civil disobedience was 'both irresponsible and insane' and since this movement 'may be the best way to serve the best interests of the Congress party … and not the country', he therefore exhorted people who did not believe in the movement to take steps to prevent it. Ambedkar's rather uncompromising stance appeared to have been influenced, if not determined, by the negligence of the Congress of the minority issue in all its political resolutions since 1940.

THE MOVEMENT AND ITS DEVELOPMENT

The Quit India Movement was the melting point of the struggle between the Raj and the Congress, which surfaced with the institutionalization of nationalist politics through the formation of the Indian National Congress in 1885. With the adoption of the 8 August resolution, the entire top leadership was incarcerated, which unleashed an unprecedented countrywide mass anti-British campaign. It is plausible to argue that the role of the Congress in mobilizing people politically was significant. Equally important was the entire atmosphere, which was already a tinderbox ready to ignite owing to the war crisis and its concomitant socio-economic and political consequences.

In general, three interrelated phases of the movement can be discerned. First, with the adoption of the 8 August 'Do or Die' resolution and incarceration of Gandhi and his lieutenants in Bombay, the all India upsurge which was massive and violent, sparked-off. Within just a week between 9 and 15 August, the movement which appeared to be a civil rebellion comparable to the magnitude of any mass revolution, was smashed fast, reassuring the Raj's hegemony in India and simultaneously warning the British ruling elite of the possible strength of any future Congress-led movement which was so well coordinated. Bombay and Calcutta were the storm centres undertaking principally the Gandhian method of opposition. There were casualties in Delhi, and Patna witnessed a violent Congress attack on the British police in front of the secretariat on 11 August. Along with urban upsurges in which students took a prominent part, labour strikes were called in Lucknow, Kanpur, Bombay, Nagpur and Ahmedabad which may not have been sympathetic strikes per se, but posed serious threats to the continuity of the empire. The Tata Steel workers, for instance, resolved not to resume work till a national government was formed. Strike at Ahmedabad textile mills which lasted for three and a half months, made the telegraph lines in order to prevent the movement of the troops; the railway track connecting Talcher with the rest of the country, was severely damaged for miles. With the consolidation of the *chasi-mula* combination as a parallel system of governance in Talcher, the Orissa government expressed concern and troops were requisitioned immediately; flag marches were conducted too in the Congress stronghold areas. Arrests, lathicharges, canning and firings were resorted to indiscriminately to dispel the popular feeling that the British were no longer ruling the country and the Congress-swaraj was established. To disperse the crowd who seized the palace, the military undertook machine gun firing from the air. In the face of an organized military attack, the movement lost its momentum considerably and it was finally withdrawn by the end of 1943.

The Prajamandal, though short-lived, projected an alternative governance drawing essentially on different considerations from those of the British. Championing what can be called 'a popular peasant utopia', the proposed *chasi-mula raj*, 'aimed to provide food, shelter and clothing to all, reduce rents, helped the unemployed with jobs and land, and improved the system of education, health and water supply'. Given the presence of mines and factories in the state, 'it also planned to increase wages and take over these from foreign companies'.

In Satara, a high point of.radicalism was reached in the setting up of what came to be known as the 'Prati Sarkar' or parallel government. Two phases may be distinguished in the unfolding of the Quit India Movement in Satara. The activity of the first phase followed the usual tactics of satyagraha with its boycotts, strikes and morchas, accompanied by underground activity – chiefly attacks on banks, government buildings, bridges, trains and post offices. The first phase of sabotage and underground resistance lasted till the beginning of 1943 with local groups functioning separately and with Y.B. Chavan as their overall leader or 'dictator' (in Congress terminology). Police repression was heavy and the end of 1942 saw 2000 people from Satara in jail.

In the next six months, the underground activists at Karad and Walva taluka led to two major decisions: to continue the movement in spite of the repression and to carry it forward with the setting-up of 'people's power' in the villages. This included the creation of a new ethic of struggle: the ideal freedom fighter was no longer to be the moral satyagrahi but one who succeeded in remaining free from British jail while continuing the work of resistance. In this second phase, the peasantry who had played only a supportive role in the first phase became directly involved through the campaign against the dacoity. Organized by the Congress activists, the peasants engaged in a struggle to curb banditry, which was undermining the underground organization of civil disobedience. It was in the struggle with the dacoits that the Prati Sarkar established itself. Dacoit power ended in the region by the end of 1943, and the path was cleared for the Prati Sarkar to focus its activity on peasant problems. It is at this point that the Quit India Movement flows into a peasant issue oriented agitation. The Prati Sarkar was thus committed to conducting a struggle on three fronts, (a) the Quit India front against the British government; (b) against dacoity; and (c) the solution of peasant problems particularly indebtedness and land disputes.

The structure of the Prati Sarkar as it evolved by 1943

was essentially a loose one comprising three village-based institutions: (a) Nyayadan Mandals, (b) Gram Samitis, and (c) Toofan Senas. The Nyayadan Mandals constituted the judicial arm of the Prati Sarkar. They were 'people's courts' which dealt with cases of fraud, land disputes between peasants, sale of land and cases of moneylenders charging exorbitant rates of interest. They also tried and punished traitors and informers. The court's decisions were taken by a popular consensus. The main function of the Gram Samitis or the village communities was constructive activities, finance and welfare. Popularly elected, the Samitis were expected to raise funds and setup cooperative societies, education societies, village libraries and health centers, and also to conduct anti-liquor and anti-untouchability propaganda. Finally, the Toofan Sena was youth militia drawn from village wrestling clubs or *Talims*. These village units were generally responsible for the protection of the peasant from the moneylenders' harassment, and though they meted out punishment to offenders they did not take decisions independently of the Nyayadan Mandals.[26]

Another successful experiment in this regard was conducted in Midnapur (Bengal) where the parallel national government survived till September 1944 despite natural devastation and British torture. The Midnapur nationalists never succumbed to the British repression and their government was dismantled only in response to a call from Gandhi.

THE AUGUST REVOLUTION: A RADICAL MOVEMENT

The August movement was probably most radical both in its attitude towards the British and in terms of methods employed. Gandhi's 'Do or Die' slogan was an ultimatum to the British leaving no space for negotiation at all. Such an attitude was not there in either the non-cooperation or civil disobedience movements when the Congress leadership was always keen to settle the disputes through some kind of compromise. Gandhi too agreed to accept this even at the cost of undermining the cause he fought for; its consequences were far reaching. On the one hand, masses who took part in the anti-British campaign felt betrayed, which was likely to adversely affect the future Congress mobilization. Just as Gandhi opposed radical social movements, which tended to disrupt social equilibrium, he was identified as a conservative political activist who declined to disturb the alien rule. On the other, the failure of the past Congress movements, led by Gandhi or his success in containing them at his will, strengthened the Raj in two ways: (a) in its drive to challenge effectively the Congress campaign, the British had in Gandhi a friend who, due to his commitment to non-violence, steered the political agitation in such a way as not to cause severe disruption in the British rule; and (b) once the major organized political force was thus neutralized, the British administration could concentrate on controlling other radical socio-political movements challenging its continuity. Thus, despite the apparent threat to the Raj, both the non-cooperation and the civil disobedience movements let lose a political process, conducive to the prevalent rule, which shaped, to a large extent, the anti-imperial movement before the onset of the open rebellion.

Whatever the implications of the past Congress-launched political movements, their significance cannot be denied especially in gradually radicalizing the Congress, which loomed large in the August revolution. The Congress had anticipated that the nature of the movement would be different and hence, it was not surprising that the instructions to the Congress workers were tuned to capture the heightened mass radicalism, evinced since the adoption of the 1940 Ramgarh resolution. In his address to the UP Congressmen, Nehru, the UP PCC president thus urged, 'Congressmen should be made to realize that the proposed movement is likely to be of a far more intense and more widespread character than any of the previous civil disobedience movements'. Aware of factional feuds impairing the Congress mobilization, he also exhorted that 'all local disputes must forthwith be ended. Complaints over petty matters should not be sent to the PCCs. Even those against whom disciplinary action has been taken are free to join the movement'.[27] While moving the 8 July resolution, Nehru thus confidently announced that 'the Congress is plunging into a stormy ocean and it would emerge either with a free India or go down. Unlike in the past, it is not going to be a movement for a few days, to be suspended and talked over. It is going to be a fight to the finish.'[28]

With this campaign, Gandhi also became far more radical than ever. As early as 9 July 1942, in a draft of the resolution, which was to be discussed in the Wardha AICC meeting (14 July), he underlined that

> the struggle thus would have to resolve itself into a mass movement on the widest scale possible involving voluntary strikes, voluntary non-cooperation on the part of all those who are in government employment or in the departments connected

> with government in any shape or form and it may involve also non-payment of land revenue and taxes.

That the August revolution was qualitatively different from the earlier campaigns was evident from the Congress circulars, reportedly distributed by the Central Congress Directorate during the movement. In order to enlist the support of various social groups confronting the British, the underground Congress Directorate took up issues, which demonstrate the extent to which the Congress was radicalized in the wake of the August campaign. For instance, in the AICC instruction to the peasants, they were asked 'to obstruct the revenue and police officers to collect the tax, [and] in fact, to enter the village unless in the form of a military invasion. The invaders can be harassed in the meantime by cutting their communications and supplies.' On another occasion, it was insisted on mobilizing the people on the immediate local grievances to launch a direct attack on the British and their supporters. While charting the programme of action, it was thus stipulated,

> Let the peasants select the initial targets of assault in each village or groups of villages. Let the rising and simmering discontent against the immediate grievances be churned-up into an angry ferment the more extreme and militant spokesmen of the peasants should be helped to take the lead and prepare the men for direct action: by organised and orderly seizure of stocks of essential goods; by refraining payment of rent and debts; by refusing to part with crops; by ignoring court processes for distraint and refusing to attend or bid at sales; by taking possession of the machinery of local administration, such as Union Boards, Chowkis, Thanas and running it themselves; by

> setting-up new machinery where necessary. If the developments can fairly be synchronized in a number of areas from the centre – and to a great extent, this will be helped by the natural infectiousness of the process – the forces of the state will be helpless to check this progress, the disturbances will be too widespread and scattered.
>
> [for the industrial workers], unrest must be brought to a head on immediate economic issues. . . . [d]earness allowances can never keep pace with prices which will soar higher and higher with a progressive inflation of the currency. Price control will show-up as the senseless deception it is. Strikes should be easy to organise in this context. Propaganda should be meanwhile passed home on the capitalist front, appealing to this class on emotional patriotic grounds to view strike programme with favour. The bourgeoisie must be exhorted to keep up political discontent at high pressure; declasse members of the petit bourgeois sections must be recruited to lead militant demonstration of students and labourers.[29]

There were innumerable AICC bulletins including the famous six commanders of message to the nation before Gandhi was taken to prison – which was interpreted as his instruction to resort to direct action in what was called the final battle for freedom. Hence, the participants were urged (a) not to acknowledge 'any power other than public'; and (b) to completely paralyse communications and transport, dislocate trams and bus services, uproot telegraphic and telephonic posts, dig-up roads, cut railways, tear out motor and bus tyres and dislocate the government machinery in every possible way.

For the participants, the message was articulated in the form of destroying the institutions of governance, means of communications and attacking those who sustained its continuity. Local police stations were thus an obvious target. The situation was worse in the district of Ballia, UP where 'all police stations except three were lost to the rebels', and the people were led to believe that 'a Congress Raj had already been established'. Thus in Ballia, 'there was a rumour that Lucknow had fallen, and the impression soon got around that the Government had collapsed'. The movement assumed massive proportions as the fragility of the colonial state gained ground. Proclaiming the downfall of the British, the rebel leaders 'made an announcement that the Congress Raj had taken over Ballia and all cases and complaints should be taken to them'.[30]

There was another aspect of the open rebellion, which requires emphasis, viz, the significance of the Congress flag. Unfurling of flag in the government buildings meant an inauguration and subsequently formalization of the Congress rule. Thus R.H. Niblett, the Azamgarh, (UP) district magistrate reported that the rebels 'had not come to fight their Indian brethren; they only wished to plant the Congress flag on the thana'. Similarly, students who captured a train fixed a flag in its engine, which, as it were, registered the arrival of the Congress. Thus, it was stated in the official report that the students turned the train 'into a Congress train with a flag and allowed movement under their direction and carried destruction to the control instruments of every railway station'. The police appeared helpless and the British administration was also largely undermined. On the part of the rebels, this was an occasion to effectively challenge the alien state; the policemen, once captured 'were made to wear Gandhi caps and carry Congress flags at the head of the crowds'. The extent of the damage and destruction of the government property clearly shows the degree to which the British state was eclipsed, at least temporarily, in the eastern UP. What is, however, significant is that despite well-entrenched radicalization manifested in the programmes of action, the newly emerged leaders draws, to a large extent, on the top Congress leaders, including Gandhi. So, it never appeared to be problematic to the rebels who labelled bombs and other explosives as 'Gandhi blasting stick', 'Jawahar grenade', 'Subhas blasting jelly', and so on. Such an endeavour reveals the importance of the incarcerated Congress leaders in mobilizing the masses resorting to means, which neither Gandhi nor other leading Congress leaders would have approved. This also demonstrates the strategic sense of the rebel leaders who articulated the anti-British feeling in the form of a different kind of movement deriving inspiration from the nationalist leaders and thus linked the campaign at the grassroots with its all India counterpart. It was therefore not surprising for the Home Department, Government of India to note that though Gandhi reigned supreme, there was not 'any master hand behind the disturbances which were largely the cumulative effect of anti-British agitation which has been deliberately intensified by the Congress leaders since the failure of the Cripps Mission'. Had the Congress leaders committed to non-violence been around, the movement would perhaps not have assumed such alarming proportions. Attributing the violent nature of the rebellion to the second rank Congress leaders, not particularly concerned with the nature of means adopted to attain the goal, the Benaras district collector thus bitterly noted, 'the well-known and mainly moderate Congressmen were escorted to gaol leaving those whom we found later to be the real plotters of the rebellion, still happily plotting away'. So, it was a battle of a different kind in which the participants undertook several measures to establish a counter authority – which may not have survived long enough though it had its symbolical value regarding the possible emergence of a free India.

The situation was thus unprecedented and the newly emerged Congress leadership strove to exploit the immediate local grievances connected with the war to organize an effective political campaign against the British, which looked vulnerable especially after the fall of Malaya and Singapore. Having prepared so carefully to stop the movement before it started, the government was appalled at the common pattern of disruption that developed almost simultaneously in widely-separated parts of the country. Hinting at the growing radicalization of the Congress, Linlithgow thus bitterly expressed that 'we have found ourselves faced with an extremely awkward situation, wholly revolutionary in character, well-organized by people working underground and deterred by non considerations of non-violence or the like.

THE NATURE OF THE MOVEMENT

The nationalist upsurge which sparked-off following the Quit India Resolution is different from both 1919-22 non-cooperation and 1930-32 civil disobedience movements[31] in a number of ways. The Quit India Movement assumed massive proportions in the absence of the top-ranking Congress leadership, thereby bringing in a new type of direction, which sustained the movement even beyond what the imprisoned leaders could perceive when they had launched it. Secondly, as in the case of leadership, the August resolution brought a new constituent of supporters to the national movement who, though they participated in the earlier anti-British campaign, asserted themselves more vigorously in what was perhaps the final battle for independence. That new groups were politically mobilized is indicative of the widening of frontiers of the freedom struggle. Not only was the campaign effective from the point of view of participation; it also introduced new dimension to the nationalist movement itself by incorporating new actors at various levels. Thirdly, although the movement absorbed anti-landlord sentiments, which had been manifest in scattered peasant attacks on the landlords, it never assumed the form of a mass-peasant uprising drawing on the age-old rift between the landlord and peasantry. This is possibly due to the intensity of anti-British feeling, which prevailed over other contradictions. Here lies the success of the Congress in containing and directing popular turbulence towards the attainment of freedom. The Quit India revolt thus perhaps provided 'a safety valve' among the peasants against the British. Fourthly, what really marks off the Quit India Movement is its continuity in Midnapur in Bengal, Talcher in Orissa, and Satara in Maharashtra, whence it had completely withered away elsewhere. Apart from indicating the autonomous nature of the movement in specific regions, it demonstrates the ability of the local Congress organizers to sustain popular zeal in the face of inhuman torture unleashed by the British to control the movement. The continuity of the movement in three different and completely unrelated geographical locations refer to a process of mass mobilization – though started earlier and drew upon the 1922 Gaya Congress resolution to incorporate peasants and workers in order to widen the Congress base – which not only integrated the disparate anti-British struggle with its national counterpart, but also brought in local Congress leaders with organic links with the grassroots political activists, onto the political scene.

Although the Quit India Movement was the final battle for India's freedom, there has been debates as regards its nature. According to Francis Hutchins, what emerged in 1942 following the adoption of the 8 August resolution by Congress was 'a spontaneous revolution' because even with the imprisonment of top Congress leaders, the movement assumed massive proportions far beyond their expectation. Inspired by the Congress call, the participation in the campaign was spontaneous. To argue his point, Hutchins strives to draw our attention to the mobilization pattern during the movement, which was done fairly quickly despite the absence of the established Congress leadership. This, in fact, is substantiated by the assertion that the mobilization pattern varied widely from one locality to another just because in the absence of specific Congress directives to the revolutionaries at the grassroots level, participants carried on the anti-British campaign primarily in accordance with the exigency of the situation.

The spontaneity thesis seems plausible in another respect: unlike the earlier movements, the Congressmen in the localities resorted to violence and justified their actions as being in tune with Gandhian thought. In the light of Gandhi's decision to halt the Non-Cooperation Movement following the Chauri-Chaura incident, whether Gandhi would have approved of violence is a matter of conjecture; it, nonetheless, refers to the autonomous nature of the uprising which started with non-violence but drifted away completely in a number of instances as the movement progressed. Here lies the role of local Congress leaders who guided the movement in accordance with their ideological preferences. As a result, in both Midnapur and Satara, where the influence of revolutionary terrorism was substantial, participants often resorted to violence, whereas in Talcher, the movement never became violent, primarily because non-violence prevailed over other ideological leanings.

In terms of its actual manifestation, the movement had the characteristics of a spontaneous outburst, though the Congress was getting ready to launch the final battle for freedom since the 1940 Ramgarh session. So, there was a preparatory phase, which culminated in the 1942 revolution. In other words, though the movement erupted following the incarceration of the Congress leaders, it was the result of consistent efforts of the Congress which led to the mass upsurge. R. Maxwell, the Home Member, who never believed in 'the spontaneity thesis' thus argued, 'the ordinary characteristics of spontaneous disturbances have almost entirely absent. The first object of riotous mob is generally loot. There have, of course, been cases of looting but on the whole this form of activity has been far less common than might have been expected.' Moreover, by referring to the simultaneous attack on railways and other communications in widely separated parts of India, he further substantiated the claim that 'these disturbances were not spontaneous outbursts arising out of the arrest of the Congress leaders'. The disturbances themselves had appearances, to start with, of being spontaneous and unregulated but remarkable resemblance of objectives of attack in different parts of India (mainly communications of various kinds) draws our attention to the presumption of pre-organization. It is possible, as an assessment of the Home Department shows, that 'activities selected were outcome more of ideas that had been spread about regarding the plans of Congress than of deliberate instigation by the Congress leaders on the spot'. The viceroy did not seem convinced and while defending the spontaneous thesis, he attributed the movement essentially to 'the highly strung and excitable character of some of these young men [who took part] and the amusement which it is so easy to get from smashing things or setting something on fire'.[32]

Given the evidence, it is difficult to conceptualize the movement in terms exclusively of 'a spontaneous outburst'. What is plausible to argue here is that the movement was the product of a process, unleashed with the 1940 Ramgarh resolution and the Congress efforts over time yielded results. So, it was the culmination of an organized attempt on part of the Congress. There were other factors too which contributed to such an unprecedented campaign: the apparent difficulty of the British after the fall of Rangoon, for instance, strengthened the idea that Raj was coming to an end; the emergence of a new set of leaders who openly appreciated 'violence' as opposed to 'non-violence' to attain independence.

Along with Hutchins' spontaneous thesis, there is a counter-thesis characterizing the Quit India uprising as mere 'disturbances intending to give notice to quit to British rule in India'. According to N.C. Chaudhuri who puts forward this view, the Quit India Movement was 'a freak and an impulsive outbursts of anger' at what the Indian people took as an exhibition of outrageous impudence on the British administration in India in arresting the Congress leaders. According to him, the movement was more or less a face-saving gesture because the Congress leaders had to counteract the impression which was growing after the rejection of the Cripps' offer that they were powerless to do anything against British intransigence. He admitted that the movement was relatively more serious in the eastern UP region because it was a backward area in which 'the blind xenophobia' was stronger than elsewhere. Attributing a movement, which was widespread at least temporarily, to economic backwardness, is bound to provoke controversy when it is more or less established that politics has autonomy of its own, and reducing politics to economic determinism invites serious methodological problems. Besides, the fact that apart from eastern UP the movement assumed gigantic proportions in areas which did not suffer economically, shows the limitation of 'the economic backwardness thesis', and substantiates the autonomy of politics.

The sudden collapse of a movement, which had the potential of surpassing the intensity of both non-cooperation and civil disobedience movements led Judith Brown, a Cambridge School exponent, to characterize Quit India as 'a flotilla of rafts colliding with a battleship'. Though the movement evaporated soon, the interpretation seems to have been derived from a particular bias. According to the available documents, not only had the rulers an access to an army; they had also a well-prepared plan for immediate imprisonment of the Congress leadership and pre-emptive strike against the Congress. Thus, the British had both the motivation and the necessary manpower to destroy the movement fast in a way they could not have thought in 1919-22 or 1930-32.

Similarly, the characterization of the Quit India campaign as nothing but 'a fifth-columnist conspiracy' is equally misleading. In order to win the world anti-fascist opinion, the British ruling elite attributed the violent nature of the movement to secret pro-Axis sympathies. The explanation which was readily acceptable by the highest level of British administration, including Churchill who found in the Quit India Movement a Japanese design to cripple the Indian economy and paralyse the state. The idea probably gained ground in view of intelligence reports that the Congress plan 'is to organize collective civil disobedience in zones immediately threatened by the Japanese'. Moreover, the British allegation may have been derived from Gandhi's original draft for the 1942 Allahabad session of the AICC (held in July) which included: 'if India were freed, her first step would probably be to negotiate with Japan . . . India bears no enmity with Japan'. Later during the session, Jawaharlal Nehru's argument clarifying that 'it is Gandhiji's feeling that Japan and Germany will win [which] unconsciously governs his decision' confirmed the British apprehension. Yet, the Congress' apparent pro-Axis tilt, which influenced its political stance temporarily was transitional because the leadership came out heavily against the fascist powers on a number of occasions. Apart from his open letter to Hitler in which he was held responsible for the devastating war, Gandhi was so emphatic in his assessment of the Japanese that he appealed to his countrymen to oppose Subhas Chandra Bose who was reported to have aligned with the Japanese. In a press interview, he thus made clear: 'well, Subhas has risked much for us: but if he means to set-up a Government in India under the Japanese, he will be resisted by us'. So, the interpretation attributing the movement to a Japanese-inspired conspiracy (JIFS) does not seem to capture the complexity of largely popular outbursts like the August revolution. And the charge was consequently withdrawn; Wavell, the viceroy thus wrote to Gandhi mentioning that 'I do not accuse you or the Congress Party of any wish to aid the Japanese. But you are much too intelligent a man ... not to have realized the effect of your resolution must be to hamper the prosecution of the war; and it is clear to me that you had lost confidence in our ability to defend India, and were prepared to take advantage of our supposed military strains to gain political advantage.'[33]

The entire top Congress leadership was put behind the bars and the oft-quoted 8 August resolution was equally vague about the details of the ensuing upsurge. And yet there was a massive counterattack in retaliation to the British policy of repression. The fact that more than fifty battalions were deployed in the early suspension of the movement confirms the extent to which it threatened the overall security of the Raj. Linlithgow thus labelled the August upsurge as 'by far the most serious rebellion since that of 1857, the gravity and extent of which we have so far concealed from the world for reasons of military security'. However, the comparison is not quite apt. The Indian sepoys who mutinied in 1857 had some arms and ammunition and training while the simple village folks of Ballia, Azamgarh and other small towns and villages in

Bihar and UP who had risen in revolt at the bidding of boys fresh from schools and colleges, wielded nothing more lethal than sticks and stones; their violence was sporadic, unplanned and suicidal. The British response was predictably ruthless. According to official figures, which could be underestimates – by the end of 1942 over 66,000 persons had been convicted or detained, and the army had fired on 538 occasions.

The movement was radical, for the Congress volunteers resorted to open violence in a number of instances. It is debatable whether Gandhi would have allowed such movement to continue in view of his strong antipathy to violence. There is evidence to show that the movement gradually became violent and that British provocation had played a significant role in it. In fact, this also introduces another dimension to the structure of politics during the open rebellion. The movement's deviation from a true Gandhian path shows the autonomy of the unorganized level where political articulation and mobilization were being carried on through different idioms, which were meaningful only in the context of a completely different ideological perception. Here lies the viability of the argument highlighting the autonomy of unorganized politics following a unique pattern and demonstrating new dimensions of the structure of grassroot politics. The argument seems convincing in the light of 8 August resolution and the transformation of the movement after the incarceration of the top Congress leadership. In fact, the Congress urged its volunteers to 'be ready, organize at once, be alert, but by no means act. ... till Mahatmaji decides'. The six stage programme mentioned in the Andhra Pradesh Congress committee circular included only the traditional

Gandhian means like salt preparation, boycott of courts, schools, colleges and government services, picketing of foreign cloth and liquor and no tax and no rent as 'the last resort'. There was just a Congress plan for disrupting communications: stopping of trains 'by pulling chains only'. Drawing on this, the Congress volunteers might have been inspired to launch a massive and violent attack on communications. Although the attack was not pre-planned, the sudden eruption seems to suggest that had the masses not been ready psychologically to fight 'the last battle', under no circumstances would the movement have assumed such alarming proportions. Given the military preparedness of the British, the Quit India campaign did not pose as serious a threat as it was apprehended. What had caused consternation was the fear that 'the movement will destroy "the will" to resist or even the very idea of resistance'. Once this was accomplished, the UP government's note underlined, 'it will be easy for the Japanese to find people to commit acts of sabotage [and to] become spies etc.' Congress was thus identified with 'the counterpart of Lavers party in France and equally, if not more, dangerous.'

The government statistics provide an indication of the extent of mass participation and an intense British repression to smash the movement fast. By the end of 1943 when the movement at the all India level waned, 91,836 people had been arrested with the highest figure coming from Bombay Presidency (24,416), UP (16,796) and Bihar (16,202); 208 police outposts, 332 railway stations and 945 post offices had been destroyed or severely damaged and there had been 664 bomb explosions. Police and army firing had killed around

1060 persons, while 63 policemen had died fighting the upsurge and 216 had defected. That the British felt threatened is evident from Linlithgow's order of 'machine gunning from air' against crowds disrupting communications around Patna and, in fact, aeroplanes were employed to fire from the air to disperse the Congress rebels in Bhagalpur and Monghyr in Bihar, Nadia and Tamluk in Bengal and Talcher in Orissa.

CONCLUSION

So, it was a confrontation of a different type, for the Congress clung to violence, if necessary to counter the British attack. It was a mismatch battle though, because the unarmed Congress volunteers fought the British forces equipped with most modern weapons. This, *inter alia,* is indicative of the spontaneity of the participants who rose in revolt despite adverse consequences of undertaking an anti-British onslaught.

Although the morale of the rebels was high, neither the British police nor the army, composed predominantly of Indians, expressed sympathy for the civil rebellion. Except for the Bihar police, which declined to cooperate with the authority when the movement was at its zenith, the force was generally loyal to the Raj. As regards the army, apart from those who defected to the Japanese to form the Indian National Army abroad, not a single instance shows that 1942 upsurge cut the ground even under the Raj's main instrument of coercion. This certainly enabled the British authority to bring the all India movement under control within a short period. The rise of dissidents among the Bihar police was, however, an indication of shifting loyalty from the imperial ruler to the indigenous Congress-led authority: it was felt even at the highest level, R. Maxwell, the Home Member noted thus, 'our officials – and especially the Hindus among them – must naturally, in considering their future prospects, look towards the rising rather than setting sun. The one thing quite certain to them is that we shall not be here to employ or protect them in future . . . and we cannot [therefore] expect our servants to do more for the present government than their duty actually requires.'[34] Change was also evident among the Indian Civil Service officers, a majority of whom were Indians by 1940: 614 as opposed to 587.

Although the loyalty of the Indian ICS men to the Raj was never in doubt, they seem to have felt threatened with the prospect of Congress coming to power, which was in the air since the arrival of the Cripps Mission. Naturally, they began to wonder what would happen to them after the winding up of the empire. Lord Wavell, who was presiding over a fast dismantling imperial authority appreciated the Indian officers' apprehension. He told his cabinet colleagues that Indian ICS men could not be expected to carry out 'a firm policy unless they were assured of the continuity of the Raj for at least a decade afterwards'.

Not only was there a prospect of the breakdown of the imperial edifice, the informal part of collaborative network of support was also beginning to show signs of collapse. The alarming proportions which the 1942 rebellion assumed, even with the pre-emptive British strike, are indicative of the extent to which British reliance on those Indians who chose for a variety of reasons to give it informal support, advice and information and to guarantee it the backing of their own followers proved abortive.

So, in the final years of the Raj, the entire British network of Indian allies both in formal and informal sectors was fast weakening. The war crisis and their adverse consequences, the prospect of British withdrawal, the communal schism affecting the law and order situation, and finally the dubious loyalty of the Indian ICS officers to the Raj itself, were the factors contributing to the decline of the empire. Viewed thus, the 1942 Quit India was an important signpost of the Raj's disintegration, for it made the ruling elite aware of the possible strength of any future Congress movement which struck at the empire's foundation, particularly if it occurred after the war when the imperial authority had neither the legitimacy nor was well-equipped psychologically or materially to ensure its continuity.

For the Mahatma, the open rebellion was a novel experiment. Launched by Gandhi, it was not guided by him as he was incarcerated once the movement was declared. However, the course of the movement confirms three important points, which are linked with the evolution of Gandhi as a mass leader. First, despite his absence from the scene, the movement continued unabated by drawing ideological inspiration from ahimsa. On occasions, there were violent eruptions that too were defended in the name of Mahatma. What it suggests is the hegemonic influence of the Mahatma over those participating in 'the last war against imperialism'. Secondly, as evident in the earlier pan-India movements, the open rebellion was sustained by the local Gandhians who remained most critical in both interpreting and executing Gandhi's message to the Congress volunteers. Their role was thus most crucial in popularizing Gandhi at the grassroots. Finally, the Quit India Movement was also a failure for the Mahatma. The withdrawal of a large section of Muslims, especially those championing the 1940 Lahore resolution for a separate Muslim state, undoubtedly weakened the nationalist platform. Gandhi failed to defuse Jinnah's separatist campaign. It would, therefore, not be ahistorical to suggest that the Quit India Movement made a dent in Mahatma's nationalist image because Muslims preferred to support the British government during the open rebellion.

---

1 Quotations are from *Harijan* unless otherwise stated. *Harijan*, 16 August, 1942.

2 Centre of South Asian Studies, Cambridge (CSAS hereafter), F.O. Bell Papers (TSS), p. 18.

3 CSAS, Benthall Papers, Box No. XIX, Benthall Diary, political situation in 1940.

4 R. Coupland, *Indian Politics. 1936-42: Report of the Constitutional Problem in India*. Part II, OUP, Madras, 1944, p. 263.

5 IOR, L/I/11777, Central Intelligence Officer, Madras to the Home Department, Government of India, 4 January, 1942.

6 TP , vol. I, London, 1970, Churchill to Linlithgow, 10 March, 1942, pp. 394-95, TP, Vol. I, A war cabinet telegram to Cripps, April, 1942.

7 IOR, L/PO/6/1O2A, L. S. Amery's broadcast in the BBC, 9 August, 1942.

8 ibid.

9 F.G. Hutchins, *Spontaneous Revolution: The Quit India Movement*, Manohar, New Delhi, 1971, p. 272.

10 Paul Greenough, 'Political mobilisation and the underground literature of the Quit India movement, 1942-44, MAS, 17.3.1983, p. 360.

11 Dwindling of the Congress membership, 1938-41:-

Congress Provinces	*1938-39*	*1939-40*	*1940-41*
Ajmer-Marwara	13,151	6,700	6,250
Assam	37,321	56,623	56,300
Bengal	4,83,158	4,40,729	2,44,064
Bihar	5,63,629	2,76,704	1,83,731
Bombay city&suburbs	6,936	60,368	18,631
Maharashtra	1,48,544	1,15,137	87,240
Karnataka	1,72,113	75,426	28,312
Gujarat	92,418	80,101	55,231
Nagpur	44,854	42,418	22,638
Mahakoshal	1,26,554	1,10	———
Vidarva	78,396	119	14,878
Delhi	19,423	44,733	7,974
Tamil Nadu	3,64,393	11,956	———
Andhra	3,35,205	2,06,152	———
Kerala	55,031	2,05771	———
NWFP	34,397	49,266	15,985
Orissa (Utkal)	1,98,325	1,26,126	45,792
Punjab	1,88,791	1,89,289	1,10,289
Sind	22,303	18,179	12,667
United Provinces	14,72,456	8,33,830	2,58,826
Total	*45,11,858*	*29,73,452*	*14,86161*

Source: NAI, Home-Poll (g), 4/7/41, Decrease in Membership of the Congress; IOR, L/I/1/885, Decrease in Membership; *The Times*, London, 31 July, 1941.

12 R. Tottenham, *Congress Responsibility,* Record of the Congress Working Committee meeting, pp. 42-43.

13 NMML, AICCG 32/1942: Working Committee draft resolution: Nehru's speech to the Congress Working Committee.

14 NMML, AICC G 32/1942: Working Committee's resolution, 14 July, 1942.

15 IOR, R/3/l/350, T. Wickenden's report on the Congress disturbances, p. 21. Nehru's statement of 20 July was quoted in the report.

16 Jawaharlal Nehru, *The Discovery of India,* Oxford University Press, Delhi, p. 475.

17 Quotations are from *The Transfer of Power* unless otherwise stated. Vol. II, London, 1971, The Quit India Resolution, p. 622.

18 *CWMG*, Vol. No. LXXVI, April, 1942 - December, 1942, Gandhi's speech at the AICC meeting, 8 August, 1942, p. 392.

19 *CWMG*, Vol. No. LXXVI, April, 1942 - December, 1942, Gandhi's speech at the AICC meeting, 8 . August, 1942, p. 403.

20 IOR, L/PO/6/1O2A Tgm, Viceroy to the Secretary of State, 9 August, 1942 - reporting the view of the Governors on the question of Gandhi's fast

21 India office Records, Mss. Eur F 125/11, Linlithgow Papers, Linlithgow to Amery, 17 August, 1942.

22 NMML, Purushottam Thakurdas Papers, File No. 178; the copy of the resolution of the Indian Chamber of Commerce, adopted on 10 August, 1942.

23 IOR, L/I/1/1116; P. C. Joshi, *The Indian Communist Party: Its Policy and Work in the War of' Liberation.* (pamphlet), Communist Party of Great Britain, London, 1942, p. 12.

24 *The Transfer of India*, Vol. II, The Muslim League Working Committee Resolution, 20 August, 1942, p. 771.

25 B.R. Ambedkar, *Pakistan or Partition of India*, Thacker and Co, Bombay, 1945, p. 407.

26 See, for details. Gail Omvedt, 'The Satara Prati Sarkar', in G. Pandey (cd), *The Indian Nation in 1942*: Livi Rodrigues, *'Rural Protest and Politics: A Study of Peasant Movement in Maharastra'*, unpublished PhD dissertation, University of London, 1984, pp. 400-19.

27 NMML, AICC P 22/1942, Jawaharlal Nehru's address to the UP PCC, 24 July, 1942.

28 NMML, AlCC G 22/1942; Nehru's speech at the AlCC meeting while moving the 'Quit India' resolution, Bombay, 8 August, 1942.

29 R. Tottenham, *Congress Responsibility.* Appendix VII, pp. 67-68.

30 IOR, R/3/1/359, The congress Rebellion in United Provinces, Government of UP, Lucknow, 1943, p.55.

31 There is a plethora of literature on these movements. See, for instance, on the Non-Cooperation movement, P.C. Bamford *Histories of the Non-Cooperation and Khilafat Movements,* Government of India. New Delhi.

1925: N, Mitra,(ed), *Indian Annual Register 1922:* Judith Brown, *Gandhi Rise to Power. Indian. Politics. 1915-1922.* Cambridge University Press, Cambridge, 1972; for Civil Disobedience:, see, Judith Brown, *Gandhi and Civil Disobedience: The Mahatma in Indian Politics.* Cambridge University Press; Judith Brown, *Gandhi: Prisoner of Hope.* Yale University Press, New Haven, 1991.

32 Mss. Eur F 125/11, Linlithgow papers, Linlithgow to Amery, 17 August, 1942.

33 *CWMG*, Vol. 39, Wavell to Gandhi, 24 March, 1944 Appendix xx, p.464.

34 *The Transfer of Power*, Vol.III, R. Maxwell to G. Laithwaite, private secretary to the viceroy 24 October, 1942, p.157.

4

~

THE MAHATMA AND THE MASSES

UNDERSTANDING GANDHI AND HIS PHILOSOPHY IS ELUSIVE. Although Gandhi had written extensively on India's socio-economic and political scenario, there were areas in his thought processes that often projected a different Gandhi altogether. In order to deconstruct Gandhian thought in the perspective in which he was involved in a gigantic nationalist struggle of the twentieth century, what is probably incumbent is to assess Gandhi in two different ways. First, Gandhian political ideas are to be related to the actual anti-British onslaught that began with the 1919-22 Non-Cooperation Movement and culminated with the 1942 Quit India campaign. In this context, Gandhi's worldview, taking into account his role as a social reformer, aimed at changing the outlook of people, was thus connected with social development. Secondly, there were events, more significant perhaps from the point of view of 'anti-imperial struggle', which though drawing upon Gandhian teachings, deviated from the well-established norm of non-violence. The implication of such deviations appeared disastrous to Gandhi himself. But for those who participated in these movements, which ran counter to non-violence, the means of political action seem to have been also derived from Gandhi.

Though there is no dearth of material written by Gandhi, understanding his ideology is not simple. There is neither a thesis nor any consistency in his arguments as the Mahatma reacted differently at different point of times in response to circumstances. Primarily a political activist, Gandhi was probably aware of inconsistency in his thoughts when he admitted,

> At times of writing I never think what I have said before. My aim is not to be consistent with my previous statements on a given question, but to be consistent with truth as it may present itself to me at a given moment. The result has been that I have grown from truth to truth. I have saved memory from an undue strain.[1]

On another occasion, Gandhi attributed his plan of action to his 'sixth sense'. As he argued, 'my sixth sense does wake up at the right moment and afterwards goes to sleep'. He further added that 'I speak under inspiration. I cannot decide as to how I shall tackle a particular situation until I am faced with it.' Moreover, he once admitted himself of doing things contrary to his previous practices. While on one occasion, he suggested the satyagrahis 'to act as model prisoners and obey every order of the officials', on another in the context of the 1942 open rebellion, he asked the participants to respond to the situation as it demanded. The volunteers responded to the situation as it demanded, and this movement became violent too. As evident, Mahatma's deeds were generally context-dependent and what appeared to be contradictory seems to be strategic.

Unlike his predecessors, Gandhi, with his well-entrenched Indianness in lifestyle and political vocabulary, mobilized the people of India and demonstrated his ability to translate popular grievances into political action. Attributing the rise of the Mahatma as an invincible leader in the nationalist struggle against the British to his physical and mental affinity with the traditions and temperament of the Indian masses, Subhas Chandra Bose, who opposed Gandhi and Gandhism almost throughout his active political career within the National Congress, thus commented,

> . . . when the Mahatma spoke, he does so in a language that [the people] comprehend not in the language of Herbert Spencer and Edmund Burke, as for instance, Sir Surendra Nath Banerjee would have done, but in that of the Bhagvad Gita and the Ramayana. When he talks to them about Swaraj, he does not dilate on the virtues of provincial autonomy or federation, he reminds them of the glories of Ramrajya [the kingdom of the mythical king Rama] and they understand. And he talks of conquering through love and ahimsa (non-violence), they are reminded of Buddha and Mahavira and they accept him.[2]

THE BASIC PRECEPTS

Gandhi's ideological interaction with the masses was always articulated around two basic precepts, namely, satyagraha and ahimsa. Most authors on Gandhi seem to conflate the two. What is rather relatively less known is the fact that during the period between his experiment in South Africa and the agitation against the Rowlatt Act, it was satyagraha – in the sense of a protest without rancour – that held the key to his entire campaign. It was only in the aftermath of the 1919 anti-Rowlatt movement, that ahimsa or non-violence was included as integral to Gandhi's satyagraha campaign. There is no doubt that ahimsa always remained a significant influence in the conceptualization of satyagraha; but it was not projected as crucial a component as it became later. In other words, despite its obvious importance, ahimsa never figured prominently in Gandhian discourse of political action. As a method, satyagraha was always informed by ahimsa though its role was not vividly articulated till 1919. From now on, the Mahatma paid enormous attention to both conceptualizing and justifying the importance of ahimsa in political mobilization by referring to the ancient scriptures in his defence. That ahimsa acquired tremendous importance following the Rowlatt Satyagraha is also suggestive of the nature of the movement that Gandhi was contemplating in its aftermath. Gandhi was preparing for a pan-Indian Non-Cooperation Movement in the satyagraha format in which ahimsa was to play a determining role in political mobilization. Thus, the micro-experiments of satyagraha in Champaran, Kheda and Ahmedabad, where ahimsa was constitutive of Gandhian model of anti-imperialism were therefore decisive in formulating Gandhi's social and political thought.

Ahimsa is central to Gandhism, which he conceptualized in the following manner: (a) non-violence is the law of the human race and is infinitely greater than and superior to brute force; (b) in the last resort it does not avail to those who do not possess a living faith in the god of love; (c) non-violence affords the fullest protection to one's self-respect and sense of honour, but not always to possession of land or movable property, though its habitual practice does prove a better bulwark than the possession of armed men to defend them.

Non-violence in the very nature of things is of no assistance in the defence of ill-gotten gains and immortal acts; (d) individuals or nations who would practice non-violence must be prepared to sacrifice (nations to the last man) their all except honour. It is therefore inconsistent with the possession of other people's countries, i.e., modern imperialism which is frankly based on force for its defence; (e) non-violence is a power which can be wielded equally by all – children, young men and women or grown-up people – provided they have a living faith in the god of love and have therefore equal love for all mankind. When non-violence is accepted as the law of life it must pervade the whole being and not applied to isolated acts; (f) it is a profound error to suppose that whilst the law is good enough for individuals, it is not for masses of mankind.[3]

For Gandhi, ahimsa meant 'both passive and active love, refraining from causing harm and destruction to living beings as well as positively promoting their well-being'. This suggests that by ahimsa, Gandhi did not mean merely 'non-injury' to others as that was a mere negative or passive connotation; instead, ahimsa had also a positive or active meaning of love and charity. As Gandhi clarified by saying that

> In its negative form, [ahimsa] means not injuring any living being whether by body or mind. I may not, therefore, hurt the person of any wrong-doer or bear any ill-will to him and so cause him mental suffering. In its positive form, ahimsa means the largest love, the greatest charity. If I am a follower of ahimsa, I must love my enemy or a stranger to me as I would my wrong-doing father or son. This active ahimsa necessarily included truth and fearlessness.[4]

As evident, Gandhi defined ahimsa in two contrasting ways: on the one hand, in its narrow sense, it simply meant avoidance of acts harming others; while in its positive sense, it denoted promoting their well-being, based on 'infinite love'.[5] Non-violence was certainly not just a negative force, it was not just non-resistance; it was rather non-violent resistance which was, as Jawaharlal Nehru characterized, 'a positive and dynamic method of action' [and] it was not meant for those who 'meekly accept the status quo'. The very purpose for which it was designed was, 'to create "a ferment in society" and thus to change existing conditions. Whatever the motives of conversion behind it, in practice, it has been' Nehru argued further, 'a powerful weapon of compulsion as well, though that compulsion is exercised in the most civilized and least objectionable manner.'[6]

Ahimsa, in its positive connotation, was based on highest moral values, epitomized in 'the unselfish self'. Gandhi thus wrote,

> our desires and motives may be divided into two classes – selfish and unselfish. All selfish desires are immoral, while the desire to improve ourselves for the sake of doing good to others is truly moral. ... The highest moral law is that we should unremittingly work for the good of mankind.

As a crucial variable in satyagraha, ahimsa not only enabled Gandhi to provide a new conception of anti-colonial politics, it also gave him an opportunity, by completely avoiding ill-feelings towards those in opposition, to politically accommodate people from all walks of life. But his approach was very cautious, as he argued,

> [a]himsa with me is a creed, the breath of life. It is [however] never as a creed that I placed it before India or, for that matter, before any one. ... I placed it before the Congress as a political weapon, to be employed for the solution of practical problems.[7]

Thus, ahimsa was complementary to Gandhi's model of conflict resolution that was certainly the most original and creative model of social change and political action even under most adverse circumstances. This was a theory of politics that gradually became the dominant ideology of a national political movement in which Gandhi reigned supreme. What lay at the root of this theory of politics was ahimsa, which was 'the organizing principle for a science of politics [that] was wholly different from the all current conceptions of politics [producing] the science of violence'. Not only was this theory effective in mobilizing people regardless of socio-economic differences, it also provided a moral framework for 'solving every practical problem of the organized political movement'.

Satyagraha meant not merely passive resistance, but 'intense activity by the people'. It denoted a legitimate, moral and truthful form of political action by the people against the brutal state power. It was a movement against various forms of injustice, meted out by the state. As Gandhi argued, 'we do not desire to make armed assaults on the administrators, nor to unseat them from power, but only to get rid of injustice'.[8] What it involved was a plan of action involving large masses of people targeting the state and vested social and economic interests. In organizing people for satyagraha, what was needed was also a level of awareness among the people linking their 'poverty' with the exploitative alien state. Gandhi was confident that the circumstances were ready and what was required was a call for campaign. Hence he argued just on the eve of the Rowlatt Satyagraha,

> it is said that it is a very difficult, if not an altogether impossible task to educate ignorant peasants in satyagraha and that it is full of perils, for it is a very arduous business to transform unlettered ignorant people from one condition into another. Both the arguments are silly. The people of India are perfectly fit to receive the training of satyagraha. India has knowledge of dharma, and where there is knowledge of dharma, satyagraha is a very simple matter. ... Some have a fear that once people get involved in satyagraha, they may at a later stage take arms. This fear is illusory. From the path of satyagraha, a transition to the path of a-satyagraha is impossible. It is possible of course that some people who believe in armed activity may mislead satyagraha by infiltrating into their ranks and later making them take to arms. ... But as compared to other activities, it is less likely to happen in satyagraha, for their motives soon get exposed and when the people are not ready to take up arms, it becomes almost impossible to lead them on to that terrible path.[9]

The Rowlatt Satyagraha translated the Gandhian deeds into action. Drawing on his faith on the spontaneous resistance of the masses to injustice, Gandhi was confident of the success of the campaign against the Rowlatt Act. There is no doubt that this satyagraha was a watershed in Gandhi's political ideology for two specific reasons, as: (a) Gandhi now realized the potential of the growing mass discontent in the anti-British struggle; and (b) this satyagraha was also a litmus test for the Mahatma who now was confident of satyagraha as a technique for political mobilization. For Gandhi, the Rowlatt Act was an unjust order that should be dis-honoured, for he argued,

> whether you are satyagrahis or not, so long as you disapprove of the Rowlatt legislation, all can join and [he was confident] that there will be such a response throughout the length and breadth of India as would convince the government that we are alive to what is going on in our midst.

With his success in this satyagraha, Gandhi was now ready for a pan-Indian political movement against the ruler, and the Rowlatt Satyagraha provided the impetus. Although Gandhi underlined the importance of ahimsa in satyagraha, he did not appear to emphasize its importance very strongly. For him, what was crucial was an organized attack on the British interest through a satyagraha campaign. As he argued,

> popular imagination has pictured satyagraha as purely and simply civil disobedience, if not in some cases, criminal disobedience. … As satyagraha is being brought into play on a large scale on the political field for the first time, it is in an experimental stage. I am therefore ever making new discoveries. And my error in trying to let civil disobedience take the people by storm appears to me to be Himalayan because of the discovery, I have made, namely, that he only is able and attains the right to offer civil disobedience who has known how to offer voluntary and deliberate obedience to the laws of the State in which he is living.[10]

Thus, Gandhi capitalized on the obvious mass discontent, which he translated, in satyagraha. Now, what were the organizational principles? In his scheme of things, a satyagrahi should know these principles before embarking on a campaign. As he mentioned, before they got involved in any political campaign against the ruling authority, 'they should thoroughly understand its deeper implications. That being so, before restarting civil disobedience on a mass scale, it would be necessary to create a band of well-tried, pure-hearted volunteers who thoroughly understood the strict conditions of satyagraha.'[11] Thus was conceptualized the notion of satyagraha as a mobilizing principle governing the behaviour of volunteers participating in nationalist campaign. And the more 'Gandhi concerned himself with the organizational norms within which a national movement had to be conducted, the more he began to elaborate upon the concept of ahimsa'.[12] A leader was responsible to direct the mass discontent into a course of action. Masses were not trained and their behaviour even in resistance was always that of a mob. The leadership was crucial in transforming the mob into an organized mass with meaningful action to undertake. As Gandhi himself confessed, 'nothing is so easy to train the mobs, for the simple reason that they have no mind, no pre-meditation. They act in frenzy. They repent quickly.'[13] He was not hesitant to characterize demonstrations during the first phase of the Non-Cooperation Movement as 'a mob without a mind'. He believed that such undisciplined demonstrations would not be able to 'procure swaraj for India'. And so, to involve the masses in meaningful political campaigns, one had to articulate satyagraha into specific courses of action, especially its 'modalities of resistance'. This is where ahimsa assumes tremendous significance. Ahimsa was that specific organizational principle that governed the behaviour of a satyagrahi. In other words, ahimsa was critical to the entire exercise of satyagraha, without which the very act of resistance would appear to be futile. Ahimsa was a foundational principle as well. Not only did it articulate the nature of the campaign, it would also structure the form of resistance by guiding those involved in it. This was indeed 'the science of non-violence' in the sense that it provided a grammar of Gandhian political mobilization in which 'civil resisters represent the non-violent army of the nation. And just as every citizen cannot be a soldier on the active list, every citizen cannot be a civil resister on the active list'. Interestingly, the onus of strictly adhering to the science of non-violence rested with the leadership and not with the masses. Just like a soldier of an army 'who does not know the whole of the military science; so also does a satyagrahi not know the whole of satyagraha. It is enough if he trusts his commander and honestly follows his instructions and is ready to suffer unto death without bearing malice against the so-called enemy. The satyagrahis must render heart discipline to their commander.' Here Gandhi was referring to mass civil disobedience where the role of the leader was immensely important in guiding the masses whereas in individual civil resistance 'everyone was a complete independent unit [and] every resister is his own leader'.

As evident, despite its significance in earlier satyagrahas in Champaran, Kheda and Ahmedabad, ahimsa was not clearly articulated by the Mahatma till the Rowlatt Satyagraha when its importance was duly recognized both in mobilizing people and also defining the goal of the campaign. Ahimsa came to the surface, as it were, and its political importance in Gandhian resistance was upheld beyond doubt. Satyagraha was thus based on the principles of satya, ahimsa and tapas (self-suffering). No definition is more apt than Gandhi's own oral submission before the Disorders Inquiry Committee, known as the Hunter Committee, on 9 January 1920.

Admitting that he was 'the author of the Satyagraha Movement', Gandhi defined satyagraha by stating that:

> it is a movement intended to replace method of violence and movement entirely upon Truth. It is, as I have conceived it, an extension of the domestic law on the political field and my experience has led me to the conclusion that that movement and that alone can rid India of the possibility of violence spreading throughout the length and breadth of the land, for the redress of grievance.

Satyagraha was not therefore identical with passive resistance. While identifying the features of satyagraha in his *Hind Swaraj*, Gandhi was of the opinion that passive resistance 'fails to convey [what he meant]. It describes a method, but gives no hint of the system of which it is only a part. Real beauty, and that is my aim, is in doing good against evil.' In other words, the similarity between satyagraha and passive resistance was just peripheral since both of them were a clearly-defined methods of political resistance, opposed to violence. Gandhi may certainly have drawn on passive resistance conceptually; but when he defined satyagraha he underlined its unique nature and characteristics. In *Hind Swaraj* he elaborated,

> Passive resistance is a method of securing rights by personal suffering; it is reverse of resistance by arms. When I refuse to do a thing that is repugnant to my conscience, I use soul-force. For instance, the government of the day has passed a law which is applicable to me. I do not like it. If, by using violence, I force the government to repeal the law, I am employing what may be termed body-force. If I do not obey the law, and accept penalty for its breach, I use soul-force. It involves sacrifice of self.

As shown, passive resistance can never be equated with satyagraha for the simple reason, as Gandhi himself stated, that it involved application of force as well, while in the latter, the application of force, of whatever nature, was completely ruled out. He defended that satyagraha was distinctly different from passive resistance while challenging the views that it was the same as passive resistance practised in England by the suffragettes and by the opponents of the 1902 Education Act. What separates passive resistance from satyagraha was the fact that while the former was compatible with mild forms of physical violence, that was an anathema to the latter, Gandhi held. In his words,

> Burning of houses by [the women involved in the Suffragette Movement in England] and ... fasting in prison ... might very well be passive resistance, but they were not satyagraha. . . . The movement in South Africa is not passive but active. The Indians of South Africa believed that Truth was their object, that Truth ever triumphs, and with this definiteness of purpose they persistently held on to Truth. They put up with all the suffering that this persistence implied.

Hence he was most categorical by saying that,

> passive resistance is an all-sided sword; it can be used anyhow; it blesses him who uses it and him against whom it is used. Without drawing a drop of blood, it produces far-reaching results. It never rusts, and cannot be stolen. Competition between passive resisters does not exhaust. The sword of passive resistance does not require a scabbard. It is strange indeed that you should consider such a weapon to be a weapon merely of the weak.[14]

Gandhi associated passive resistance with internal violence. It unleashed 'forces of prejudice and separatism rather than compassion and inclusiveness'. While emphasizing this dimension, he further argued,

> Everybody admits that sacrifice of self is infinitely superior to sacrifice of others. Moreover, if this kind of force is used in a course that is unjust, only the person using it suffers. He does not make others suffer for his mistakes. Men have before now done many things which were subsequently found to have been wrong. No man can claim to be absolutely in the right, or that a particular thing is wrong, because he thinks so, but it is wrong for him so long as that is his deliberate judgement. It is, therefore, [meant] that he should not do that which he knows to be wrong, and suffer the consequences whatever it may be. This is the key to use soul-force.

In the Gandhian mode of conflict resolution, self-suffering was crucial but resorted to sparingly. Once reasoning with the opponent failed, the satyagrahi was allowed to resort to self-suffering. Satyagraha was therefore a device recognizing the limits of reason in resolving amicably fundamental social, religious, political and economic conflicts. So, for Gandhi, satyagraha was not to be immediately launched; instead, it was the last resort of action when other usual processes or reasoning with the opponents or oppressors completely failed. Gandhi was categorical in this respect, as he argued,

> since satyagraha is one of the most powerful methods of direct action, a satyagrahi exhausts all other means before he resorts to satyagraha. He will, therefore, constantly and continually approach the constituted authority, he will appeal to public opinion, educate public opinion, state this calmly and coolly

> before everybody who wants to listen to him; and only after he has exhausted all these avenues will he resort to satyagraha.

Two points are very clear now. First, Gandhi was not anarchic in his approach. While elaborating the stage of the campaign, the lawyer in Gandhi was not prepared to plunge into satyagraha at the outset; instead, he would exhaust all possible channels of conflict resolution before satyagraha was launched. Secondly, as a liberal, the Mahatma also underlined the importance of public opinion as a powerful device to persuade the authority. In his words, 'public opinion, for which one cares, is a mightier force than gunpowder'. In the formation of public opinion, the role of a satyagrahi was immensely important for 'the satyagrahi strives to reach the reason through heart'. Once reasoning failed, satyagrahi was allowed to undertake tapas or self-suffering that was now justified as the last straw to change the 'heart' of the opponents or oppressors. When 'appeal to reason does not answer', 'self-suffering' is the only means available, to the satyagrahis as this would create conditions for reason to triumph. The conviction rapidly grew within him that 'things of fundamental importance to the people are not secured by reason alone, but have to be purchased with voluntary suffering'. Thus, self-suffering was integrally linked with Gandhi's theory of conflict resolution because of its obvious importance. He argued that self-suffering and through it moving your opponent's heart was more powerful than war.

Self-suffering was a force to inculcate reason in the opponents that constituted a significant dimension in Gandhi's social and political thought. Satyagraha was thus not merely a conceptual construction, but was also 'designed as an effective substitute for violence', based on certain fundamental theoretical tenets in contrast with those informing the Western civilization. His opposition to violence was more fundamental than assumed simply because he believed that violence distorted the Western civilization by defending exploitation of human beings. Not only did Gandhi shape satyagraha as a plan of action, he also provided 'a strong institutional base for the expression of dissent' within colonialism despite the obvious adverse consequences of opposition. Satyagraha translated 'the voice of protest' in effective terms. It thus 'provides a means through which … the personal is made political' in the sense that satyagraha was simultaneously a device for Truth and freedom from colonial rule.

Gandhi's satyagraha had several forms. During the nationalist movement in India, the most frequently employed methods of campaign were 'non-cooperation' and 'civil disobedience', apart from submitting memorandum of demands to the authority. While non-cooperation (hartal, strikes, boycott, and fasts unto death) was a mechanism for indirect pressure on the opponent, civil disobedience (picketing, non-payment of taxes and defiance of specific laws) entailed several positive steps to confront the ruling authority face-to-face. Non-Cooperation appears to pave the way for civil disobedience, which was a form of non-violent rebellion. Simultaneously with these two contrasting designs for political action, Gandhian satyagraha also entailed constructive programme (for the promotion of communal harmony, removal of untouchability, adult education, promotion of social and economic equality, devolution of power through schemes of political and economic decentralization). Taken together, satyagraha was not merely a political weapon to challenge the British rule, it was also a detailed scheme to rid Indian society of the age-old social and economic prejudices. In other words, satyagraha was a continuous exercise with clear social and economic messages, relevant to the dis-privileged and exploited, apart from the political opposition to the British rule. As Gandhi described,

> the satyagraha struggle in British India had two aspects, non-violent non-cooperation with the Government, and co-operation among the people themselves. Both these aspects should constantly be kept [in mind]. The constructive programme that I have set before you necessitates perfect co-operation among all sections.

In Gandhian satyagraha, fasting, which was purificatory as well, was defined 'as a great weapon in the armoury of satyagraha'. Gandhi undertook fasts also to put pressure on the opponents when persuasion failed to yield results. This was a device to inflict pain on himself, a process that Gandhi believed was to persuade the opponents to appreciate the goals for which fast was undertaken. Fast was to be sparingly resorted to since 'there is', according to Gandhi 'violence behind … fasting'. He made a subtle distinction between fasting and hunger strike. While the latter is a serious political weapon with tremendous impact on the opponents, the former was a soul-purifying exercise. Hunger strike was thus an innovative tool of action directed against the opponents once the usual processes of satyagraha were aborted. As it required tremendous mental strength, hunger strike had to be resorted, Gandhi warned, carefully because withdrawal was not possible unless its aim was fulfilled. As he stated,

> unscientific experimentation with [hunger strike] is bound to be harmful to the one who fasts, and it may even harm the cause espoused. No one who has not earned the right to do so should, therefore, use this weapon. A fast may only be undertaken by him who is associated with the person against whom he fasts. The latter must be directly connected with the purpose for which the fast is being undertaken.

There are three points for consideration here: (a) fasting was to be undertaken as a last resort; once the usual available tools of satyagraha were exhausted, the satyagrahi was allowed to plunge into fasting; (b) the individual action in this regard would be justified only when the satyagrahi was convinced that fasting was the only option available under the circumstances and he completely endorsed the goal; and (c) fasting was allowed to be undertaken against those with whom one was connected with the ties of love. Its implications are quite clear. Gandhi, therefore, set limits to the way fasting was to be resorted. Furthermore, although it was a crucial form of opposition, fasting was 'an adjunct to other forms of satyagraha'. This was a form in which individuals articulated protests by inflicting injury on to one's self. Gandhi argued that fast was a form of love, articulated in self-suffering, and had a fourfold purpose. First, it was his expression of a deep sense of sorrow and hurt at the way in which those, against whom this was directed, had degraded themselves and disappointed him; secondly, as their leader, he was responsible for them and his fast was his typical way of atoning for their misdeeds; thirdly, it was his last desperate attempt, 'an intense spiritual effort' to bring the moribund masses into action and to mobilize their moral energies; finally, fast was his technique to defuse the communal tension between the Hindus and Muslims by deepening the sense of community and foster mutual respect for each other.

As shown, Gandhi's satyagraha was a well-defined plan of action with both social and political implications. The steps that constituted satyagraha were not only well-designed, but also organically linked with his theory based on love. Hence satyagraha needed to be guided not by 'minds' but by 'hearts'.[15] While writing on satyagraha, the Mahatma always insisted on certain basic principles. Gandhi publicized 'some rules of satyagraha' in *Young India* (27 February, 1930), which were as follows: 'as an individual (a) a satyagrahi, i.e, a civil resister will harbour no anger; (b) he will suffer the anger of the opponent; (c) in so doing he will put up with assaults from the opponent, never retaliate; but he will not submit, out of fear of punishment or the like, to any order given in anger; (d) when any person in authority seeks to arrest a civil resister, he will voluntarily submit to the arrest, and he will not resist the attachment or removal of his own property, if any, when it is sought to be confiscated by authorities; (e) if a civil resister has any property in his possession as a trustee, he will refuse to surrender it, even though in defending it he might lose his life. He will, however, never retaliate; (f) non-retaliation excludes swearing and cursing; (g) therefore a civil resister will never insult his opponent, and therefore also not take part in many of the newly coined cries which are contrary to the spirit of ahimsa; (h) a civil resister will not salute the Union Jack, nor will he insult it or officials, English or Indian; (i) in the course of the struggle if anyone insults an official or commits an assault upon him, a civil resister will protect such official or officials from the insult or attack even at the risk of his life. The second set of rules is applicable to a satyagrahi when in prison: (a) as a prisoner, a civil resister will behave courteously towards prison officials, and will observe all such discipline of the prison as is not contrary to self-respect; as for instance, whilst he will *salaam* (show respect) officials in the usual manner, he will not perform any humiliating gyrations and refuse to shout 'victory to *Sarkar*' or the like. He will take cleanly cooked and cleanly served food, which is not contrary to his religion, and will refuse to take food insultingly served or served in unclean vessels; (b) a civil resister will make no distinction between an ordinary prisoner and himself, will in no way regard himself as superior to the rest, nor will he ask for any conveniences that may be necessary for keeping his body in good health and condition. He is entitled to ask for such conveniences as may be required for his physical or spiritual well-being; (c) a civil resister may not fast for want of conveniences whose deprivation does not involve any injury to one's self-respect. Rules are different for a satyagrahi when he is a part of a unit. In a unit, (a) a civil resister will joyfully obey all the orders issued by the leader of the corps, whether they [are pleased] with him or not; (b) he will carry out orders in the first instance even though they appear to him insulting, inimical or foolish, and then appeal to higher authority. He is free before joining to determine the fitness or the corps to satisfy him, but after he has joined it, it becomes a duty to submit to his discipline, irksome or otherwise; if the sum total of the energy of the corps appears to a member to be improper or immoral, he has a right to sever his connection but being within it, he has no right to commit a breach of its discipline;

(c) no civil resister is to expect maintenance for his dependents. It would be an accident if any such provision is made. A civil resister entrusts his dependants to the care of god. Even in ordinary warfare wherein hundreds of thousands give themselves up to it, they are able to make no previous provision. How much more, then, should such be the case in satyagraha? It is the universal experience that in such times hardly anybody is left to starve. Finally, there are also clear rules for a satyagrahi during communal fights involving Hindus, Muslims and other communities. In communal fights, (a) no civil resister will intentionally become a cause of communal quarrels; (b) in the event of any such outbreak, he will not take sides, but he will assist only that party which is demonstratively in the right. Being a Hindu he will be generous towards Mussalmans and others, and will sacrifice himself in the attempt to save non-Hindus from a Hindu attack. And if the attack is from the other side, he will not participate in any retaliation but will give his life in protecting Hindus; (c) he will, to the best of his ability, avoid every occasion that may give rise to communal quarrels; (d) if there is a procession of satyagrahis they will do nothing that would wound the religious susceptibilities of any community, and they will not take part in other processions that are likely to wound such susceptibilities.' Before embarking on a satyagraha, one had to be convinced that the situation warranted a campaign and its objectives were clear to the participants; as it was an open call, the opponents were to be given an opportunity for negotiations if they wanted to avoid oppositional campaign; Hence, satyagraha should not be resorted to 'lightly', and that if satyagraha was not to be abused, it must be resorted to by those individuals who were qualified to embark on it 'must have already acquired the habit of willing obedience to laws without fear of their sanctions', [and] those who have not learnt to obey laws for the right reasons do not have the right to obey the law'. This is what Gandhi insisted when he mentioned that 'disobedience without civility, discipline [and] non-violence is certain destruction'. Gandhi never foreclosed the channel of communication with the adversaries presumably because the attitudes on either side, he believed, should not be allowed to be rigid. This was the grammar of satyagraha as a campaign in which a satyagrahi was required to take a pledge not to harm the opponents even by nurturing any ill feelings towards them. The primary duty of a satyagrahi was to convert the opponent by self-suffering and not by causing pain. Even while in prison, a satyagrahi was to behave in an exemplary manner without asking for facilities 'whose deprivation does not involve any injury to his self-respect'.

Gandhi's satyagraha was not only a political doctrine directed against the state, it has also social and economic thrusts relevant to and drawn on human nature. In contrast with the constitutional and extremist methods of political mobilization, satyagraha was a highly original and creative conceptualization of social change and political action. Opposed to violence, Gandhi's preferred way was ahimsa that drew on the strength of persuasion. Once persuasion failed, Gandhi was not hesitant to adopt fasting that was a slightly stronger means in the sense that it affected the opponents by moral blackmailing. The principles governing satyagraha and its participants are illustrative of his endeavour to organize the mass protest within a strict format that clearly stipulates the duties and responsibilities of an individual satyagrahi. So, not only did he creatively define the nature of the struggle for freedom he also provided a well-designed structure for political mobilization. In the narrow sense, satyagraha was strictly a method of political struggle, drawn on moral reasoning; in the wider sense, this was an extremely humane and creative way of dealing with disagreements and conflicts involving the ruler and the ruled and also socio-economically dis-privileged and their *bete noire*. What is most distinct in Gandhi's conceptualization was the importance of 'rational' discussion and persuasion and also their obvious limitation in radically altering the existent moral relationships between individuals in different socio-economic locations. Hence satyagraha was to be a continuous process seeking to transform the individuals by appreciating the humane moral values that had remained captive due to colonialism and various social prejudices, justified in the name of religion.

Satyagraha was a theoretical construct of conflict resolution as well as a practical doctrine of political mobilization. Though there were competing ideologies in the anti-British campaign, their influence did not appear to be as significant as satyagraha. Even for those who sought to provide a creative alternative ideology, Gandhi was a constant referent. In other words, Gandhi remained critically important both as a discourse and a practical model for organizing people for political action. And, also the possibilities for a different ideological route for freedom were always nipped in the bud presumably because it was suicidal for the multi-class nationalist mobilization. Hence, Gandhi and his colleagues always endorsed the national democratic ideology. Satyagraha appeared appropriate in an effort to sustain, if not strengthen, Gandhi's ideological character without radically disrupting its core. It was therefore obvious that although peasants and workers emerged as separate constituencies in the nationalist politics by the early 1920s, they were always represented by the Congress and mobilized for the Gandhi-led political campaign for freedom. In other words the issues relevant to the workers and peasantry were appropriated to advance the national democratic goal of the Indian National Congress. For instance, the commitment to national democracy was so genuine and firm that the Congress involvement in the working-class movement for better deal from the industrialists was always half-hearted. As a result, the workers were alienated just like the peasantry that never became an integral part of the nationalist platform, at least examples from Bengal clearly illustrate where the peasant response was articulated in both communal and ideologically radical terms. Gandhism thus provided the conception of a national framework of politics 'in which the peasants are mobilized but do not participate, of a nation of which they are a part, but a national state from which they are forever distanced'.

GANDHI: THE LEADER AND THE METAPHOR

There is no doubt that Gandhism was a hegemonic influence in the Indian nationalist movement. On most occasions, the Mahatma authored and scripted the anti-British political campaign in accordance with what he stood for ideologically. This is one part of the story. The other equally important part concerns with the diverse nature of the movements, which purportedly drew on Gandhian satyagraha. In other words, there was a clear hiatus between the actual articulation of the movements at the grassroots and the ideology that appeared to have inspired the participants. Suggestive of 'autonomy of politics', the Gandhian instructions were translated differently by those involved in satyagraha that ran, on occasions, counter to the basic precepts of Gandhism. Although Gandhism was the most effective organizing principle for the mass movement, its texture varied from one location to another within a particular movement. What it suggests is the fact that in the articulation of a movement, Gandhian intervention was crucial and yet, its ability to shape the movement at the grassroot was highly restricted showing probably the role of the local organizers in demarcating its ideological contour. Gandhi was highly significant in defusing fear from the grassroot activists who dared to defy the authority in the name of the Mahatma. But when movements were articulated they, on various occasions, flouted the core idea of ahimsa, for instance thus justifying the autonomy of Gandhi's social and political ideas. Gandhi was interpreted creatively by the participants keeping in mind the importance of the locally relevant social, political and economic issues that easily mobilized the people for the nationalist cause. Despite undermining the basic precepts of Gandhism, Gandhi always remained a significant referent even in the movements which were hardly Gandhian either in content or spirit and yet they were justified as having derived from the Mahatma.

It is difficult to deal with the remarkably large number of socio-political movements in India during the nationalist struggle in which Gandhi figured prominently either as a leader or as one providing the ideology. Hence, I shall be selectively dealing with three major pan-Indian nationalist campaigns – the Non-Cooperation, the Civil Disobedience and the Quit India Movements. What is theoretically innovative and intellectually refreshing is the way these movements were articulated at the grassroots by the local political activists in accordance with their priorities by redefining the core ideas of Gandhi's social and political philosophy. In other words, as in organizing movements, Gandhi remained crucial in their sustenance as well, though their nature was at variance with what the Mahatma stood for.

NON-VIOLENCE AS A MEANS OF POLITICAL ACTION

Is non-violence as a means of political action a product of a particular historical conjuncture? The answer is probably 'yes'. In the midst of the 'extremist challenge', which was confined to the noble deeds of the revolutionary terrorists, non-violence appeared to be a unique method of involving the masses regardless of religion and caste, thus extending the constituency of the nationalist politics. Hence, Gandhi's arrival on the political scene was well-tuned to the requirements of the day for reasons connected with the peculiar historical circumstances. What is argued here is that Gandhi, with his method of non-violence, appeared invincible probably due to a peculiar combination of socio-economic and politico-cultural forces in which no method other than non-violence gained currency.

Gandhi as a phenomenon is an offshoot of a process, which began in South Africa in the late nineteenth century. Like any other political activist, nurtured in the enlightenment tradition of knowledge, Gandhi also found himself as a colonial subject, fashioned in the loyalist discourse. Interestingly, the speeches and writings in which he justified his role as a colonial subject constitute what can be termed as 'a classic text of collaborationist nationalism'. The following excerpts again seem apt in this context:

> If an unflinching devotion to duty and extreme eagerness to serve our sovereign can make us of any use in the field of battle, we trust, we would not fail . . .
>
> The motive underlying this humble offer is an endeavour to prove that, in common with other subjects of the Queen Empress in South Africa, the Indians too, are ready to do duty for their Sovereign on the battlefield. The offer is meant to be an earnest of the Indian loyalty.[16]
>
> . . . the English-speaking Indians came to the conclusion that they would offer their services unconditionally and absolutely without payment . . . in order to show the colonists that they were worthy subjects of the Queen.[17]

Besides defining self-subjection of the colonized, these excerpts, with phrases like, 'eagerness to serve' and the offer of 'their services without pay unconditionally' are both a description and measure of the social distance between the colonizer and the colonized. What is evident here is that Gandhi, who grew up in the tradition of loyalist discourse, defended his argument by reference to the duty of the subject race to the empire in crisis. Even as a subordinated nation, Gandhi championed unequivocally the demands for the rights of South African Indians because as British subjects, Indians were entitled to basic rights. This was probably a watershed in Gandhi's political thinking, because he was no longer prepared to be unconditionally loyal to the British dominance. What can be argued here is that the South African experience appeared significant in identifying the limitations of a racist administration *vis-a-vis* the subject race. Here began the transformation of Gandhi from a loyalist whose 'loyalty to the empire drove him to the side of the British during the Boer war in the teeth of opposition from some of his countrymen', to the most effective political leader challenging the continuity of the empire. By asserting the rights of the subject people, Gandhi moved from loyalism to opposition to the British rule. Hence, what had begun as a stray reference became an important feature of Gandhian political ideology that was to unfold later. Similarly non-violence as a means of political tool acquired new dimensions in the light of changes in Gandhi as a leader who asserted, though within the constraints of bargaining and pressure politics, the people's right to rebel.

NON-VIOLENCE: DEFINITION

Semantically, non-violence means refraining from causing harm and destruction to others and is thus a negative concept. For Gandhi, however, non-violence connotes positive resistance – probably an appropriate method to politically mobilize Indians against the British at a particular juncture of history. Not only is the method well tuned to the Indian situation, it is also a means to build character in conformity with the well-entrenched Indian tradition. So despite its apparent negative content, non-violence, in its positive and active sense, results in organization for political action, which is grounded in compassion and love. Drawing on the Hindu,

Buddhist, and Jainist tradition, Gandhi seems to have arrived at an all-encompassing definition of non-violence by means of three crucial steps: (i) non-violence, in Gandhi's explanation, is compassion which is equated with love; (ii) like all other emotions, love constitutes a formidable force; and (iii) love is thus an alternative to the prevalent ideology for political mobilization. While endorsing these basic characteristics, Gandhi elaborated,

> [b]efore you aspire to drive the British from this country, you must drive every vestige of violence from your system. Remember that it is not going to be a fight with sticks and knives or guns, but only with love. Until you are sure you have an overpowering love at heart for your enemy, don't think of driving him out. You must generally forget the term "Enemy". You must think of him as a friend who must leave you. You must train yourself to become a 100 per cent ahimsa soldier. You must become so sensitive that it is not possible for you to wear sandals of the hide of slaughtered animals; you should prefer to go barefoot rather than wear the hide of an animal killed for your sake, that is if you are unable to secure the skin of an animal that had died a natural death.[18]

What is significant here is Gandhi's ability to translate natural human emotions and feelings into an all-pervasive and powerful ideology, which broadened the base of Indian nationalism by incorporating new social groups into nationalist politics.

Although non-violence is derived from the traditional Indian concept of ahimsa, in Gandhi's view it is different from the age-old connotation. He was categorical on a number of occasions by arguing that 'complete non-violence means complete cessation of all activity. Not such, however, is my definition of non-violence.' On another occasion, the Mahatma emphatically defended the view that non-violence is not merely an individual value but could also be a rule of conduct for the collectivity. In his words, 'non-violence is not cloistered virtue to be practised by the individual for his peace and final salvation, but a rule of conduct for society if it is to live consistently with human dignity.' He carried forward the argument further by making non-violence obligatory for all. Gandhi observed that non-violence was not only meant for the *rishis* and saints. It was also for the common people. Gandhi had no doubt that 'the power of unarmed non-violence is any day far superior to that of armed force. Its superior strength [he realized] in South Africa where [he] had to pit it against organized violence and racial prejudice' of the South African government.

Gandhi was not merely arguing for non-violence as a practicing ideal. As an activist who challenged the mighty imperial power, he defined non-violence as a political ideology, designed to inspire and mobilize the masses irrespective of caste, class, and religion, for the counter-offensive against the British. Insisting on the active participation of the people in the Congress-led nationalist struggle, he exhorted: 'Yours should not be a passive spirituality that spends itself in ideal meditation, but it should be an active thing which will carry war into the enemy's camp.' Non-violence, Gandhi thus argued, 'does not mean meek submission to the will of the evil-doer, but it means the pitting of one's whole soul against the will of the tyrant'. As he further elaborated in his response in *Harijan*,

> non-violence is not mere disarmament. Nor is the weapon of the weak and impotent. A child who has no strength to wield the lathi [stick] does not practise non-violence. More powerful than all the armaments, non-violence is a unique force that has come into the world. He who has not learnt to feel it to be a weapon infinitely more than brute force has not understood its true nature. This non-violence cannot be "taught" through word of mouth. But it can be kindled in our heart through the grace of God, in answer to earnest prayer.

Non-violence was therefore the weapon of those with tremendous mental strength. Adoption of non-violence was not strategic consideration contingent on the circumstances because Gandhi never allowed space for violence in his conceptualization of satyagraha. Hence those 'who harbour violence in their breasts and simply await opportunity for its display' had no place in his political campaign. It was necessary, therefore, Gandi insisted for every Congressmen to individually and collectively, 'examine the quality of their non-violence. If it does not come out of real strength, it would be best and honest for the Congress to make such a declaration and make the necessary changes in its behaviour.' Central to his civil disobedience campaign was non-violence on which Gandhi never compromised, because for him, 'the acid test of non-violence is that one thinks, speaks and acts non-violently, even when there is the gravest provocation to be violent'.

Gandhi's defence of non-violence seems a derivative course in the sense that he drew upon the Hindu, Buddhist, and Jainist traditions, besides the European influence, while developing his ideology. By consistently arguing for non-violence, the Mahatma developed a political discourse in which non-violence was always championed against violence. His preference for ahimsa was a conscious choice because, according to him, the use of violence was futile, as it does not secure a genuine change at all. In his words, 'violence may destroy one or more bad rulers, but like Ravana's head, others will pop up in their places for the root lies elsewhere. It lies in us. If we reform ourselves, the rulers will automatically do so.' Gandhi's undiluted faith in changing the attitude of the rulers may not sound plausible in the context of the British atrocities unleashed in the wake of the nationalist struggle by discarding violence altogether. What Gandhi probably hinted at was its limitation in transforming social relations simply because hatred and enmity, instead of containing animosity, create and sustain a situation for violence only.

Although Gandhi was a true supporter of non-violence, he, on occasions, upheld violence in preference to cowardice. He observed: 'where there is only a choice between cowardice and violence, I would advise violence'. Non-violence, he asserted, 'is not a cover for cowardice, it requires far greater bravery than swordsmanship'. For a coward, bravery is incomprehensible because, 'he is less than man' and he therefore 'does not deserve to be member of a society of men and women.' Having distinguished the act of cowardice from non-violence, Gandhi justified the application of violence if an individual 'cannot protect himself or his nearest and dearest or their honour by non-violently facing death, he may and ought to do so by violently dealing with the oppressor. He who can do neither of the two is a burden.' Explicit in Gandhi's statement is his unequivocal support for violence as a means under specific circumstances. Here probably lies the root of

Gandhi being evoked to justify happenings in which violence had triumphed despite constant vigil by the Congress High Command, which, true to the spirit of non-violence, never approved political campaign opposing the Gandhian creed. It perhaps illustrated either the limitation of non-violence as an effective ideology at the all-India level or the autonomy of politics at various levels of nationalist movement where ahimsa, in contrast to other prevalent ideologies, failed significantly in so far as political mobilization was concerned. There were occasions, as the discussion below shows, when the Congress nationalists consciously resorted to violence with the understanding that Gandhi would have approved of violence under those circumstances. A remarkable twist in the shape of an irony of history is thus evident. Gandhi the leader was readily acceptable and political action defying non-violence was justified too in his name. Gandhism the ideology, however, was both being questioned and jettisoned as well in several cases where ahimsa eclipsed and other ideologies blossomed.

Notwithstanding arguments and counter-arguments, non-violence remained integrally connected with Gandhi's value system despite heavy odds. Justifying convincingly that non-violence meant active involvement in India's freedom struggle, Gandhi had thus introduced a new dimension to India's nationalism, which had hitherto failed to provide a united resistance because of the infighting among the nationalists on ideological grounds. Therefore, Gandhi's appearance on the political scene transformed the nature of the anti-British campaign. Not only did he put forward a new ideology in otherwise adverse circumstances, he also personified in himself the qualities of a political leader who transcended the limitations of the day by his charisma. What seems significant here is Gandhi's capacity to absorb the traditional Indian value system in order to construct an ideology in which Indians, regardless of religion and other primordial schisms, found themselves well represented. Politically, it appears, no other ideology was likely to reinvigorate the freedom struggle as ahimsa did in the context of the British repression and the feud among the nationalists due to ideological crosscurrents.

NON-VIOLENCE AS A METHOD

For Gandhi, the adoption of non-violence as a method of political action was probably most expedient because, as he himself admitted: 'We do not know how to handle arms. It is not our fault, it is perhaps our misfortune that we cannot'. In the course of his direct involvement in the Congress-led nationalist movement, he both tested and consequently perfected the method which became a singularly important yardstick to the Mahatma in judging the nature of the movement. A deviation from ahimsa, as was evident in the latter part of the Non-Cooperation Movement of 1919-22, was enough to withdraw an otherwise successful anti-British political campaign. With hindsight, his apparent obsession for non-violence was justified in the light of the failures of both the moderates and the revolutionary terrorists who, despite their dedication and sincerity to the cause of national emancipation, failed to emerge as a formidable political force. Moreover, in the context of the British repression neither the terrorist nor the moderate method appeared effective.

Between 1920 and 1942, Gandhi was most powerful and

probably the only acceptable leader in the faction-ridden Congress Party. Although his first interaction with the Indian political scene was through the Non-Cooperation Movement, he began effective political activity in 1906 in South Africa where he organized non-violent resistance against the white settlers' racist policies. By mobilizing Indians for a direct but non-violent confrontation with authority, he launched bonfires of registration documents and an Indian march into the prohibited territory. The campaign saw a remarkable unity among the variety of Indians in South Africa ranging from Muslim traders to low-caste indentured labourers. The South African experience between 1907 and 1914 had thus provided Gandhi with an effective tool in the form of non-violence for mass mobilization in otherwise adverse circumstances.

Before he launched the 1919-22 Non-Cooperation Movement, Gandhi undertook non-violent campaign in three different localities against injustice. In Champaran, he launched non-violent confrontation to redress the grievances of the peasant-tenants who were being forced to grow indigo at disadvantageous terms by white planters. By mobilizing peasants in Kheda against the enhancement of land revenue, the South Africa rebel gave a new twist to the nationalist movement, which soon expanded its constituency by upholding the Ahmedabad Cotton Mill workers' demand for wage increase in 1918. Despite failure in Kheda, his success in Champaran and Ahmedabad highlighted the effectiveness of non-violent campaign in the face of large-scale atrocities.

Non-violence attained all-India publicity in the wake of Gandhi's campaign against the Rowlatt Bills. He offered non-violent civil disobedience in the form of satyagraha and sought the cooperation of moderates on the ground that 'the growing generation will not be satisfied with petition, etc. We must give them something effective. Satyagraha is the only way, it seems to me, to stop terrorism. From this point of view, I am justified in seeking your help'. The Rowlatt Satyagraha was a failure, but notwithstanding Gandhi's disappointment, the Rowlatt campaign was a breakthrough for him who was so far a stranger in Indian politics. Besides putting him on the centre-stage of nationalist politics, dominated by revolutionary terrorism and moderates, the 1919 satyagraha projected the extent to which ahimsa as a means of political action could be effective.

What began in the 1919 Rowlatt Satyagraha seems to have set the tone of the anti-British campaign. Between 1920 and 1942, not only did Gandhi consolidate his position in the Congress, non-violence also appeared invincible both as an ideology and as a method of political struggle. The 1919-22 non-cooperation was Gandhi's answer to those who clung to violence and the Western style of politics. Like the Rowlatt Satyagraha, Gandhi called off the Non-Cooperation Movement because of a vicious attack on a police station in Chauri Chaura. However, during the period between August 1920 and February 1922, Gandhi rose as the most powerful leader in the struggle for freedom who through non-violent non-cooperation infused a new zeal into an otherwise stagnant nationalist politics. In the official correspondence, it was thus noticed:

> The outstanding feature of the 1920 Nagpur Congress has been the personal domination of Gandhi over all political leaders and followers alike. He has carried through the policy that he had decided for this Congress without any material modification. All

opposition to his views has been overcome without difficulty owing to his strong hold over the bulk of the delegates and visitors with whom his word is law.

Gandhi's remarkable success in the 1920 political offensive can partly be attributed to the Hindu-Muslim consolidation, which was possible due to the merger of the Non-Cooperation Movement with the Khilafat cause. The decision to incorporate the Khilafat demands in the Congress-launched non-cooperation campaign was the offshoot of the practical consideration of eliciting Muslim support, which would have been impossible otherwise. Although the merger was the last instance of a combined Hindu-Muslim challenge to the British, it nonetheless draws our attention to the consolidation of Muslims as a separate political identity in the nationalist politics. The 'two-nation theory', so far a mental construct, became a reality with the organization of Muslims following the Khilafat ideal, which percolated down to the villages, though the Caliph was a distant object to the Indian Muslims. Both the Hindus and Muslims, therefore, agreed to the merger because of completely different political considerations. For the Hindus, the non-cooperation was a direct nationalist challenge, whereas, for the Muslims, it meant an assault on the British who had undermined the institution of the Caliph elsewhere.

After the collapse of the Non-Cooperation Movement, India seemed to have lapsed into 'political torpor', the Hindu-Muslim unity went to pieces, the Raj seemed firmly in the saddle, and 'the heady goal of Swaraj in a year lay in ruins'. Gandhi's decision to stay away form the nationalist politics in the aftermath of the non-cooperation campaign was probably determined by his awareness that 'with the present temper of many Congressmen, with our internal dissensions, with the communal tension . . ., it may be impossible to offer civil disobedience at this stage in the name of the Congress.' In March 1930, Gandhi, however, was prepared to launch the Civil Disobedience Movement which lasted between 1930 and 1934 with an intermission for most of 1931 'when the Congress negotiated with the Raj'.

During the civil disobedience campaign, non-violence had its manifestation in attacks on the government's salt monopoly and the boycott of foreign cloth. The Salt Satyagraha was all-pervasive affecting almost all the provinces, though for geographical reasons, there was little opportunity for making salt in some areas except token gestures. Bombay Presidency witnessed the most successful salt campaign where salt was produced under the protection of a human chain, formed by the Congress volunteers, thereby making it virtually impossible for the police to intervene without resorting to force – thus creating the moral outrage towards the alien administration, which the Congress had long been striving. In contrast, the boycott of foreign cloth appeared a more forceful campaign, in that not only did it seal the respect of selling foreign cloth in India, it also helped cultivate a constituency among the indigenous manufacturers. In fact, the boycott caused economic hardship as far as the British interest was concerned. Anticipating the adverse consequences of the Congress campaign in this regard, the government expressed concern and accordingly suggested steps to nip the movement in the bud.

Ahimsa had triumphed as a means of political action,

though its impact varied in style and intensity from region to region. Bombay and Gujarat were hit the hardest compared with other provinces for reasons connected with the physical location of these provinces. Unlike the non-cooperation, civil disobedience posed a serious threat to the Raj on a continental scale in terms of numbers, areas, and the types of the people involved. Despite being a successful anti-British campaign, the 1930-34 movement was a failure, in the sense that the Hindu-Muslim unity, evident during the non-cooperation days, was almost absent, except on the Frontier where, under Khan Abdul Gaffar Khan's stewardship, Gandhi's non-violence received a favourable response. In the Muslim-majority provinces like Bengal and Punjab, the campaign lost its vigour due to the lack of participation of the Muslims. The imperial divide-and-rule policy thus paid off in these two politically vibrant provinces. Alarmed by the consolidation of Hindu-Muslim schism, the Congress adopted measures which were neutralized, if not defeated, by the internecine feud among the Congressmen in Bengal and the lack of organization in Punjab.

Non-violence, which was so far a guiding force in the Congress-led freedom struggle, seems to have been largely undermined in the wake of the 1942 Quit India Movement due to circumstances, which went beyond Gandhi's control. Although the movement had shown symptoms of a mass upheaval, it collapsed under a fierce imperial retaliation, which was possible owing to the military preparedness of the British in the context of the Second World War. In the absence of the major Congress leaders, including Gandhi, the movement, though short-lived, took a violent turn, which *inter alia* provoked ruthless military intervention by the British.

Whatever the achievements of the Congress in the Quit India Movement, it projected a different Gandhi who, in a rather belligerent mood, seemed to have justified any means for fighting the British, especially in his passionate 'do or die' speech. Although the need for non-violence was reiterated, the famous 8 August Resolution espoused the call for 'mass struggle on non-violent lines on the widest possible scale' under the leadership of Gandhi with the instruction that if the Congress leadership was removed by arrest, 'every man and woman who is participating in this movement must function for himself or herself'. Apart from this resolution, Gandhi's statements urging people to fight till death inspired them to resort to means other than ahimsa. In his public statements, the Mahatma appeared to have appreciated violence if circumstances so demanded. For instance, in a press interview, he urged that 'this orderly disciplined anarchy (in the shape of the British administration) should be removed at any cost and if as a result, there is a complete lawlessness, I would risk it.' In another interview in August 1942, he defended a general strike by exhorting 'if a general strike becomes a dire necessity, I shall not flinch', thus undermining his well-argued justification for trusteeship.

The Quit India campaign, though assumed massive proportions, waned rather quickly at the all-India level. It, however, continued unabated at least for two years in Midnapur, Talcher, and Satara where both violence and non-violence were resorted to in the name of Gandhi. In the case of Midnapur, as discussed earlier, the Congress volunteers drew upon Gandhi to justify violence as it meant a contribution to the cause of freedom. *Biplabi,* the Congress journal published from Midnapur, exhorted that the Mahatma would have approved violence in the name of serving the motherland. There are instances of inflicting death penalty on those who committed a heinous crime, like raping the village women to terrorize. Though the Congress decision ran counter to Gandhi's ahimsa, it was nonetheless justified by drawing attention to his writings in which he was reported to have defended violence for protecting women's honour.

The events during the Quit India Movement show that on occasions, Gandhi the person appears insignificant in comparison with the Mahatma, the idea which was thought out and reworked in popular vision in a completely different way, which Gandhi and the Congress high command would never have approved. In an in-depth study of the events in Gorakhpur, subsequent to Gandhi's visit in February 1921, it has been demonstrated that 'Gandhi's Swaraj . . . appears to have taken shape quite independently of the district leadership of the Congress Party.' Similarly, in Champaran, where the Mahatma launched a successful non-violent resistance against the illegal exaction by the planters, he was reported to have been 'sent into Champaran by the Viceroy, or even the King to redress all the grievances of the *raiyats*'. He was said to be about to abolish all the unpopular obligations, which the planters imposed on their *raiyats*, so that there was no need to obey the word of any planter any more. A rumour was also in the air that the administration of Champaran was going to be handed over to the Indians and that the 'British would be cleared out of the district within a few months'. Taking note of the tremendous influence of Gandhi in shaping the popular psyche, the British administration seemed perplexed in a rather quick dissemination of Gandhian ideas in the remote areas. That Gandhi was identified as a saviour of the poverty-stricken masses was evident in a police report mentioning that 'the real power of his name is perhaps to be traced back to the ideal that he who got *bedakhli* (illegal exaction) stopped' in Pratapgrah in UP. Accordingly, the UP peasants were reported to have believed that Gandhi would 'provide holdings for them through ahimsa'. These illustrations indicate and probably justify the role of rumour in underscoring the institutionalized form of politics in the context of a transitional society like India. Underlying this is probably the explanation as to why the Gandhi-type leadership, exemplified, for instance, in Swami Prajnananda in Bengal, Swami Darsanananda in Bihar or Baba Ramchandra in Pratapgarh, had strong religious overtones. Besides arguing that these outsiders established the crucial link between the upper and lower courses of the nationalist struggle which had its manifestation in both the organized and unorganized worlds of politics, they have brought out another interesting dimension of the Gandhi-led freedom movement, that is, the peasants still needed an outsider to organize themselves in a society going through a period of acute strain and tension due to peculiar circumstances. This argument, if pursued with vigour, is likely to identify significant lapses in the analysis of some of the early writings of the subaltern school which, while challenging the so-called elitist historiography, tends to somewhat romanticize the revolutionary potential of the rural masses.

CONCLUSION

There was no doubt that Gandhi was able to galvanize the people into action because he articulated the voice of protest in a much more comprehensible language than anyone else in the past. He was also able to involve more people in the nationalist intervention because of an easy acceptance of his model of conflict resolution by the Indian masses. Gandhism remained politically relevant simply because of its organic roots in India's social, economic and political circumstances. This was evident time and again. Whatever the ramifications in leadership, non-violence had an easy acceptance among the Indian populace at large probably because ahimsa articulated the anti-British feeling, in the form of Satyagraha, better than the prevalent ideologies. Furthermore, Gandhi's strategic sense made satyagraha a viable mode of protest. As Ravinder Kumar in his book *Essays in Social History of Modern India* argued, Gandhi pursued 'class politics' in the struggles he led in Champaran, Kheda and Ahmedabad, but shifted to 'communitarian politics' in the larger national movement, which he launched against colonialism. The explanation lies in the logic of national democracy that Gandhi and Congress religiously pursued during the freedom struggle. Class-issues were divisive while moral issues appear to be integrating. Thus from the Rowlatt Satyagraha onwards, Gandhi mobilized people on moral issues rather than class-issues 'to cement a grand alliance of Hindus and Muslims, rich and poor … the working class and the industrial magnates … the zamindars and peasants, in a great struggle against the British Government'.

Moreover, the fact that Gandhi was able to mobilize the

masses with his Indianness in lifestyle and political vocabulary, demonstrated his ability to translate the popular grievances into political action in the face of imperial oppression and atrocities. This is just one part of the story narrating the rise of Gandhi in the context of the freedom struggle. In order to grasp the quintessence of the Mahatma as an organic leader of the nationalist movement, attention should be drawn to the process projecting Gandhism as an ideology, which developed through a dialogue with rapidly changing socio-economic and political arrangements. What is noticeable in such a construct is the absence of familiar Gandhian ideas, which are justified, in turn, as being in tune with non-violence and its concomitant value system. So what had happened in Chauri Chaura in 1922 and during the Quit India Movement, which defied the fundamental precepts of Gandhism, seems to be an offshoot of a peculiar interpenetration between ideology and reality. That Gandhism had a firm grip over the mass psyche despite tendencies otherwise was evident with the unconditional submission of those, believing in violence, to the Mahatma in both the cases. Therefore, the eclipse of non-violence and its subsequent triumph merely identify the relative weakness of the contesting ideologies, which, though posed a serious threat to non-violence in Punjab, Maharashtra and Bengal, appeared peripheral at the national level. Hence, the historical impact of Gandhism on the evolution of nationalism was immensely significant.

There were innumerable occasions when the Congress-led anti-British campaign largely deviated from non-violence and yet the participants justified their action as being inspired by the Mahatma. So there are several Gandhis – each being interpreted differently reflecting the priorities of the participants. Translating Gandhism in such a way as to gain maximum mileage, the grassroot leaders articulated the political agenda by attributing the popular grievances to imperialism. Furthermore, the interpretation of Gandhi's idea also varied in accordance with the preference of the leadership involved in the mobilization for an anti-British offensive.

The 'science of non-violence' was the form in which Gandhism addressed itself to the question of nationalism. By sincerely championing ahimsa, the Mahatma provided a format for articulating the anti-British sentiments in the form of satyagraha, which was probably the most appropriate strategic method of struggle at a particular juncture of India's nation-building. Unlike other prevalent ideologies, Gandhism thus succeeded in providing for the first time in nationalist politics an ideological basis for including the whole people, irrespective of caste, class, and creed, into an imaginary construct called 'political nation'. Gandhi's greatest contribution to political mobilization was, thus argued Rudolphs, 'helping India to acquire national coherence and identity, to become a nation, by showing Indians a way to courage, self-respect and political potency'.[19] In other words, not only did Gandhian non-violence put up an effective challenge to the British domination, it also created conditions for the inclusion of the largest segment of the nation, namely the peasantry, into the Indian state that was to emerge with the eclipse of imperialism. Gandhism with its concomitant value system, however, appropriated the peasantry only in so far as it contributed to the nationalist struggle, conceived and directed by the Indian National Congress. Although Gandhi introduced new constituencies in the anti-British political campaign by including both the peasantry and the workers, his endeavour in an otherwise elite-dominated freedom struggle aimed not to train the masses in self-conscious attainment of power by themselves, but to solicit their cooperation in the Congress-led struggle for swaraj. That Gandhi succeeded in reinvigorating the 'otherwise sterile' nationalist movement despite the ideological limitations of what he offered through non-violence indicated the extent to which 'national democracy' triumphed and other ideologies were marginalized. Notwithstanding the anti-Gandhi wave in independent India, Gandhi appeared invincible in whatever he undertook between 1920 and 1942, primarily because of his physical and mental affinity with the traditions and temperament of the Indian masses, which yielded results in the context of a volatile socio-economic and political order.

---

1 *Harijan*, 30 September, 1939.

2 Subhas Chandra Bose, *The Indian Struggle, 1920 - 42*, Asia Publishing House, London, 1964 (reprint), p. 293.

3 M.K. Gandhi, 'God of love, not war', *Harijan*, 5 September, 1936, *CWMG*, Vol. 63, p. 262.

4 Gandhi's letter in *Modern Review*, October, 1916 – reproduced in Raghavan Iyer, *The Moral and Political thought of Mahatma Gandhi*, Oxford University Press, Delhi, 1973, pp. 179-80.

5 Gandhi defined ahimsa as 'infinite love' while elaborating the role of women in nationalism. M.K. Gandhi, 'What is woman's role?', *Harijan*, 12 February, 1940.

6 Jawaharlal Nehru, *An Autobiography (with musings on recent events in India)*, John Lane and Bodley Head, London, 1941, p. 540.

7 Gandhi's letter to editor, *The Modern Review*, October 1916 -

reproduced in Raghavan Iyer, *The Moral and Political thought of Mahatma Gandhi*, Oxford University Press, Delhi, 1973, pp. 179-180.

8 M.K. Gandhi, 'Satyagraha – Not Passive Resistance', *CWMG*, Vol. 13, p. 523. Gandhi further stated, '[w]e can … free ourselves of the unjust rule of the Government by defying the unjust rule and accepting the punishment that go with it. We do not bear malice towards the Government. When we set its fears at rest … they will at once be subdued to our will.'

9 ibid., p.524.

10 M.K. Gandhi, 'The Duty of Satyagrahis', *CWMG*, Vol. 15, p.436.

11 M.K. Gandhi, *Autobiography*, *CWMG*, Vol. 39, p. 374.

12 Partha Chatterjee, 'Gandhi please stand up?', *Illustrated Weekly of India*, 15-21 January, 1984, p. 27.

13 Quoted in Partha Chatterjee, 'Gandhi please stand up?', *Illustrated Weekly of India*, 15-21 Janaury, 1984, p. 27.

14 M.K. Gandhi, 'Satyagraha in South Africa', Chapter 13, *CWMG*, Vol.29, pp.93-97.

15 M.K. Gandhi, 'Talk with ashram inmates', 22 March, 1934, *CWMG*, Vol. 57, p. 301.

16 *CWMG*, Vol. 3, pp. 113-14 and 119-20.

17 ibid., p. 129.

18 Cited in R.K. Narayan, *Waiting for the Mahatma*, Indian Thought Publications, Chennai, 2003 (reprint), pp. 77-78.

19 Susanne Hoeber Rudolph and Lloyd I Rudolph, *Gandhi: The Traditional Roots of Charisma,* Orient Longman, New Delhi, 1987, pp. 64-65.

5

~

GANDHI AND HIS COLLEAGUES: RABINDRANATH TAGORE AND B.R. AMBEDKAR

IDEAS DO NOT EMERGE IN A VACUUM. THE CONTEXT SEEMS TO play a significant, if not a determining role in the dialogue that unfolded in pursuance of the freedom struggle in India. In other words, political ideas of Gandhi, Rabindranath Tagore and B.R. Ambedkar were rooted in the larger socio-economic and political processes in the nineteenth and twentieth century. The socio-historical and cultural perspective of British India remained, for obvious reasons, a constant reference to Tagore and Ambedkar. Gandhi conceptualized a model that, for a variety of reasons, gained currency both as a nationalist strategy for political mobilization and a blueprint for India's future. Drawn on their respective beliefs and ideas, Tagore and Ambedkar put forward their views both in contrast and juxtaposition with that of Gandhi and in that sense, the Mahatma appears to have broadly set the discourse and its articulation. Although the ideologically inspired critiques of Gandhi by Tagore and Ambedkar articulated different voices, they nonetheless were largely theoretical because neither Tagore nor Ambedkar was involved in the nationalist movement as organically as Gandhi was. What was unique about Gandhi was his ability to guide the nation towards a goal following a model, based on his experience as a practitioner of different kinds of politics.

The chapter draws on the critiques of Rabindranath Tagore and B.R. Ambedkar simply for the reason that not only were they refreshing theoretical interventions, they also helped Gandhi reformulate some of his ideas that were held so dear in his earlier writings. While Ambedkar evaluated Gandhi on the basis of his conceptualization of distributive justice that privileged 'the untouchables' or dalits over others, Tagore's critique of Gandhi is perhaps the most creative response, which is both indigenous and West-influenced. These varied critiques dialectically influenced Gandhi and also transformed his ideas on occasions. So the blueprint of future India that the Mahatma sought to articulate was reflective of various different but authentic influences. Herein lies the significance of the dialogue that Gandhi had with his colleagues on issues of socio-economic and political importance. One can thus safely argue that the communication between Gandhi and his colleagues is illustrative of India's age-old tradition of 'arguments and counter-arguments spread over incessant debates and disputations'.[1] There is no doubt that this tradition sustains and is enriched by another equally powerful tradition of 'heterodoxy'. Gandhi was perhaps a neat example of 'an argumentative Indian', engaged in debates and disputations probably to grasp the socio-economically peculiar Indian reality in the context of colonialism.

Notwithstanding the significant contribution of M.A. Jinnah in articulating a sovereign state for the Muslims, the chapter does not deal with his critique of Gandhi for two reasons: (a) the critical literature on this theme is plenty and hence the discussion will merely be repetitive; and (b) since both Jinnah and Gandhi were primarily political activists it would be improper to deal with the dialogue without contextualizing the issues that figured in their discussion. Just like Gandhi, Jinnah too carved out an independent place in the Indian freedom struggle that culminated in the bifurcation of British India following his two-nation theory. The aim of the following discussion is therefore two-fold: (a) to underline the distinctive issues that figured in the dialogue; and (b) to identify, if possible, the conceptual basis of the arguments which they made either in their defence or to counter the Mahatma.

GANDHI AS A COMMUNICATOR: RABINDRANATH TAGORE AND GANDHI

In the evolution of India as a civilization, both Tagore and Gandhi have played significant roles. They represented 'two types entirely different from each other, and yet both of them typical of India'. This is the reason why the communication between them is so creative. Tagore admired Gandhi by saying that 'great as he is as a politician, as an organizer, as a leader of men, as a moral reformer, he is greater than all these as a man, because none of these aspects and activities limits his humanity. They are rather inspired and sustained by it.'[2] But he had serious disagreements with him on a number of issues. Gandhi also appreciated Tagore critically, but stuck to his point of view despite having even 'annoyed' the poet. These differences, argues Amartya Sen, 'have a clear and consistent pattern, with Tagore pressing for more room for reasoning, and for a less traditionalist view, a greater interest in the rest of the world, and more respect for science and for objectivity generally'.

Rabindranath Tagore built his critique of Gandhi on India's cultural heritage and plurality of life. His evaluation was based on a certain reading of Indian civilization and actual political processes that unfolded in the context of the struggle against imperialism. Not only did they interact regularly on various philosophical issues pertaining to India as a civilization – either through personal correspondence or through the media – they also exchanged views on the mundane political agenda of the Indian National Congress. So Tagore's critique was an offshoot of a dialogue, rooted in the contemporary milieu. As a poet who was not directly involved in the nationalist agitation, Tagore sought to articulate the un-articulated concerns of Indian public consciousness. Tagore was transcendental in his conceptualization presumably because he drew more on civilizational values about human society and less on worldly socio-political and economic ideas.

Tagore was perhaps the first to emphatically argue against the belief that identity in the subcontinent was uni-dimensional. Challenging the concept of 'nation' as it undermines the multi-layered Indian identity, Tagore reminded people of the combined role of the 'little' and 'great' traditions in shaping what he loosely defined as the Indian nation. India's diversity, Tagore felt, was her 'nature [and] you can never coerce nature into your narrow limits of convenience without paying one day very dearly for it'.[3] Not only 'have religious beliefs cut up society into warring sections . . . social antagonisms (between the Hindus and Muslims) have set up impassable barriers every mile – barriers which are guarded night and day by forces wearing the badge of religion'. For Tagore, the gulf between the different communities was largely due to 'the cultural forces', released by British colonialism that 'fractured the personality of every sensitive exposed Indian and set up the West as a crucial vector within the Indian self'. As India's social system got distorted, '[l]ife departed', argued Tagore, 'from her social system and in its place she is worshipping with all ceremony the magnificent cage of countless compartments that she has manufactured'.[4] While Tagore was critical of artificial division among the communities, created and consolidated by forces supporting colonialism, he was equally alarmed by the drive to gloss over India's diversity for the sake of creating a nation-state as in Europe since it would strike at the very foundation of a civilizational society that flourished in India over centuries. Interrogating the 'totalizing' dimension of the nationalist project – where a single entity, called nation, always prevails over other forms of identity – Tagore sought to provide an alternative to an 'essentialistic' invocation of identity in the shape of a nation. According to him, in articulating the civilizational identity of India, the importance of underlying cognitive and ethical claims, which are invariably lodged in and emanate from contradictory social locations, could never be undermined. So the European modular form of nation was conceptually futile and politically inapplicable presumably because India's civilizational identity was not singular but multiple and thus difficult to capture on a single axis.

Like Tagore, Gandhi rarely used the term, nation, in the sense Jinnah referred to it. Yet, Gandhi failed to halt the historical processes whereby the Indian Muslims soon became a nation and bargained successfully for a separate Muslim state. Jinnah's role was equally significant. In the penultimate year of the transfer of power, the Jinnah-led Muslim League secured parity with the Congress and in the 1946 Shimla conference, the League and Congress representation was equated. What came in the form of the 1940 Lahore resolution became feasible. And, Jinnah's appeal to 'unsettle the settled notions of Muslims being a minority [that] had been around for so long' was finally translated into reality. So, not only did the *Quaid-i-Azam* succeed in dramatically altering the role of the Muslims in the over-all constitutional settlement on the eve of the Great Divide, he also transformed the Muslim community into a nation by ascertaining 'territorial sovereignty to a heterogeneous community turned homogeneous nation'. The Muslim community for Jinnah was, therefore, not 'an abstract historical-political entity . . . but a separate nation with distinct interests [which] could not be treated only as a minority'.[5]

Gandhi's opposition to the concept of a separate nation was based on two specific arguments: first, he put forward a contextual argument by saying that the logic of creating religion-based nation state was faulty because religion could neither be 'a stabilizing nor a unifying factor in humanity', but 'divisive'. So, by seeking to gloss over the obvious diversities among the Indian Muslims for a sovereign state, Jinnah ignored the long-drawn historical processes in the community formations. For Gandhi, nation was hardly a criterion to conceptualize the complex and deeply heterogeneous communities in the subcontinent regardless of religion. Couched in a humanitarian fashion, the second argument dwells on the devastating consequences of conceptualizing Hindus and Muslims as separate nations. Holding politics responsible for the Hindu-Muslim schism, Gandhi pledged to 'rescue people from this quagmire and make them work on solid ground where people are people.' Therefore his 'appeal was not to the Muslims as Muslims, nor to the Hindus as Hindus, but to ordinary human beings who had to keep their villages clean, build schools for their children and take many other steps so that they could make life better'. To Gandhi, as the passage demonstrates, nation, as a categorizing device, was perhaps the narrowest in its manifestation ignoring the inherent diversities of the communities. Nation is a project of homogenizing people regardless of historical space and time. Conceptually non-viable and practically inappropriate, the application of nation as a category weakened the anti-British struggle because of the clash of interests between the Hindus and Muslims once they were characterized as separate nations.

What was common between Tagore and Gandhi was the idea that the concept of nation was absolutely inapplicable to Indian people. Both regarded nationalism as a by-product of Western nation-state system and of the forces of homogenization let loose by the Western worldview. To them, 'a homogenized universalism', itself a product of the up-rootedness and deculturation brought about by British colonialism in India struck at the root of Indian civilization. In contrast with an imported category like nationalism, their alternative was 'a distinctive civilizational concept of universalism embedded in the tolerance encoded in various traditional ways of life in a highly diverse, plural society'. This conceptualization within an absolutely non-nationalist philosophical framework defused the arguments in favour of Hindu nationalism in the context of the freedom movement in India. So, not only was this critique of nation and nationalism morally acceptable and politically effective, it also laid the foundation of community-based society drawing on the resources of a civilization which it was a part of.

But the honeymoon was short-lived and differences between the poet and the Mahatma loomed large in course of time. When Gandhi launched the Non-Cooperation Movement, it was based on the idea that since the continuity of the British government depended on the cooperation of the Indian subjects it would collapse once the Indians withdrew their support. The campaign involved resignation from the government jobs, refusal to participate in the government institutions and schools, and later to pay taxes and burning of foreign clothes. His idea of burning foreign clothes provoked much unease with Tagore who wondered if Gandhi was not encouraging the flames of narrow nationalism and xenophobia. As he argued,

> the clothes to be burnt are not mine, but belong to those who most sorely need them. If those who are going naked should have given us the mandate to burn, it would, at least, have been a case of self-immolation and the crime of incendiarism would not lie at our door. But how can we expiate the sin of the forcible destruction of clothes which might have gone to women whose nakedness is actually keeping them prisoners unable to stir out of the privacy of their homes?[6]

Similarly, withdrawal from the schools and colleges never appeared to be a wise call. Tagore refused to endorse the campaign because 'the great injury and injustice which had been done to those boys who were tempted away from their career before any real provision was made, could never be made good to them'. He was not persuaded to believe that Western education 'injured' the young minds and be altogether rejected. The root of the misconception lies elsewhere. As Tagore pointed out, 'what has caused the mischief is the fact that for a long time we have been out of touch with our own culture and therefore the Western culture has not found its prospective in our life, very often found a wrong prospective giving our mental eye a squint'. Tagore adopted a nuanced argument vis-à-vis the Non-Cooperation Movement, which was a relatively successful political campaign involving a wider section of the population across the length and breadth of India.

While Tagore was convinced that this programme would alienate the masses since mill-products were cheaper and hence affordable, Gandhi defended the agenda as he felt that it would not only harm the British commercial interests but also foster the cultural self-confidence of the masses. In *Young India*, he elaborated:

> Non-cooperation is the nation's notice that it is no longer satisfied to be in tutelage. The nation had taken to the harmless, natural and religious doctrine of non-cooperation in the place of the unnatural and irreligious doctrine of violence. ... Non-cooperation is intended to give the very meaning that the poet is yearning after. An India prostrate at the feet of Europe can give no hope to humanity. An India awakened and free has a message of peace and goodwill to a groaning world. Non-cooperation is designed to supply her with a platform from which she will preach the message.

On another occasion, he further added,

> Our non-cooperation is neither with the English nor with the West. Our non-cooperation is with the system the English have established, with the material civilization and its attendant greed and exploitation of the weak. Our non-cooperation is a retirement within ourselves. Our non-cooperation is a refusal to cooperate with the English administrators in their own terms.[7]

Similarly, Gandhi did not endorse Tagore's criticism of boycott of English education. While appreciating English learning, the Mahatma was critical of the pernicious effect of English education on the Indian minds. According to him,

> English is being studied because of its commercial and political value. ... English is being made mother tongue in families. Hundreds of youth believe that without a knowledge of English, freedom of India is practically impossible. ... The only meaning of Education is a knowledge of English. ... All these are for me signs of our slavery and degradation. It is unbearable to me that the vernaculars should be crushed and starved as they have been.[8]

As shown, Tagore's critique of the aim of the non-cooperation with the Raj drew on his own perception of the 'constructive work' that he experimented during the 1905-08 Swadeshi Movement in Bengal. He was opposed to the coercion because his experience of the swadeshi mobilization had shown its adverse consequences. When the movement was at its zenith, Tagore denounced its reliance on coercion and the alienating impact it had on the masses it claimed to enthuse and activate. His critique of the non-cooperation techniques followed the same logic. The pervasive use of social boycott and other forms of coercion was therefore 'regarded by him as evidence of the swadeshi activist's failure to persuade people to their cause'. He thus argued that 'we have not been patient enough to work our way gradually towards winning popular consent'. That was at the root of the nationalist failure to unite all Indians in 'a grand patriotic mobilization'. The debate between Gandhi and Tagore brought out the contrasting perspectives on this subject that had, as shown, its root in the Swadeshi Movement as well. While Gandhi was confident that the non-cooperation agenda was most appropriate socio-politically, Tagore expressed his doubts on the ground that the 'narrow political aim' of the movement was likely to jeopardize its wider goal and objectives. The debate remained inconclusive, but raised certain major questions on Gandhi's social and political ideas that appeared to have decisively influenced Indian minds.

Just like the debate over the strategy of non-cooperation, the exchange of views between Gandhi and the poet on charkha and khadi was reminiscent of different perspectives in which they were conceptualized. Tagore was not persuaded, let alone impressed by the campaign for charkha. As he admitted,

> the depths of my mind have not been moved by the charkha agitation ... for its inherent weaknesses [and he therefore apprehended] that all intense pressure of persuasion brought upon the crowd psychology is unhealthy for it [because] it will create blind faith on a very large scale in the charkha ... which is liable to succumb to the lure of short cuts when pointed out by a personality about whose moral earnestness they can have no doubt.[9]

In two articles, published in the *Modern Review*, Tagore summarized his arguments to question the applicability of charkha in the context of the colonial India. First, he was confident that charkha was not a competitive substitute for machine and given the complex problems that masses confronted both due to colonialism and other obvious social and political constraints. For Tagore, 'no wealth is greater than lightening man's material burdens'. Stating it figuratively, he further argued that 'wheel in the shape of the spinning wheel, or the potter's wheel or the wheel of a vehicle, the wheel has rescued innumerable men from [poverty] and [reduced] their burden'. Symbolizing wheel as the growth of science, Tagore thus concluded by underlining the importance of wheel in augmenting resources for human civilization. As he articulated, 'man gradually realized that his wealth has gone on compounding itself in the ever-increasing rotation, refusing to be confined to the limited advantage of the original charkha'. As an archaic, but useful at a particular historical juncture, charkha appeared to have exhausted its potential to contain poverty effectively. His second argument against charkha was built on this. He was unambiguous in believing that the charkha was not a capable tool to bring swaraj, or remove India's poverty because it was based on the false expectation that people would be naturally drawn to spinning. Seeking to delink swaraj from charkha, Tagore further argued that

> to give the charkha the first place in our striving for the country's welfare is only a way to make our insulted intelligence recoil in despairing inaction. A great and vivid picture of the country's well-being in its universal aspect, held before our eyes, can alone enable our countrymen to apply the best of head and heart to

> carve out the best way along which their varied activities may progress towards their end.[10]

Swaraj was self-fulfilment of people regardless of differences in ethno-religious terms. It was not simply an act of spinning thread, weaving khadi or holding discourses; it was a plan of action involving the masses with a vision of society, free from exploitation of all kinds. So, Tagore, not persuaded by the narrow conceptualization of swaraj merely in terms of charkha, highlighted both the depth of swaraj as a socio-economic blueprint for future India and also its significance in inculcating mass interest in certain specific meaningful programmes relevant to the people of British India. The third argument that Tagore made in opposition to charkha relates to the realistic feasibility of this device when imposed on the people without their consent. Gandhi felt that the success of charkha lay in utilizing the surplus time of the cultivator; the more the cultivators involved themselves the more effective the charkha would become. But Tagore believed otherwise, simply because the basic assumption behind the argument concerning the profitable employment of the surplus time of the cultivator was flawed unless the cultivators themselves spontaneously accepted charkha. But this was most unlikely because first, the cultivator acquired a special skill with his hands, and special bent of mind by dint of consistent application to his particular work. Hence 'to ask the cultivator to spin is to derail his mind; he may drag on with it for a while, but at the cost of disproportionate effort and therefore waste of energy'. Secondly, if charkha was imposed on the cultivators who might not have the inclination it would lose its significance and effectiveness. In other words, the acceptance of charkha was not spontaneous and hence the consequence could be devastating because as Tagore most eloquently put that

> it would be wrong to make the cultivator either happier or richer by thrusting aside, all of a sudden, the habits of body and mind which have grown upon him through his life. ... To tell the cultivator turn the charkha instead of trying to get him to employ his whole energy in his own line of work is only a sign of weakness (sic). We cast the blame for being lazy on the cultivator, but the advice we give him amounts rather to a confession of the laziness of our mind.

According to Tagore, spinning was not creative, for 'by turning its wheel man merely becomes an appendage of the charkha; that is to say, he but does himself what a machine might have done; he converts his living energy into a dead turning movement. [In the process] he becomes a machine, isolated, companionless.' Critical of this mechanical involvement that was of no consequence for swaraj, Tagore suggested some concrete steps, which were organically linked with our life. For instance, as he perceived, the village that was self-sustained economically and supported each of its inhabitants in distress could lay the foundation of swaraj in the true sense of the term. As he most unambiguously put, 'the village of which people come together to earn for themselves their food, their health, their education, to gain themselves the joy of so doing, shall have lighted a lamp on the way to swaraj'.

Gandhi responded to the poet's critique in his rejoinders in the *Young India*. Instead of countering Tagore's arguments, the Mahatma, defended charkha as something indispensable for India's economic well being. In response to the charge that he insisted on spinning to the exclusion of all other activities, Gandhi argued that this was far from the truth because he never wanted 'the poet to forsake his muse, the farmer his plough, the lawyer his brief and the doctor his lancet. [Instead], he asked the famishing to spin for a living and the half-starved farmer to spin during his leisure hours to supplement his slender resources'.[11] The idea based on sound logic articulated a device for supplementary incomes for the starving peasants and their families. Juxtaposed with this idea was his unequivocal condemnation for machine. He was not opposed to machine per se; what he apprehended was the consequence of machine civilization that would make human labour redundant, a consequence most devastating where human labour was in abundance. As Gandhi argued,

> machine must not be allowed to displace the necessary human labour. An improved plough is a good thing. But if by some chance one man could plough up by some mechanical invention of his the whole of the land of India and control all the agricultural produce and the millions had no other occupation, they would starve, and being idle, they would become dunces, as many have already become. ... [i]t is therefore criminal to displace hand labour by the introduction of power-driven spindles unless one is at the same time ready to give millions of farmers some other occupation in their homes.

The other part of the argument is equally significant where charkha was a symbol of involvement with the day-to-day life of the poor and thus was a powerful device to conceptualize the reality. As he suggested to the poet that 'if [he] spun half an hour daily his poetry would gain in richness [for] it would then represent the poor man's wants and woes in a more forcible manner than now'. Furthermore, Gandhi replied to the charge that the charkha was calculated to bring about a deathlike sameness in the nation. For Gandhi, charkha was a powerful symbol to unite the disparate Indian masses. Hence charkha to him was 'intended to realize the essential and living oneness of interest among India's myriads'. Charkha was not simply an economic activity, instead, it brought people together by involving them in an activity that was (a) a source of supplementary income; and (b) a device to link them automatically with the rest of India politically. In other words, although articulated as an economic activity it was an organizing device with a clear political message to those involved in Gandhian satyagraha. Spinning for Gandhi was therefore a symbolic form of identification with the masses while Tagore, as discussed, was suspicious of any such appeal that tended to gloss over the inherent diversity among the Indian people.

Apart from these major issues, an interesting debate took place following Gandhi's characterization of the Bihar earthquake in February 1934 as 'divine chastisement' for the great sin committed against those known as harijans. Tagore took a serious note of this by saying that 'it has caused me painful surprise to find Mahatma Gandhi accusing those who blindly follow their own social custom of untouchability of having brought down gods' vengeance upon certain parts of Bihar'. Since it came out from the most revered political leader of the country, the statement, he felt, was most devastating for its obvious impact on inter-personal relationship between harijans and others. So, it should not go 'unchallenged'. Tagore prefaced his critique of this superstitious view of Gandhi by saying that 'it is all the more unfortunate, because this kind of unscientific view of things is too readily accepted by a large section of our countrymen'. Underlining that 'physical catastrophes [like earthquake, etc.] have their inevitable and exclusive origin in certain combination of physical facts', he further argued that

> if we associate ethical principles with cosmic phenomena, we shall have to admit that human nature is morally superior to Providence that preaches its lessons in good behaviour in orgies of the worst behaviour possible. ... What is truly tragic about it is the fact that the kind of argument that Mahatmaji uses by exploiting an even of cosmic disturbance far better suits the psychology of his opponents. ... [He thus felt] profoundly hurt when any words from [Gandhi's] mouth may emphasise the elements of unreason ... which is a fundamental source of all the blind powers that drive us against freedom and self-respect.

Gandhi retorted against Tagore's views equally strongly. Reiterating his views on the Bihar earthquake, the Mahatma argued,

> to me, the earthquake was no caprice of God nor a result of a meeting of mere blind forces. ... Visitations like droughts, flood, earthquakes and the like, though they seem to have only physical origins, are, for me, somehow connected with man's morals. Therefore, I instinctively felt that the earthquake was visitation for the sin of untouchability. [He firmly believed] that our sins have more force to ruin the structure than any mere physical phenomenon.

On this occasion, both of them held diametrically opposite views. A scientific Tagore upheld reason, while a moralist Gandhi privileged reason over his faith. Tagore insisted on debate on every issue and distrusted 'conclusions based on a mechanical formula, no matter how attractive that formula might seem in isolation. ... It is in the sovereignty of reasoning – fearless reasoning in freedom – that we can find Rabindranath Tagore's lasting voice.' Perhaps the best description of the differences between these two great Indians happens to be the one which Tagore himself articulated. As Tagore explicitly stated,

> [w]e who often to glorify our tendency to ignore reason, installing in its place blind faith, valuing it as spiritual, are ever paying for its cost with the obscuration of our mind and destiny. I blamed Mahatmaji for exploiting irrational force of credulity in our people, which might have had a quick result [in creating] a superstructure, while sapping the foundation. Thus began my estimate of Mahatmaji, as the guide of our nation, and its fortunate for me that it did not end there.

The point here is not to ascertain the validity of their respective arguments objectively, but to dig-out their appropriateness in the context of India's struggle for swaraj that was more than mere political freedom from imperialism. Tagore's was a reasoned argument with a limited application while Gandhi's had a wider application given his influence over the masses. It was, as it were, a Gandhian preemptive measure, based on his wider acceptability as a political leader. What informed Gandhi was perhaps his confidence in dissuading those practicing untouchability because of impending god's wrath. For Gandhi, the linking of the Bihar calamity with the sin of untouchability, which, though unscientific logically, was a significant step in his battle against untouchability. In other words, the statement on the Bihar earthquake acquired completely different connotations, which one may not comprehend without gauging Mahatma's popularity among the masses. So, given the typical Gandhian methodology of mass mobilization for freedom, it was just another method to launch an effective and meaningful campaign against untouchability.

As evident, the difference between Tagore and Gandhi was fundamental on specific political strategies for mass mobilization. Unlike Gandhi, Tagore never appreciated the non-cooperation strategy, for instance, for its in-built weaknesses. Similarly, on charkha and khadi, the poet was critical of the Mahatma since they neither provided an appropriate alternative to the masses nor adequately addressed the problem of poverty. It was largely 'a hollow political slogan', as Tagore believed, given the obvious adverse political and economic consequences on the masses if forced on them. Despite the validity of Tagore's argument in a wider perspective, there is no doubt that charkha and khadi instrumentalized the Gandhi-led mass movement; they, in other words, became symbols of mass involvement in the anti-imperial struggle. While they differed with regard to politico-economic strategies, they held uniform views on nationalism. Given the nature of disparate Indian masses, nation, to both of them, never appeared to be a viable organizing principle. Tagore was perhaps first to confront the devastating consequences of the application of the principle of nationalism in the context of the Swadeshi Movement of 1903-08 in Bengal when the schism between the Hindus and Muslims was articulated in a nationalist language. The growing strength of the Muslims, defined later as a separate nation by Jinnah, caused a permanent fissure between these two major religious communities – that ultimately led to the 1947 partition of the subcontinent. Articulating their views in a non-nationalist language, Gandhi and Tagore, perhaps the finest product of the Indo-British cultural encounter, provided the most creative and also challenging response to the nationalist 'oneness' of the Western world.

GANDHI AS A NEGOTIATOR: AMBEDKAR AND GANDHI

The complexities of Gandhi's social and political ideas owe largely to various different ideological discourses, articulated by his colleagues in the Indian freedom struggle. M.N. Roy for instance drew on a creative interpretation of Marxism to critique Gandhian ideas while Tagore privileged his faith in humanism to assess what constituted the core of Gandhi's social and political philosophy. Bhimrao Ramji Ambedkar (1891-1956), popularly known as Babasaheb Ambedkar, introduced a new critique by drawing on 'the dalit' perspective. Critical of the nationalist movement that upheld caste and untouchability at the behest of Gandhi, Ambedkar sought to articulate an alternative political ideology by challenging the very foundation of the 'Hinduised' nationalist movement. One of the most significant arguments that Ambedkar made against Hinduism was that caste and untouchability struck at its foundation and hence it was inherently divisive. Gandhi by clinging to the basic philosophy of caste never seriously challenged, as Ambedkar accused, untouchability in Hinduism. According to him, Gandhism was 'a paradox' because 'it stands for freedom from foreign domination [and] at the same time it seeks to maintain intact a social structure, which permits the domination of one class by another on a hereditary basis which means a perpetual domination of one class by another'.[12] For Ambedkar, Gandhi's loyalty to Hinduism amounted to supporting 'untouchability' because it also evolved as integrally linked with Hinduism and was thus justified. This assumption, however, stands in contradiction with what the Mahatma sincerely believed. According to him, 'untouchability is not a sanction of religion; it is a device of Satan. ... There is neither nobility nor bravery in treating the great and uncomplaining scavengers of the nation as worse than dogs to be despised and spat upon.'

Ambedkar criticized Gandhi further for having eulogized the Indian villages as illustrative of a unique unit of social, economic and political equilibrium. Instead, Ambedkar argued that the Indian villages

> represent a kind of colonialism of the Hindus designed to exploit the Untouchables. The untouchables have no rights. They are there only to wait, serve and submit. They are there to do or to die. They have no rights because they are outside the village republic and because they are outside the so-called republic, they are outside the Hindu fold. This is a vicious circle. But this is a fact which cannot be gainsaid.

For Gandhi, the village was the basis for building a republican society, not polluted by colonialism while for Ambedkar it was 'the black hole' of Indian civilization. Village, for Gandhi, was not merely a geographical location where people lived in small settlement drawn on land. For him, in essence it reflected the essence of Indian civilization. The Indian village had a design, a way of life, which had the potential of becoming 'an alternative to the city-based and technology-driven capitalist

West'. His conception of village was not anchored 'on the modern notion of development but on the post-modern perspective of quality life'. And, yet for the dalits 'the village … could never be an embodiment of justice since to remain in village meant remaining tied to the same humiliating occupation that had so far been their fate'. So, for Ambedkar, the structure of village settlements reflected the basic tenets of Hinduism that never recognized dalits as its integral part. In other words, village contributed and simultaneously sustained the divisive nature of the Hindu society where the untouchables always remained 'outside the fold'. As he most eloquently put,

> the Hindu society insists on segregation of the untouchables. The Hindu will not live in the quarters of the untouchables and will not allow the untouchables to live inside the Hindu quarters. … It is not a case of social separation, a mere stoppage of social intercourse for a temporary period. It is a case of territorial segregation and of a cordon sanitaire putting the impure people inside the barbed wire into a sort of a cage. Every Hindu village has a ghetto. The Hindus live in the village and the untouchables live in the ghetto.

In contrast with Gandhi, Ambedkar conceptualized village as a model of the oppressive Hindu social organization, a microcosm of the overall demeaning circumstance in which dalits were located. It was 'the working plant of the Hindu social order' where one could see the atrocities of Hinduism. Given the obvious role of the villages in sustaining the atrocious social circumstances of the dalits, Ambedkar never, as evident, endorsed Gandhi's eulogy for Indian villages because they represented an exclusive domain for the touchables at the cost of the untouchables who invariably were pushed into the ghetto.

The conflict between Gandhi and Ambedkar on the issue of the separate electorates for untouchables and the depressed classes was an articulation of two contrasting perspectives that fundamentally altered the nature of political participation by the scheduled castes and tribes in the British India and its aftermath. Once the separate electorate for the Muslims was conceded by the Congress while accepting the 1935 Government of India Act, Ambedkar argued, on behalf of the dalits, that they must be allowed to constitute a separate electorate and elect their own representatives to the central and provincial legislatures. He further defended the claim by saying that since voting was severely restricted by property and educational qualifications, the geographically highly disparate depressed classes were unlikely to have any influence in the decision making process. So, the solution lay in separate electorate for them. Ambedkar held the view that untouchables were absolutely separate from Hinduism and hence he tried 'to find a solution to their problem through political separatism'.[13] In order to substantiate, he further argued that the Hindus 'had much to lose by the abolition of untouchability, though they had nothing to fear from political reservation leading to this abolition'. The matter was therefore 'economic' rather than 'religious'. Unable to appreciate Ambedkar's demand, Gandhi declined to accept that the untouchables were a community separate from the Hindus and instead was prepared to have reserved seats for them in general constituencies. For him, the matter was highly 'religious', as he stated, 'for me the question of these classes is predominantly moral and religious. The political aspect, important though it is', he further added, 'dwindles into insignificance compared to the moral and religious issue'. He reacted strongly when a charge was labelled that the upper-caste Congress leaders could never properly represent the untouchables. When his attention was drawn to the Congress acceptance of the 1932 Communal Award, Gandhi insisted that unlike the question of religious minorities, the issue of untouchability was a matter internal to Hinduism and had to be resolved within it. Underlining the adverse consequences of such division on the Hindus, the Mahatma thus emphatically argued that

> I cannot possibly tolerate what is in store for Hinduism if there are two division set forth in the villages. Those who speak of the political rights of untouchables do not know their India, do not know how Indian society is today constructed, and therefore I want to say with all the emphasis that I can command that if I was the only person to resist this thing I would resist it with my life.

Gandhi's protest against the extension of the separate electorate for the dalits was double-edged: on the one hand, Gandhi sincerely believed that the separate electorate would also split them from the Hindu society and absolve the latter of its moral responsibility to fight against the practice of untouchability. There were clear political calculations, as Bhikhu Parekh argues, that governed Gandhi's mind for 'the separate electorate would have reduced the numerical strength of the Hindu majority, encouraged minority alliance against it, and fragmented the country yet further'.[14] So, the Gandhian intervention was the result of a skilful political strategy as well as of his passionate concern for Indian unity. Ambedkar was equally assertive and insisted on separate electorate as the best device to protect the social, economic and political interests of the dalits. As he stated, 'I trust [that] the Mahatma would not drive me to the necessity of making a choice between his life and the rights of my people. For I can never consent to deliver my people bound hand and foot to the caste Hindus for generations to come.' No solution was visible. For Gandhi, the separate electorate for the untouchables was to divide the Hindu society further, perpetuating their inferiority. Ambedkar denounced this as a strategic argument for using the untouchables as 'weightage for the Hindus against the Muslims'. When the British government endorsed the separate electorate in the Communal Award of August 1932, Ambedkar had an edge over his rival. Now, the only course of action open to Gandhi was to embark on a fast. He went on a fast rather than approve the demand of the separate electorate for the depressed classes. Gandhi who was in Yervada prison in Poona began his fast on 20 September that ended only on 24 September once Ambedkar agreed to accept the reservation of seats for dalits within the caste-Hindu constituencies. An agreement between Gandhi and Ambedkar, known as the Poona Pact, was signed in 1933 and the depressed classes were given a substantial number of reserved seats but within the Hindu electorate. The Poona Pact accorded reservation of seats for the untouchables in exchange for Ambedkar's conceding to a joint rather than separate electorates. The 1932 Communal Award had granted untouchables 78 seats in the legislature, along with the right to elect their own candidates as well as vote for general seats.

Under the revised arrangement, they were granted 148 seats, with 18 per cent reservation in the central legislature. Only untouchables could contest in these seats; however, their right to elect their own candidates was withdrawn, the disheartening implication for untouchables being that their representation would still remain in the hands of the majority community since their legislators would be chosen by the general electorate.[15]

The Poona Pact represented a victory for the Mahatma in two ways: (a) it was accepted that untouchability was 'a social' and not 'a political problem'; and (b) it was a problem of Hindu religion and not of the Hindu economy. Nonetheless, what was unique about the Pact was that it, for the first time, placed the backward classes, later classified as the Scheduled Castes in the 1935 Government of India Act, on the centre stage of Indian politics with a separate identity. From now on, the scheduled castes invariably figured in any discussion on national identity. Although in Ambedkar, the scheduled castes found a powerful leader, they continued to remain a politically significant 'minority' with narrow social, economic and political goals. As a dissenter bent on dismantling an oppressive caste system, Ambedkar therefore 'fulfilled the historical role of dissent not only to question the hateful religious dogma but also unbuckle the consolidating ambitions of the secular state within which former religious orthodoxies are subsumed'. What is striking is that despite having opposed Hindu orthodoxy, manifested in caste rigidity of which he was a victim, Babasaheb attempted to steer a steady course between a separatist, sectarian stance and unconditional citizenship function in which identity of untouchables would be subsumed within Hinduism. It would be, however, wrong to suggest that Ambedkar believed that the problem of untouchability would be solved not through legislative feats but through institutionalized social measures. As he argued,

> any electoral arrangement, I believe, cannot be a solution of the larger social problems. It requires more than any political arrangement and I hope that it would be possible for you to go beyond this political arrangement that we are making today [of joint electorate] and devise ways and means whereby it would be possible for the Depressed Classes not only to be part and parcel of the Hindu community but also to occupy an honourable position, a position of equality of status in the community.

Despite Ambedkar's reservations, the 1932 Poona Pact is the first well-articulated arrangement in which the scheduled castes were identified as a separate group within Hinduism. Their emergence with a distinct political identity significantly influenced the provincial elections that followed the 1935 Act. Apart from the Muslims who had already asserted their existence as a significant community, the ascendancy of the scheduled castes clearly indicated the complexity of the future course of Indian history, which, so far, had glossed over the well-entrenched fragmented identities within both the Hindus and Muslims. In fact, the Pakistan demand that drew upon Jinnah's 'two nation theory' hinges on the exclusive identities of both the principal communities, Hindus and Muslims, despite sharing the same socio-economic and politico-cultural milieu. For the nationalists, the idea of separate Hindu and Muslim identity had no natural basis and also the two communities were politically separated through the manoeuvers of communal forces and imperial *divide-et-impera*.

For Jinnah and the Muslim League, the demand for a sovereign and independent Muslim state was logical since Muslims constituted a separate nation with a different religious philosophy, social customs and literature. Hindus and Muslims belong to two completely different civilizations, which drew on conflicting ideas and conceptions. The Hindu counterpart of this logic was articulated by V.D. Savarkar who argued strongly for a separate Hindu identity because of distinctive features separating Hindus from Muslims though its root can be traced back to the eighteenth century when the English writing on India clearly provided the Hindus with a distinct identity 'in racial, religious and linguistic terms'.

That Muslims constituted a self-determining political community was always emphasized to completely dissociate from the Hindus seeking to establish 'a Hindu Raj'. The Hindu-Muslim schism was not merely based on religious differences but also on certain fundamental principles guiding their respective lives. As Muslims drew upon completely different socio-cultural values it was unthinkable that they could live as 'a mere minority in a Hindu-dominated India'. While explaining the Hindu-Muslim chasm in colonial India, Ambedkar thus argued that the Hindu-Muslim 'antagonism . . . is formed by causes which take their origin in historical, religious, cultural and social antipathy of which political antipathy is only a reflection. These form', he further elaborated, 'one deep river of discontent which, being regularly fed by these sources, keeps on mounting to a head and overflowing its ordinary channels.' So, Ambedkar held the Hindus equally responsible for the rise of Muslims separatism that was finally resolved in the emergence of Pakistan as a nation.

B.R. Ambedkar, in his *Pakistan or the Partition of India*, endorsed the claim for Pakistan in terms of realist politics. According to him, partition was possibly the best solution to resolve the constitutional impasse in India for two reasons. First, given the hostility of the Muslims to the idea of a single central government, inevitably dominated by the Hindu majority, it was certain that if there was no partition, the animosities and suspicion between the communities would remain: 'burying Pakistan is not the same thing as burying the ghost of Pakistan'. Furthermore, given the demographic composition of what was proposed as Pakistan, there was no doubt that it would be a homogeneous state and hence free from communal bickering and mutual distrust. Secondly, Ambedkar felt that in united India where more than a third of the population was Muslim, 'could Hindu dominance be a serious threat to the very existence of the polity'. In such a state, Muslims apprehending the tyranny of the Hindu majority were likely to organize themselves into 'a theocratic party' provoking in turn the rise of Hindu fundamentalist forces seeking to establish 'a Hindu raj'. Partition would radically alter the situation where Muslims in Hindustan would be a very small and widely scattered minority force joining different political parties in accordance with what they consider 'as most protective' of their socio-economic and political interests. As a result, a party like Hindu Mahasabha that drew on the principle of 'a Hindu raj' would gradually disappear. Persuaded by the logic of his argument, Ambedkar suggested that the lower of Hindu society should join hands with the Muslim minority to fight the Hindu high castes for their rights of citizenship and social dignity.

The Poona Pact was a political response that triggered off debates on the relevance of caste in Indian society. While Gandhi's faith in caste was unquestionable, Ambedkar attributed untouchability to caste and other obnoxious and archaic practices, justified in the name of Hinduism. According to Ambedkar, caste system 'is a hierarchy in which the divisions of labour are graded one above the other. ... This division of labour is not spontaneous, it is not based on natural aptitudes ... in so far as it involves an attempt to appoint tasks to individuals in advance, selected not on the basis of trained original capacities, but on that of the social status of the parents.'[16] Since the caste system was based on ascription of status by birth, it was inherently exclusive losing its publicness. As Ambedkar argued, 'caste has killed public spirit. Caste has destroyed the sense of public charity. Caste has made opinions impossible. To the Hindus, virtue has become caste-ridden and morality has become caste-bound'. By attacking *Chaturvarnya*, the basic institution holding the caste system in tact, Ambedkar countered Gandhi's argument defending that the former was an innocent typology of human beings on *guna* (worth). By dividing the Hindu society into four different categories – *Brahmins*, *Kshtriya*, *Vaishya* and *Shudra* – on the basis of birth, *Chaturvarnya*, argued Babasaheb,

> sanctions not only a differentiation of persons but also their gradation. [The labels, Brahmin, Kshtriya, Vaishya and Shudra] are names which are associated with a definite and fixed notion in the mind of every Hindu. The notion is that of a hierarchy based on birth. So long as these names continue, Hindus will

> continue to think of the Brahmin, Kshtriya, Vaishya and Shudra as hierarchical divisions of high and low, based on birth, and act accordingly. The Hindu must be made to unlearn all this. But how can this happen if the old labels remain and continue to recall to his minds' old notions. ... To continue the old name is to make reform futile. To allow this Chaturvarnya, based on worth to be designated by such stinking labels of Brahmin, Kshtriya, Vaishya, Shudra, indicative of social divisions based on birth, is snare. ... To, this Chaturvarnya with its old labels is utterly repellent and my whole being rebels against it.[17]

As evident, Ambedkar advocated a total rejection of *Chaturvarnya* simply because of its justification of division within the Hindu society on the basis of birth. Appreciating Ambedkar for his critique of caste, Gandhi made his defence in the columns of *Harijan*. He reiterated his faith in Hinduism and its institutions, including the *Chaturvarnya*, presumably to avoid further divisions within the Hindu society. Instead of taking Ambedkar head-on, Gandhi simply provided an interpretation of caste and *varnashrama* to defend his point of view. He believed in *varnashrama* of the *Vedas,* which in his opinion was based on absolute equality of status, notwithstanding passages to the contrary in the *smritis* and elsewhere. Defending *varnashrama* as a mere social arrangement of universally-applicable division of occupation, he thus argued,

> [The four] Varnas ... have been sanctioned by the Shastras [holy books]. Whether or not people are conscious of them, they do exist all over the world as we see. There are everywhere these four classes: one to impart knowledge of god for the welfare of the world, another to protect the people against manifold dangers, a third one to carry on the work of farming, etc., to

sustain the community and one class to work for these three classes. There is no feeling of high and low to this division.

Integrally linked with Hinduism, *Chaturvarnya*, he believed, was

> based on absolute equality of status, notwithstanding passages to the contrary in the smritis [the holy scriptures] and elsewhere. ... There was no prohibition of intermarriage and inter-dining. Prohibition there is of change of one's hereditary occupation for purposes of gain. The existing practice is, therefore, doubly wrong in that it has set up cruel restrictions about inter-dining and intermarriage and tolerance about choice of occupation ... it must be left to the unfettered choice of the individual as to where he or she will marry or dine.[18]

On another occasion, he was critical of the ways caste evolved as a social system governing inter-personal relations by saying 'restrictions as regards inter-marriage and inter-dining which defy reason ... are very harmful and stand in the way of the community's progress. It has nothing to do with religion.' He thus made a distinction between caste and *varnashrama*; while the former by endorsing various kinds of social restrictions was distorted, the latter was 'a cooperative society with its members divided into occupational groups, each fulfilling their own functions, but all of equal status'; and it was this ideal of caste to which Gandhi adhered throughout his life.

For Ambedkar, this was an attempt to scuttle the contentious issue. Furthermore, his critique of the caste system was misleading if it was juxtaposed with his defence for the *Chatruvarnya*, the core of the caste system. This conformed to the endeavours of other Hindu leaders who criticized the practice of caste discrimination to fulfil their own narrow political agenda at the cost of the dalits. As he argued,

> Hindu leaders became filled with an illicit passion for their belief when any one proposes to rob them of their companionship. The Mahatma is no exception. [He] appears not to believe in thinking. He prefers to follow his saints. ... One must sympathise with him. ... But ... dependence on saints cannot lead us to know the truth. ... In so far as he does think, to me he really appears to be prostituting his intelligence to find the reasons for supporting this archaic social structure of the Hindus. He is the most influential apologist of it and therefore the worst enemy of the Hindus.

Why was Gandhi in favour of the caste system despite its divisive nature? Ambedkar attributed this to Mahatma's narrow political calculations. He thus bluntly placed, on record, his views by saying that

> the reason why the Mahatma is always supporting Caste and Varna is because he is afraid that if he opposed them he will lose his place in politics. Whatever the source of his confusion the Mahatma must be told that he is deceiving himself and also deceiving the people by preaching Caste under the name of Varna.

Ambedkar's diatribe against Gandhi and Hindu society in his lecture entitled 'Ranade, Gandhi and Jinnah', has two clearly defined parts. On the one hand, Ambedkar evolved his critique of Hinduism by drawing extensively on Ranade's view on Hinduism. The second part dwells on his criticism of the role of Gandhi and Jinnah as political leaders of Hindus and Muslims in India. While appreciating Ranade for his critique of Hinduism, Ambedkar stated that Ranade was the first

Indian politician who argued that 'there were no rights in the Hindu society, … there were privileges and disabilities, privileges for a few and disabilities for a vast majority'. Linking this argument with his criticism of Gandhi, Babasaheb felt that there was no alternative for the Mahatma but to support Hinduism and caste system simply because 'Mr Gandhi wants the untouchables to remain as Hindus … [n]ot as partners but as poor relations of Hindus'. Characterizing Gandhi as 'a Tory by birth as well as faith' because of his rigid views on social and religious issues, he accused the Mahatma of 'demoralizing' his followers and also 'politics'. Like Jinnah, he made 'half of his followers fools and the other half hypocrites'. He attributed the rise of Gandhi rather simplistically to 'the aid of big business and money magnates'. As a result, Indian politics,

> at any rate the Hindu part of it, instead of being spiritualized has become grossly commercialized, so much so that it has become a byword of corruption. … Politics has become a kind of sewage system intolerably unsavoury and insanity. To become a politician is like going to work in the drain.

The debate between Gandhi and Ambedkar is significant for two important reasons. First, Ambedkar's sharp critique has not only problematized the twin concepts of justice and freedom by taking into account the dalit point of view, it has also posed before us new social, economic and political issues involving the peripheral sections of Indian society. Ambedkar's intervention captured a serious gap in the nationalist socio-political thought. Gandhi, despite being universal in his approach, failed to incorporate the specific dalit issues while organizing the campaign for freedom. That Gandhi represented all regardless of class, caste and creed was based on assumptions inflating the claim of the Mahatma to amicably settle the conflicting socio-political and economic interests of diverse Indian population. Not until the 1932 Poona Pact, Gandhi effectively negotiate with the dalits as an emerging and socially formidable constituency of the nationalist politics. Only after this Pact, the Congress leadership formally accorded a legitimate space to the dalits who, so far, had not actively participated in the struggle for freedom. The role of the British government here was not insignificant either. By accepting Ambedkar as representative of the dalits in the 1932 Round Table Conference, the ruling authority deflated Gandhi's claim to epitomize India as a whole. Gandhi was pushed to the periphery and Ambedkar was brought in presumably because of his success in articulating the issues concerning dalits, which though important, were never adequately addressed either by the nationalist political leadership or by the colonial government. So, justice and freedom acquired new connotations in the changed milieu when dalits had already emerged as a politically significant constituency under the stewardship of Ambedkar. By providing a new conception of emancipatory politics, Babasaheb went beyond a comprehensive 'de-legitimation' of slavery, which was but another name of untouchability. It entailed, as discussed, a wide-ranging programme of equality and equity measures seeking to fulfil a wide variety of material and non-material needs of those, identified as untouchables. It is this total programme of societal transformation that constituted his conception of swaraj, which was not just freedom from colonialism; it was a freedom which was just. Swaraj, thus defined, was not merely political and economic freedom from colonialism, as conceptualized by Gandhi, but a significant socio-political package striving to ameliorate the conditions of those 'outside the fold'. It would not be wrong to argue therefore that the Gandhi-Ambedkar debate is theoretically innovative and politically crucial in grasping the most volatile phase of Indian nationalism when the Mahatma no longer remained the undisputed leader of the nationalist articulation of the freedom struggle.

Secondly, it is alleged that Ambedkar manipulated dalit agenda in order to undermine the effort of the Indian National Congress to achieve freedom. His 'separatist ideology' caused a fissure in the nationalist campaign, for obvious reasons. Ambedkar was not persuaded because he regarded 'with great suspicion all attempts, [including that by Gandhi], to portray democratization as a process independent of caste manipulation'. His sustained criticism of Gandhi for supporting the *Chaturvarnya*-based Brahminical social order has wider theoretical implications. According to him, the collusion between Brahminism and colonialism was possible because of the support, accorded by Gandhi. His analogy between a colonial government that drained resources from the colony and a caste ideology that lived off the labour of outcaste groups are 'consistent with his rhetorical strategy of conflating disparate historical moments within a single frame, in order not only to illuminate the interchangeability of British colonialism and Brahminism, but also to expose the claims of an ideology negated by its own practices'. The debate between Gandhi and Ambedkar is therefore most instructive in both grasping relatively non-visible dimensions of Indian reality and also in conceptualizing the dalit intervention in the nationalist discourse that so far had failed to address the dalit issues most conclusively.

CONCLUSION

There is no doubt that Gandhi remained a constant referent to those seeking to articulate an ideological alternative to what constituted Gandhism. The Mahatma had an edge over the other leaders and compatriots because of two important reasons: first, Gandhi was undoubtedly the organic leader of the nationalist movement that acquired completely different characteristics once its constituencies went beyond the metropolis and other urban centres of political activities. Whatever the immediate response to Gandhi's arrival on the Indian political scene, it was he who galvanized the masses into action despite the obvious adverse consequences of challenging a well-entrenched colonial power. The Mahatma was perhaps the first to have realized the political inadequacies of the urban-centric national movement in a diverse society like India. Indian nationalism became mass-based and geographically widespread in contrast with its earlier phases when the national movement had a very narrow base. The territorial expanse of nationalism was directly linked with the gradual, but steady expansion of the Indian National Congress that was no longer a platform for mere constitutional opposition to the British rule, but also a forum for well-organized campaigns for freedom. By involving the so-called peripheral sections of India, he also let lose another significant process empowering them to endorse and also challenge the nationalist articulation of freedom struggle by Gandhi and his colleagues in the Indian National Congress. So, the Gandhian hegemony in conceptualizing even his critique can never be undermined.

Secondly, despite their roots in Gandhism, these critiques also provide alternative to what the Mahatma stood for. It is true that neither Rabindranath Tagore nor B.R. Ambedkar was involved in the nationalist struggle as organically as the Mahatma. Hence they missed the wider story which Gandhi both scripted and directed. There is no doubt that the Mahatma paid less attention to some of the major social evils, including the caste system, presumably for the political goal that was prior to any other goals. Furthermore, the issues that figured in critiques of Gandhi were contingent on the contemporary socio-economic and political circumstances. For instance, Tagore's critical response to nation and nationalism owed largely to his own experience of the 1903-08 Swadeshi Movement when the flirtations with the idea of nation alienated the Muslims completely. Hence, he was not appreciative of this conception that was likely to be divisive in the context of multi-cultural India. By drawing on the civilizational resources, not only did he create a stable constituency for the nationalist cause, he also sustained it by providing a proper organizational backing involving people irrespective of class, clan and religion. Despite the success of the Muslim League in carving out an independent space for the Muslims, Indian National Congress under Gandhi's stewardship maintained its secular character even in circumstances where exclusive ideologies seemed to have flourished. In other words, Gandhi's strength lay in his ability to sustain a multi-class nationalist platform seeking to primarily attain political freedom from the British rule, which would allow the nationalists then to properly address the relevant social and economic issues crippling the nation. This is where the intervention by Ambedkar was very important. Insisting on 'a just swaraj' for all, Babasaheb was the first to have identified a major flaw in Gandhi's conceptualization of dalit and the issues, relevant to their social, political and economic existence. Whereas Gandhi was, in a typical Brahminical way, accommodative of the dalit issues in the nationalist agenda, Ambedkar endeavoured to carve-out an independent space for the dalits while negotiating with the British government as well as the dominant nationalist groups, including the Gandhi-led Indian National Congress. More specifically, through a serious contestation of Gandhi's social and political ideas, Ambedkar drew out a new mental map, based on a redefinition of 'freedom' and 'justice' that remained ideologically constrained if conceptualized in caste terms.

Drawn on different, if not contrasting perspectives, these critiques are illustrative of creative nationalist responses to imperialism suggesting the theoretical inadequacies of the so-called modular forms that tend to homogenize the nationalist discourses. In other words, because the modular forms gloss over the peculiar socio-economic and political milieu in which the nationalist response is articulated, they fail to grasp, let alone conceptualize, the ideological basis of most of the nations involved in anti-imperial struggles. As evident in the discussion, instead of approximating to the Western modular forms of nation and nationalism, the Afro-Asian nationalist responses remain always innovative presumably because of the dialectics of anti-imperial movements, the nature of which vary, for obvious reasons, from one location to another. Moreover, the nationalist discourse is neither uniformly structured nor evenly poised. Gandhi was certainly a dominant strand, but not the only one. Hence, the importance of the critiques which provide an alternative, based on different ideological perspectives and also differently articulated. So, the modular forms appear to be inappropriate within a particular nationalist discourse. In that sense, the alternative points of view of Tagore and Ambedkar are theoretically innovative and practically useful to understand the inner tension within the nationalist discourses, in which Gandhism was certainly dominant. They provided critiques within a critique since the Indian response (sic) was a critique of the larger nationalist discourses defending the modular forms. Therefore, the argument defending that the nationalist discourses regardless of location are nothing but 'derivative' does not seem to be plausible by any stretch of imagination. Furthermore, even Gandhism, which remained one of the major forms of nationalist articulation had varied manifestations at different levels of the anti-British struggle in India. The major nationalist discourse was, as evident, not only differently textured due perhaps to diverse participants, but also articulated differently underlining the importance of the context. So, both Gandhism and the critique, provided by those who critically evaluated Gandhi and Gandhism, constitute an important pillar of the nationalist discourse that was neither derivative nor imitative, but creative and innovative.

---

1 Amartya Sen, *The Argumentative Indian: Writings on Indian History, Culture and Identity*, Allen Lane, London, 2005, p. 3.

2 Rabindranath Tagore, 'Gandhi the Man' (1938) – quoted in Amartya Sen, *The Argumentative Indian: Writings on Indian History, Culture and Identity*, Allen lane, London, 2005, p. 99.

3 Rabindranath Tagore, *Nationalism*, Rupa, Delhi, 1994 (reprint of the collection, originally published in 1917). p. 89.

4 ibid., p.90.

5 Jinnah's presidential address in the 1940 Lahore session of the All India Muslim League – reproduced in S.S. Pirzada (ed.) *Foundations of Pakistan*, Vol.II, National Publishing House, Karachi, p.337.

6 Rabindranath Tagore, 'The call of truth', reproduced in Sabyasachi Bhattacharya (compiled and edited) *The Mahatma and the Poet: Letters and Debates between Gandhi and Tagore, 1915-1941*, National Book Trust, New Delhi, 1997, pp. 83-84.

7 M.K. Gandhi, 'The great sentinel', *Young India*, 13 October, 1921.

8 M.K. Gandhi, 'The Poet's Anxiety', *Young India*, 1 June, 1921.

9 Rabindranath Tagore, 'The cult of Charkha', *The Modern Review*, September 1925, pp.101-2.

10 Rabindranath Tagore, 'Striving for Swaraj', *The Modern Review*, September 1925, p.118.

11 M. K. Gandhi, 'The Poet and the Charkha', *Young India*, 5 November, 1925

12 B.R. Ambedkar, 'Gandhism', reproduced in Valerian Rodrigues (ed.), *The Essential Writings of B.R. Ambedkar*, Oxford University Press, New Delhi, 2002, p. 165.

13 Judith Brown, 'The Mahatma and modern India', *Modern Asian Studies*, 3 (4), 1969, p. 331.

14 Bhikhu Parekh, *Gandhi*, Oxford University Press, Oxford, 1997, p. 18.

15 For details see Ravinder Kumar, 'Ambedkar, Gandhi and the Poona Pact', Occasional Paper on Society and History, No. 20, Nehru Memorial Library and Museum, New Delhi, 1985; and also, M.S. Gore, *The Social Context of an Ideology: Ambedkar's Political and Social Thought*, Sage, New Delhi, 1993, pp. 136-39.

16 B.R. Ambedkar, 'Annihilation of Caste', reproduced in Valerian Rodrigues (ed.), *The Essential Writings of B.R. Ambedkar*, Oxford University Press, New Delhi, 2002, p. 262. Ambedkar articulated his critique of caste in his address at the annual conference of the Jat-Pat-Todak Mandal of Lahore which was entitled '*Annihilation of Caste*' in its published form.

17 ibid., p.275.

18 *Harijanbandhu*, 19 January, 1936, *CWMG*, Vol 62, pp.142-43.

6

~

THE MAHATMA AND THE MARGINAL GANDHI

HISTORIANS ARE BAFFLED OVER THE QUESTION WHY GANDHI accepted the 1947 partition of India when he had always vehemently opposed Jinnah's two-nation theory. In other words, how did Gandhi who never believed that Hindus and Muslims were two nations accepted partition that drew on the conceptualization of Hindus and Muslims as separate nations? There is no straightforward answer except that one can find cues in the dwindling importance of Gandhi in the historical processes that finally culminated in the division of the continent. Yet, the Mahatma remained the most effective nationalist leader to contain 'the mass fury' of competing religious communities during the communal holocaust just on the eve of the transfer of power. Gandhi's presence in the riot-torn regions of Bengal reduced the communal brutality dramatically. Even the provincial Muslim League leadership that failed to quell the situations, especially in Calcutta, joined Gandhi in various peace rallies in the city. The effect was most dramatic and Gandhi proved once again his mantle as 'the Mahatma in Indian politics'. The aim of this chapter is to dwell on this paradox in the last two years of his life: on the one hand, he was absolutely marginal in the negotiation between the nationalists and British for the transfer of power, and on the other he still remained perhaps the only organic leader of the masses capable of mobilizing as well as guiding them in accordance with his priority.

THE MARGINAL GANDHI

The last two years of Gandhi's life were most significant for India's freedom struggle. The 1946 communal riots in Calcutta and Noakhali convinced the leading Congress stalwarts, including Nehru and Patel, of the need for partition despite the fact that none of them endorsed the two-nation theory. What is also striking is the conspicuous absence of Gandhi in the final negotiation for the transfer of power. Gandhi had no alternative, it seems, but to accept the decision of other younger leaders. Was Gandhi strategic in his response or was persuaded by the arguments, made in favour of partition, one wonders. The doubt persists because the Mahatma was never at ease with the idea of Pakistan, Jinnah's separate Muslim state. In his prayer meeting in June 1947, he thus argued, 'Pakistan is a bad thing. … What is there to rejoice over it? Our country has been divided. What is there in it to celebrate. … our land has been divided; does it mean that we should divide our hearts? How can the people of a country become two people? India can have only one people.'[1]

Gandhi might have thought that partition was a temporary arrangement for the transfer of power, and would lose its significance once Hindus and Muslims realized themselves the importance of the communal amity. This argument can easily be justified by Gandhi's assertion that a satyagrahi is always an optimist and pessimism has no place in him. His optimism is based on his belief that people and situations can radically change. His non-violent emancipatory struggle is based on the belief that one's oppressors are temporary 'foes', but potential friends. So, Gandhi's definitions of 'friends and foes' are primarily 'contextual'. There is, therefore, a mixture of both in every one of us. Gandhi demonstrated that by activating the forces of good in their opponents, 'the non-violent resisters can reduce or eliminate basic conflicts without causing any damage to the Truth or *ontic* relationship between the oppressed and the oppressor'.[2] This is probably 'the cycle of life' in which Gandhi had full trust. He witnessed the changes in 1947, and freedom came marking the withdrawal of the British from India. Freedom was won, but was accompanied by the trauma of partition and the mayhem that followed immediately before the transfer of power was formally articulated. The Gandhi-led nationalist movement led to freedom, but failed to avoid partition. Despite Gandhi's vehement opposition to the division of the country on the basis of religion, the Congress leadership accepted partition as the best probable solution to the communal animosity. The day for which Gandhi 'had longed and laboured had come, but he felt no joy because India's freedom ushered in at the cost of her unity'. Gandhi alone was troubled by feelings of disillusionment, despair and deep foreboding while the British government was relieved at the prospect of an orderly transfer of power. He felt totally marginalized in the entire negotiations for the transfer of power. No longer critical to the nationalist articulation of freedom, he confessed,

> I find myself all alone. Even the Sardar and Jawaharlal think my reading of the situation is wrong and peace is sure to return if partition is agreed upon. ... They wonder if I have not deteriorated with age. I can see clearly that the future of independence gained at this price is going to be dark. Everybody is today impatient for independence. Therefore, there is no alternative.[3]

When the tricolour was unfurled in Delhi on 15 August 1947, the optimist Gandhi was in Calcutta to quench the flames of hatred and revenge through his endless vigil, his fasts and in general his sincere commitment to the fundamental precepts of ahimsa. He was truly 'a prisoner of hope'.

By 1946, Gandhi was hardly a decisive force in the Congress and he perhaps realized, as evident in his conversation with his friend G.D. Birla. He sensed 'the dwindling of his authority' when he stated that 'I do not like the shape that things are taking and, I cannot speak out'. He further expressed his helplessness unambiguously in his prayer meeting by saying that '[w]hatever the Congress decides will be done; nothing will be according to what I say. My write runs no more. ... No one listens to me any more. ... I am crying in wilderness'. Gandhi became insignificant in the decision-making process involving the transfer of power. The nucleus of the CWC seemed to have shifted to 'a coterie' dominated by Nehru and Patel. The Congress, according to Gandhi, lost its momentum because 'a rot has set in the Congress' that virtually became an organization of 'white-clad goondas who appear respectable, but goondas at heart'. He was anguished but seemed helpless, as he wrote,

> I know that today I irritate everyone. How can I believe that I alone am right and all others are wrong? What irks me is that people deceive me. They should tell me frankly that I have become old, that I am no longer of any use and that I should not be in their way. If they thus openly repudiate me I shall not be pained in the least.[4]

'Is it really time for me to retire to the Himalayas', thus wonders Gandhi. He seemed to have accepted 'the ebbing of his authority' within the Congress. No statement is explicit than the following one where Gandhi reconciled to his secondary role in shaping the nature of the transfer of power. Once Gandhi's proposal to ask Jinnah to form the Interim Government was turned down by the CWC, Gandhi thought it fit to withdraw from the deliberations over the transfer of power and he thus conveyed his decision immediately to Mountbatten by underlining that

> I felt sorry that I could not convince [the CWC] of the correctness of my plan from every point of view. Nor could they dislodge me from my position although I had not closed my mind against every argument. Thus I have to ask you to omit me from your consideration. Congressmen, who are in the Interim Government, are stalwarts, seasoned servants of the nation and, therefore so far as the Congress point of view is concerned, they will be complete advisors.[5]

Why did the Congress accept partition despite its consistent challenge to its very foundation, the two-nation theory? With his first-hand experience of the dismantling of the Raj, Nicholas Mansergh explains this in terms of three reasons. First, the Congress always favoured a strong government that was not possible so long as Muslims remained within a united India. Hence they 'sacrificed' the unity of India for 'a strong central government'. Secondly, the perception, held both by Patel and Nehru that Pakistan 'would not endure long' may have influenced the Congress leaders to support India's bifurcation. Thirdly, the Congress leaders were believed to be 'impatient'. As they were 'aging' they were not prepared 'to delay independence further'.[6]

The acceptance of partition by the Congress leadership is perhaps illustrative of a distinct change in its assessment of the Congress Party that failed to represent the Indian Muslims at large. The acceptance was also the final act of a process of step by step concession to the League's communally orchestrated demand for a sovereign Muslim state. Each concession by the Congress consolidated communalism further. On the one hand, it had strengthened the claim of the Muslim League as the 'true' representative of Muslims; it had, on the other, weakened its position vis-à-vis the secular Hindus paving the ground for the Hindu communalists, particularly the Hindu Mahasabha, to thrive. One of the direct results of the communal tension, as an official report underlines, was 'the growth of communal organizations like the Rashtriya Swyam Sevak Sangh and the Muslim National Guards in most of the provinces'.

THE MAHATMA AND COMMUNAL RIOTS IN BENGAL

As evident, Gandhi was no longer important in institutional politics. The fate of India was decided even without concurrence of perhaps the tallest of Indian nationalist leaders. Gandhi was completely ignored which he seemed to have conceded since he hardly challenged his colleagues involved in the negotiation for the transfer of power. This is one side of the story. The other equally important side concerns with the critical role that the Mahatma played in defusing communal tension in Bengal in the penultimate year of independence. That the Mahatma hardly lost his appeal as a mass leader was amply demonstrated when his mere presence in the riot-affected areas of Bengal temporarily quelled the tension between the Hindus and Muslims. Partition could not be avoided, but 'the one-man boundary force', as Gandhi was described by Mountbatten, accomplished a miracle though he was not sure, at the outset, whether he was strong enough 'to put up with the flames of communal hatred' given the fact that his 'physical powers are waning'. By helping to avoid bloodbath in Bengal, Gandhi succeeded in achieving what the British army failed to do. So, despite his dwindling role in 'high politics', the Mahatma remained a significant force at the grassroots.

THE 1946 RIOTS IN BENGAL

The riots broke out in Bengal even before 1946. What distinguishes these riots from the earlier ones is the scale of violence and the communal character, so meticulously nurtured even during the height of mayhem. Hindus and Muslims indiscriminately killed one another to probably fulfil the grand design of the politicians to which they hardly contributed. It is thus historically inaccurate to suggest that the decision to partition Bengal along religious-demographic lines actually involved the participation of the masses of people. The actual decision was made in the Bengal Legislative Assembly that was constituted by a very restricted franchise. The decision was undoubtedly crucial in formally articulating partition of the province. What significantly influenced the course of events were, in fact, the communal killings in Calcutta in August 1946 and those in Noakhali just seven weeks later. These were probably the most powerful mass actions (sic), planned by Hindu and Muslim communalists, contributing to the second partition of Bengal. Those who were drawn to the riots appeared to have been swayed by what was projected as the goal of these unprecedented events. Some understood the 1946 communal violence as 'the cataclysmic sign of a general transition of power with its associated feelings of anxiety as well as of anticipation; [while] others took it to mean that Pakistan, whatever its precise legal or constitutional form, was inevitable'.

How did the riots begin? In its Bombay meeting, held on 29 July 1946, the Muslim League adopted to observe 16 August as the direct action day 'to get rid of the present slavery under the British and contemplated future caste-Hindu domination'. According to Jinnah, 'Direct Action was a weapon of self defence.' The Bombay resolution was, as he further added, 'a reaction to the Congress direct action [that always aimed at] coercing and blackmailing the British to bypass the Muslim League and surrendering to the Congress'.

16 August was declared a public holiday. Because a public holiday would enable 'the idle folk' to successfully enforce hartals in areas where the League leadership was uncertain, the Bengal Congress, in a debate in the Assembly, condemned the League ministry for having indulged in 'communal politics' for a narrow goal. The League sought to organize a general

hartal while the Hindus tried to keep up a normal life. The city was in the grip of tension as everybody was apprehending trouble. In his diary notes of Major L.A. Livermore, an officer of the Eastern Command, thus wrote,

> there was a curious stillness in the air. The maidan was deserted and that artery of Calcutta, the famous Chowringhee, was as a street of the dead: not a vehicle or person in sight until about noon when a few people gathered in the vicinity of the Ochterlony Memorial. . . . the silence was that of the air before the storm and that the crack of thunder would reverberate through the city at any moment.[7]

Minor confrontations were reported in the morning, but disturbances started on a large scale in the afternoon in the aftermath of the meeting, organized by Huseyn Shaheed Suhrawardy to observe the Direct Action Day.

Attributing the participation of Muslims in the hartal to 'a holy duty' to Islam, the following leaflet proclaims,

> Awake, arise and unite under the banner of the Muslim League and make this hartal a success. . . . Lead the procession [to Ochterlony Monument] with such strength and enthusiasm that even the blind, deaf, dumb can appreciate their strength and determination.[8]

The situation deteriorated in the afternoon of 16 August as the chief secretary requested the governor of Bengal to call the army at once. The governor did not call the army because he was not constitutionally authorized to do so without a formal request from the ministry. The League ministry finally asked for its intervention on the second day. This force of about 8000 soldiers, if deployed in advance, could easily have stopped the carnage before it became unmanageable. The government's unwillingness to call the army was characterized as 'intentional' especially when the situation deteriorated in the afternoon of 16 August. It is also possible that they asked for army help 'when they saw the game of killing (sic) was going against the Muslims'.

The 1946 riot was distinctly different from its earlier manifestations in Bengal. It was more organized, directly connected with institutional politics and hence, in the prevailing circumstances, 'more exclusively related to communal politics as well'. As evident, the League utilized the government machinery to mobilise the Muslims for the Direct Action Day. While both the communities had, as an American intelligence report suggests, 'made preparations for self-defence, it was Muslim provocation followed by instant Hindu retaliation' that caused the devastation. The Muslims came off 'very much the worse through the Direct Action', as a contemporary report indicates, presumably because the population of the city was predominantly Hindu. So the chief minister made 'a tactical error in selecting Calcutta for his attack'. The scene now shifted to Noakhali in east Bengal where 85 per cent of the population was Muhammadan.

Trouble began in Noakhali on 10 October 1946 and spread to the villages of the Noakhali district, Sandwip island and south-west Tippera district. The League ministry underplayed the nature of events almost for a week as the Bengal governor was enjoying his holiday in Darjeeling. Killings, conversions by force, abductions of women and loot were common. The pattern was uniform: at the head of the group were ex-servicemen who organized the raids on the villages 'in quasi-military fashion'. The roving bands looted shops, burned houses, exhorted money and booty under threats, abducted women, forcibly converted Hindus and brutally murdered people wherever there was even a slight resistance. What affected the Hindu sensibilities most both in Bengal and outside was the mass forced conversion of Hindus in these areas. These conversions took place *en masse* and, as an official report elaborates,

> appear to have been carried out in several forms. In some cases, it appears to have been a fairly formal perfunctory affair involving merely the reading of Kalma and wearing a lungi instead of a dhoti. In other cases, initial conversion was steadily followed up and converts were made to say their prayers regularly as Muslims and eat beef – anathema to Hindus. The women folk were generally herded into some central places like the village school and after the menfolk had signified their acceptance of Islam, the women were brought-out, their tikka mark on the forehead (the sign of a Hindu wife) rubbed out and their conchshell bungles broken. They were thus deprived of the outward symbols of their faith.

It is difficult to ascertain the exact number of those who were forcibly converted during the riot because of their reluctance to admit that they have been converted to Islam. The horror of such events in the eyes of orthodox Hindus must not be underrated. It seems clear, as the Bihar riot had shown, that they were greatly exaggerated and subsequent excesses in other provinces were largely influenced by stories of Hindu women being abducted and bought and sold by Muslim.

Hindus were invariably the targets of attack. After his tour of the district, the Bengal governor confirms that 'the Hindus were mostly affected and the Muslims were carefully left untouched'. While reporting on an incident in a village, called Charhaim, the governor had no doubt that the mobs had done work 'thoroughly and systematically'. 'This village had', as he elaborated further, 'a prosperous bazaar which was the economic centre of the neighbourhood. The bazaar stood on government land and the government revenue office was untouched, as were a few Muslim-owned shops; but the rest was a desolate ruin of charred timber and twisted corrugated iron sheets'.

The Muslim League may not have participated directly in the riot, but the main organizer of the mayhem happened to be Ghulam Sarwar, a former League member of the Bengal Legislature. Exhorting the Muslims to avenge the Calcutta massacre, Sarwar urged the Muslims to join the National Guard and impose an economic boycott on Hindus. Muslims buying goods from Hindus were abused and beaten. There were reports that Sarwar had conducted well-planned attacks on Hindu temples desecrating idols and sacrificing cows in the lawn of these temples.[9] 'An uncrowned king' of the Muslims, he received support of the local school teachers, mollahs, and the union presidents. What Sarwar succeeded in doing was largely possible because of the involvement of the mollahs who easily swayed the 'religious Muslim villagers' by their appeal, couched 'in Islamic terms'.

The Noakhali-Tippera riot was neither sudden nor spontaneous, but had been deliberately planned with support and encouragement from the leaders of institutional politics. Thus the *Times* wrote,

> Noakhali was the outcome of enmity, aroused by the happenings in Calcutta. These feelings were played by certain local Muslim leaders of doubtful reputation but with a large following whose motives were partly religious fanatacism and partly the desire to profit from the expulsion of Hindu elements. Disturbances took the form of seeking to establish a local Pakistan wholly Muslim in composition.[10]

Gandhi's presence in Noakhali for more than a month (6 November 1946 – 2 March 1947) temporarily quelled the situation but did not radically alter the circumstances in which both the communities were placed. Sucheta Kripalani who went to Noakhali and stayed there for seven months on Gandhi's request felt that because 'the poison of ill-will and hatred, preached by the Muslim League leaders, the Mullas and Maulvis had gone so deep',[11] Gandhi's hope that people would 'cast off their fear and return to their homes was 'unrealistic'. It was unrealistic, she further added, because Gandhi 'did not realize that this was too much to expect from the Hindus who suffered so much and so grievously'. By December, the Mahatma came to terms with the reality because, as he himself admitted, 'distrust has gone too deep for exhortation'. Disheartened by his failure to bring back those who had left, Gandhi articulated his emotions by saying that 'in spite of efforts exodus continues and very few persons have returned to their villages. They say that the guilty parties are still at large . . . that sporadic cases of murder and arson still continue, that abducted women have not been returned, that burnt houses are not being re-built and generally the atmosphere of good-will is lacking'. While explaining the rapid deterioration of communal amity between the Hindus and

Muslims, Gandhi felt that 'the poison of mutual hatred' between the two communities led to the disappearance of 'fraternalization' that figured so prominently during the Non-Cooperation-Khilafat Movement.

The Muslims did not like Gandhi's presence in Noakhali. Attempts were made to prevent those from attending the regular prayer meetings by throwing night soil and glasses on the path approaching where he lived. Initially the local Muslims had shown enthusiasm in his prayer meetings, but later, especially from January onwards, the number had suddenly dropped. The Muslim League leaders of Noakhali felt that since Gandhi's presence prevented restoration of peace he should immediately quit the district and the local Hindu and Muslim leaders should be 'left alone'. While retorting to this, Gandhi firmly stated that 'if the presence of anyone is a bar to the restoration of normal conditions, such a person or persons should be dealt with by the Government under its powers. ... If [his] prayer meetings are disliked by Muslims, they have but to abstain from attendance.' Suhrawardy and his League colleagues were critical of his decision to stay in Noakhali and charged him 'with the desire to make political capital out of an unfortunate happening'. In his address to the students in Delhi, Suhrawardy accused Gandhi of being biased towards the Hindus, otherwise, he would have gone to Bihar, which was tormented by communal riots following the Noakhali outbreak 'to see what his own nation had done to the members of the minority community' there. Despite serious campaign in the Muslim press against Gandhi, there is no denying the fact that 'his presence acted as a soothing balm on the villages in East Bengal; it eased tension, assuaged anger and softened tempers'.[12] So, the Mahatma lived up to his reputation by remaining perhaps the most critical in shaping the mass response even under circumstances, charged with communal hatred and animosity.

CONCLUSION

The Mahatma is a paradox of history. He epitomized success and failure simultaneously. He was perhaps the most successful leader of political mobilization in the twentieth century. What he had initiated in South Africa while opposing the racist government loomed large in India when he challenged the colonial British government. Satyagraha rose to prominence not only in the context of nationalist struggle, but also in innumerable protest movements in the contemporary world when Gandhi always remains the reference point. There is no doubt that the Gandhian non-violent emancipatory ideology continues to remain viable even after more than half a century of his death. Various reasons can be cited: most of them stem from the growing popularity of Gandhi because of his moral and psychological affinity with the masses. He virtually became organic to the Indian nationalist movement, which, despite being ideologically diverse, was largely governed by ahimsa. This is where Gandhi remained unique. Not only did he articulate a mass-based ideology in the form of ahimsa he also re-wrote the history of Indian nationalism by changing its contour radically. As discussed, the Non-Cooperation Movement, though abortive, introduced various new constituencies in the freedom struggle, which remained absolutely peripheral in the pre-Gandhian days. The pattern continued. Both the civil disobedience and Quit India movements created history not only in terms of their distinct ideological character, but also in terms of the diverse social constituencies that got involved.

Was India's freedom struggle a true nationalist movement? If judged from the primary ideological goal, one can argue that it was a movement, which was nationalist in character. Gandhi was undoubtedly its principal architect. It may not be a correct answer if one draws attention to the social character of the Indian nationalist movement. The Gandhi-led anti-British campaign was not exactly nationalist presumably because significant minorities, especially the Muslims and dalits held views opposed to Gandhi. Since the 1906 Lucknow Pact with the Congress the Muslim League, for instance, sustained its independent existence as a separate politico-ideological bloc in the struggle against colonialism. Participation of the Muslims in the Non-Cooperation Movement was largely possible for the merger of the Khilafat cause with that of the non-cooperation campaign. That was perhaps the only example when Hindus and Muslims held the fort together against a common foe, though due to different political considerations. In the later Gandhi-launched movements, namely the Salt Satyagraha and open rebellion, Muslims hardly participated and that undoubtedly created conditions for the divide and rule strategy to strike roots. Given the conspicuous absence of the Muslims in these two pan-Indian movements, it would not be wrong to argue that the Gandhian ideology was perhaps restricted since the Muslims happily clung to Jinnah's two-nation theory supporting a separate Muslim state. Gandhi never endorsed Jinnah's theory and yet the 1947 transfer of power steered the subcontinent towards setting up of two successor states to the Raj. This is perhaps the most difficult historical riddle, which no one can easily solve. With the formation of Pakistan in the aftermath of decolonization, one can, however, safely argue that a large section of Muslims felt alienated and Gandhi failed to assuage their feelings, while Jinnah succeeded in articulating their voice for an independent Muslim state. The reasons are multiple. What it suggests is the failure of the Mahatma to successfully challenge the arguments defending the clamour for Pakistan. And, hence he never became a nationalist leader capable of uniting Hindus and Muslims in his battle against colonialism. It is also true that Gandhi defused communal tension in the riot-ravaged Calcutta and Noakhali. As shown already, Gandhi was never accepted by the local Muslim leadership just like the provincial Muslim League leaders condemned his presence in Bengal. There is no doubt that Gandhi stopped the bloodbath, though he could hardly put a brake to the political processes that finally culminated in the division of the country.

Gandhi fell to an assassin's bullet. Presumably because of his policy of appeasement of the Muslims, the killer of Gandhi justified this extreme step. Gandhi was perceived by those involved in his assassination to be 'pro-Muslim' for he had suggested Jinnah as the prime minister of independent India and had undertaken a fast to ensure that India fulfilled the fiscal obligations to Pakistan arising out of partition. It is true, as Gyanendra Pandey has shown, that Gandhi's fast did something like 'a miracle'. The demand for driving every Muslim out of every part of Delhi lost its immediate appeal. Many Muslims were able to return to their homes and mohallas, and perhaps for the first time since late 1946, the people of Delhi began to return to the business of living and of re-building their lives, their uprooted city and their future.

Just as Gandhi failed to mitigate the campaign for Pakistan, he was also ineffective in persuading his Congress colleagues to reject partition completely. Gandhi appeared to be a burden to the Congress stalwarts in his last days. He became, to borrow his own expression, 'a back number' in the Congress. With his strong views against partition, it might well have been expected that Gandhi would resist the 3 June plan of Mountbatten of dividing the country into two independent nations. Gandhi decided not to oppose presumably because the Mountbatten plan was perhaps the only mutually-agreed scheme to settle the communal imbroglio in India. Notwithstanding his vehement opposition to the partition, Gandhi approved the Congress decision for acceptance of the plan. By this act of 'self-abnegation', Gandhi saved 'a split in Congress at a crucial moment, without compromising his own independence'. This was perhaps the most appropriate alternative that Gandhi had at the critical juncture of India's political history. He accepted his 'marginality' seemingly most gracefully when he could have spanned the wheel to radically alter India's political history. Why the Mahatma restrained himself at this historical juncture is a puzzle that historians have hardly solved conclusively.

---

1 Gandhi's speech at prayer meeting, 24 June, 1947, *CWMG*, Vol. 88, p. 204.

2 Thomas Pantham, 'Emerging Perspective', *The Hindu*, 21 August, 2005.

3 *Mahatma: The Last Phase*, Gandhi Smriti, Ahmedabad, 1958, pp. 210-11.

4 Fragments of a letter, *CWMG*, Vol.90, p. 253.

5 Gandhi to Mountbatten, 11 April 1947, *The Transfer of Power*, Vol.X, pp.197-98.

6 Diana Mansergh (ed.), *Independence Years: The Selected India and Commonwealth Papers of Nicholas Mansergh*, Oxford University Press, Delhi, 1999, pp. 232-33 .

7 Personal Reports on the killing on the Great Calcutta killing (extracts from the diary of major L. A. Livermore), Francis Tuker, *While Memory Serves*, Cassell, London, 1950, Appendix V, p. 597.

8 G. D. Khosla, *Stern Reckoning: A Survey of the Events Leading up to and Following the Partition of India*, Oxford University Press, Delhi, 1989 (a reprint of the 1949 edition with a new introduction), pp. 51-53.

9 The tour diary of the District Magistrate, E. F. McInerney, published in *The Statesman*, is replete with examples of the activities of Ghulam Sarwar during and before the riot. The *Statesman*, 23 October, 1946.

10 IOR, L/PJ/8/573, The *Times*, London, 10 February, 1947.

11 Sucheta Kripalani, *An Unfinished Biography*, Navajivan Publishing House, Ahmedabad, 1978, p. 50.

12 B.R. Nanda, *Mahatma Gandhi*, Oxford University Press, Delhi, 1996, p. 250.

CONCLUSION

GANDHI VIRTUALLY BECAME SEVERAL IMAGES THAT WERE BUILT around the human Gandhi during the nationalist movement in India. In a peculiar unfolding of the freedom struggle, Gandhi redefined 'politics' that was not confined to 'a defined sphere' but invades everyday life instead. Gandhi was not merely a leader, he also became a part of the masses. His simple attire, use of colloquial Hindi, reference to the popular allegory of Ramrajya 'had made him comprehensible to the common people'. In popular myths, he was invested with supernatural power, which could heal pain and deliver common people from their day-to-day miseries. The masses interpreted Gandhi in their own ways drawing meanings from their own lived experiences and made him a symbol of power for the weak and under-privileged. As evident on various occasions, the masses 'crossed the boundaries of Gandhian politics and deviated from his ideals of non-violence, while believing at the same time that they were following their messiah into a new utopian world of Gandhi raj'.

I

The British government expressed surprise at the growing popularity of Gandhi during the Non-Cooperation Movement when he was still not so well known to the Indian masses. An intelligence report of 1921 underlined the unprecedented quality of his appeal among the people in a small town in UP when they were informed of Gandhi's probable visit. As soon as the announcement was made it was a sight, the report goes,

> to see Hindu and Moslem villagers coming from long distances – on foot, with their bedding on their heads and shoulders, on bullock carts, on horse back, as if a great pilgrimage was going on, and the estimate that nearly a lakh of persons had come and gone back disappointed. It was simply touching to see how eagerly they inquired if there was any hope of his coming. Never before has any political leader, or perhaps even a religious leader, in his own lifetime stirred the masses to their very depths throughout the country and received the homage of so many people. ... His influence is certainly phenomenal and quite unprecedented.[1]

How was it possible? Gandhi emerged as the supreme leader of the nationalist movement presumably because of his capacity to mobilize people regardless of caste, creed and clan. His appeal was universal and was interpreted differently by different sections of society. As Judith Brown argues,

> to the really poor and illiterate, Gandhi's message and appeal was social and religious. To the more prosperous peasants and the traders and the professional men of small towns his appeal became more overtly political; while at the highest level of political participation he could couch demands in the language of legislature and constitution.[2]

As a leader, he was most appealing perhaps due to his success in addressing several social constituencies at the same time. The issues that he raised were not always exactly political, but social and religious as well which probably helped Gandhi expand his constituencies of support. By linking the political struggle with fight against various kinds of injustice, meted out to the people in the name of religiously-defended social equilibrium. His appeal was thus two-fold. Apart from resisting foreign rule, he also undertook several steps to fight against well-entrenched social evils, justified in the name of religion and religious prejudices. This is where the Gandhian charisma is located. So, it was not possible for the British administration to gauge Gandhi when he appeared on the scene. Recognizing the 'unusual' significance of Gandhi in nationalist political mobilization in the context of the Non-Cooperation Movement, Lord Willingdon, the tough governor of Madras who hardly had appreciation for what Gandhi was pursuing thus commented, 'Gandhi is here with the whole of his gang. It is amazing what an influence this man is getting. One of my ADCs came from Calcutta with them in the train and was tremendously impressed with the huge crowds at every station, their orderliness, and absolute devotion to their leader. … Now I admit [that] the position is becoming one of extraordinary difficulty. There is no doubt that Gandhi has got tremendous hold on the public imagination.'[3]

Gandhi was thus described by Jawaharlal Nehru as 'a powerful current of fresh air that made us stretch ourselves and take deep breaths; a beam of light that pierced the darkness and removed the scales from our eyes; a whirlwind that upset many things, but most of all the working of people's minds'.[4] The essence of his teaching was 'fearless and truth, and action allied to these always keeping the welfare of the masses in view'. Unless 'the system that produces misery and poverty of peasants and workers' was totally removed, freedom appeared futile. Nehru attributed the meteoric rise of Gandhi on the national scene to his capacity of being as a part of the masses 'speaking their language and incessantly drawing attention to them and their appalling conditions'. Gandhi was never an outsider. He seemed to have emerged from millions of India. Organically linked with the mass psyche, ahimsa acquired different connotation when it became an ideological weapon in the nationalist struggle. Similarly, satyagraha, a technique with roots in Indian tradition, appeared most devastating to the colonial rulers when endorsed by the masses. Unable to gauge the effectiveness of ahimsa and love as political weapons, Lord Reading, the viceroy, dismissed the Gandhi-led anti-British non-cooperation campaign by saying that Gandhi's views bordered on 'fanaticism that non-violence and love will give India its independence and enable it to withstand the British government. Hence he found it difficult to understand his practice of them in politics.' That the viceroy misread Gandhi was proved beyond doubt as the nationalist movement in India had unambiguously demonstrated how effective was 'the gospel of love' than hatred and also the fragility of 'brute force' against 'soul force' that informed Gandhi's technique of satyagraha. There is no doubt that Gandhi reinvented India's freedom struggle by introducing the ideology of non-violence in the anti-British campaign. However, he failed to transcend in the early stages of the new dispensation, the limitation of his environment. It was thus stated in a confidential report from the American Embassy in Madras that 'far off indeed yet is the day when non-violence or love will be the ruling factor in determining the relations between man and man and nation and nation, the day that signifies unalloyed love for living beings'.

To the British government, Gandhi remained an explosive force, and to the people of India, he was perhaps the most effective political leader who swayed the masses both as a persona and as an ideological messiah. His charisma had a cultural referent. Gandhi's effectiveness as 'a peripatetic teacher was related less to his oratorical or theatrical skills', thus argue Rudolphs, 'than to the reputation that preceded him and the ideal that he embodied'.[5] While underlining the magical capacity of Gandhi in defusing tension between Hindus and Muslim even during the height of the 1946 Calcutta riot, the Calcutta-based Counsellor of the American Embassy was struck by his popularity by stating that

> he is constantly besieged in his temporary home [in Calcutta] by people seeking his advice on all sorts of political and personal problems. The assembled crowd always insisted on his appearing at a window briefly to speak to them. The noise and clamour caused him to hold his ears: in explaining his action, he remarked that he hoped that brain was still young but that his ears were getting old.[6]

Gandhi was also widely credited 'with being the wizard responsible for the magical transformation of Calcutta'. The peace rallies that were organized at Gandhi's behest attracted people from all parts of the city. There was no doubt that Gandhi's presence in the riot-torn Calcutta, as the report suggests, quelled the tension between Hindus and Muslims.

II

There are three Gandhis that appeared to have emerged in the India during the freedom struggle. First, the Gandhi of South Africa who rose to prominence after his successful satyagraha campaign in Natal and Transvaal against the racist Asiatic Registration Act. Not only did he articulate satyagraha, his personality as a leader fighting for the people's cause took shape in South Africa. There is no doubt that Indian freedom struggle was conducted on a much larger scale and on much bigger issues, but his experiment in South Africa immensely contributed to his ideology that gradually evolved in the context of his struggle against colonialism in India. The second Gandhi was crystallized during and after the 1919-22 Non-Cooperation Movement in India. What he learnt in South Africa was applied on a wider scale involving Hindus and Muslims in his satyagraha campaign. Although what brought the Muslims to the nationalist campaign was largely the Khilafat cause, there is no doubt that this was perhaps the most significant mass movement where the centre of gravity shifted to the villages unlike in the past when the anti-British movements were confined mostly to the urban centres of Calcutta and Bombay. For whatever reasons, the strength of the non-cooperation lay in the Hindu-Muslim amity. The third Gandhi, perhaps the most complex and thus theoretically innovative, was shaped by the events and socio-economic and political processes of the period following the withdrawal of the Non-Cooperation Movement in wake of the Chauri Chaura incident. Muslims rose as a distinct political group demanding their share by virtue of their demographic preponderance in Bengal and Punjab. The harijans have found in B.R. Ambedkar an able leader who could confront the leading nationalist forces, including the Congress and the British to accord them a legitimate place in society and politics. The Congress was not as united as it was earlier; it was fractured due to ideological incompatibility among those who remained loyal to Gandhi in the past. The 1939 Tripuri session of the Congress in which Subhas Chandra Bose, a *bete-noire* of Gandhi, defeated the official Congress candidate for presidency, brought out the rivalry between the left and right wings in the Congress. Gandhi was placed in a peculiar situation where he appeared to have lost control of the organization. Despite the temporary hiccups that undoubtedly affected the Congress adversely, Gandhi regained control with the support of the right-wingers that gradually shifted their loyalty away from the Mahatma as India's freedom struggle drew to close. This was the phase when Gandhi, so far the supreme leader of India's freedom struggle, spoke in a vocabulary that redefined some of his basic precepts concerning for example, non-violence. Furthermore, he upheld views that ran counter to what he held in the past especially before the 1930-34 Civil Disobedience Movement. Apart from the transformed nature of the imperial power, one possible explanation of changes in Gandhi's social and political ideas is to be located in his interaction with his colleagues who held views, contrary to what the Mahatma upheld. Not only did he negotiate with the ruling authority with his reformed political agenda, he engaged in regular dialogues with those who while appreciating Gandhi's contribution to the nationalist struggle, critiqued his conceptual framework to analyse India's complex socio-economic reality. It would be difficult, if not impossible, to study all those who expressed views on Gandhi. Even during the nationalist movement, Gandhi was constantly constructed by the participants. 'The Mahatma of his rustic protagonists was thus not as he really was, but as they thought him up.' Gandhi's followers imagined that Gandhi was endowed with extraordinary 'magical power' enabling them to effectively counter the ruthless British state. It was not therefore surprising that those who led the mob against the police in Chauri Chaura during the days of non-cooperation believed that 'bullets have turned into water by the grace of Gandhi' and thus urged the volunteers to proceed without fear. The idea gained ground because there was no casualty after the police firing in the affected areas presumably because firing was more symbolical than actually targeted. This was not an isolated incident. During the height of the 1942 Quit India campaign, the Congress rebels in Midnapur (Bengal) sincerely upheld the idea that if they chanted Gandhi's name, police bullets would not harm them. Not only did Gandhi emerge as a symbol strengthening the morale of the nationalist rebels while confronting the British administration, he was believed to have possessed 'extraordinary occult power'. Matongini Hazra who fell to the British bullet on 29 September 1942 when she led the procession to attack the local thana in Midnapur during the Quit India days expressed her firm belief that by drinking water in the name of Gandhi she would be relieved of her painful gout.

Unlike his predecessors, Gandhi redefined the character of the nationalist movement by linking 'the masses' with his campaign against the British. By bringing 'new actors' on the political scene, not only did the Mahatma enlarge the constituency of the freedom struggle, he had also initiated a process whereby local issues figured significantly in the nationalist agenda. Thus, B.N. Sasmol successfully mobilized people against the introduction of the union boards in Midnapur, which by increasing taxation affected the rural people adversely. The anticipated economic hardship as a result of new taxation was clearly attributed to the imperial power and the Sasmol-led local Congress could easily direct mass discontent against the foreign state. That the same Congress was not prepared to pursue a movement challenging the prevalent socio-economic structure in which the hegemony of the well-to-do cultivators was not contested, was evident in its refusal to undertake a campaign against the Congress-minded local zamindars in the Jungle Mahal areas. Even at the cost of a split within the organization, not only did the Congress oppose agrarian radicalism, but also expelled those responsible for 'instigating the innocent tribals' to attack the zamindari property for fear of diluting the freedom struggle and to counter the threat to vested interests. Furthermore, since moral bonds of patronage were a principal mechanism of cohesion in rural society, there developed a symbiotic relationship between the wealthy and poor which largely contributed to the Congress strength.

Between 1920-44, the Congress played a decisive role in articulating anti-British sentiments because the Congress' political basis had been consolidated with the incorporation of a large section of tenure holders who articulated their anti-British role through participation in the institutions of colonial governance in the localities. The fact that these institutions lacked both resources and substantial power meant that the Congress despite being willing could not execute programmes benefiting the people. In other words, since the livelihood of the people was controlled by forces and powers beyond the reach of the district Congress, the local political activists could easily channelize the popular grievances against colonial power by highlighting its exploitative nature. By articulating the class interests of the broad range of tenure holders or jotedars, the Midnapur Congress postulated its own version of political struggle which, though militant *vis-a-vis* imperialism, opposed movements potentially harmful to the existing socio-economic order. This phenomenon accorded the Midnapur Congress a special characteristic, which was well-articulated in its stance towards the 1928 Bengal Tenancy (Amendment) Act. All this also gave the Midnapur Congress a definite ideological orientation distinguishing from the dominant tendency within the Bengal Congress; such a feature largely accounts for its success in avoiding the highly personalized factionalism that crippled the Bengal Congress. As a result, the local Congress based on rural property successfully conducted anti-British movements that displayed considerable militancy without correspondingly upsetting the existent pattern of class relationships in rural society. Interpreted thus, the Midnapur Congress did not deviate from the basic tenets of Gandhism or what the Congress stood for during the freedom struggle which while gradually expanding its political audience never allowed movements challenging the ideological hegemony of indigenous capital and the landed interests.

III

The Gandhi of the 1942 Quit India movement seemed to have

paid less attention to the question of means especially in his passionate 'do or die' speech. Although the need for non-violence was reiterated, the famous 8 August Resolution espoused the call for 'a mass struggle on the widest possible scale' under Gandhi's leadership with the instruction that if the Congress leadership was removed by arrest 'every man and woman who is participating in this movement must function for himself or herself'. Apart from the resolution, Gandhi's statement urging the people to fight till death inspired them to resort to means other than ahimsa. In his public utterances too, the Mahatma appeared to have appreciated violence if circumstances so demanded. For instance, in a press interview, he exhorted, 'this clearly disciplined anarchy [in the shape of the British administration] should be removed at any cost and if as a result, there is a complete lawlessness, I would risk it.' On another occasion, he defended a general strike by arguing that 'if a general strike becomes a dire necessity, I shall not flinch' thus undermining his own concept of trusteeship.

The open rebellion though assumed massive proportions waned quickly at the all-India level; it however continued unabated for almost two years in Midnapur where violence too was resorted to in the name of Gandhi. There are innumerable instances to show that the Congress volunteers drew upon Gandhi to justify violence as it meant a significant contribution to the cause of freedom. *Biplabi* declared that the Mahatma would have approved violence in the name of serving the motherland. There are instances of the inflicting of death penalty on those who committed a heinous crime like raping the village women to terrorize the participants; though the Congress decision ran counter to Gandhi's ahimsa, it was nonetheless justified by drawing attention to his writings in which he was reported to have conceded violence for protecting the honour of women.

Whatever the attainment of the Congress in the open rebellion, 'the location of the Mahatma image' within the existing pattern of popular beliefs and the way it informed direct action, was 'often at variance with the standard interpretation of the Congress creed'. While explaining the role of Gandhi in galvanizing the masses into action in the 1919-22 non-cooperation campaign it has thus been argued that 'there was no single authorized version of the Mahatma to which [the participants of the non-cooperation movement] may be said to have subscribed in 1921. Indeed, their ideas about Gandhi's 'orders' and 'powers' were often at variance with those of the local Congress-Khilafat leadership and clashed with the basic tenets of Gandhism itself. The violence of Chauri Chaura was rooted in this paradox'.[7] The events during the Quit India Movement demonstrate that on various occasions, Gandhi, the person, appeared insignificant in comparison with 'the image of Mahatma' which was constantly reworked in popular vision in a completely different way which neither Gandhi nor the Congress High Command would have approved. For instance, during the height of the Quit India Movement, several images of Gandhi gained currency. To the people of Contai, the Mahatma, endowed with divine power, could never be killed; people believed that Gandhi was not 'hurt' even when the British police fired bullets at him. Gandhi could not be kept in jail since, according to a rumour, he, with his power, could escape the prison as soon as he wanted. In Tamluk, the participants believed that 'if you uttered the name, Gandhi, before the British police they would lose the capacity to fire'. Thus it was not merely coincidental that the slogan - *Gandhiji ki jay* (victory to the Mahatma) – became very popular in the course of the movement. The British administration taking note of the tremendous influence of Gandhi in shaping the popular psyche seemed perplexed at the rapid dissemination of his ideas in remote areas of the district. What probably drew people to Gandhi's ideas was his image as 'a saviour' of the poverty-stricken masses. In a contemporary police report, it was mentioned that 'the real power of [Gandhi's] name is perhaps to be traced back to the ideal' that the Mahtama devoted his life to the cause of the poor Indians. The Congress mobilization for the thana attacks on 29 September 1942 demonstrated the effectiveness of the image of Gandhi which significantly contributed to popularizing the August campaign at the grassroots. Behind its success thus lay the ability of the local Congress to meaningfully explain and translate Gandhi's agenda. Although the movement was launched by the Congress, its success can be attributed largely to the role of a new group of political activists.

So, there were several Gandhis – each being interpreted differently reflecting the priorities of the participants. Translating Gandhism in such a way as to gain maximum mileage, the local leaders articulated the political agenda by attributing the popular grievances to imperialism. Furthermore, the interpretation of Gandhi's ideas also varied in accordance with the preferences of the leadership involved in the mobilization for anti-British offensive. Thus, for instance, one type of leadership exemplified in Swami Prajnananda in Bengal, Swami Darsanananda in Bihar or Baba

Ramchandra in Pratapgarh, invested the Gandhian message with particularly strong religious overtones. The participation of such outsiders also points to the fact that the peasants still needed an outsider to organize themselves in a society going through a period of acute strain and tension due to peculiar circumstances. This argument, if pursued a little further, is likely to identify significant gaps in the analysis of some of the early writings of the subaltern historians which in challenging the so-called elitist historiography tended to somewhat romanticise the revolutionary potential of the rural masses.

GANDHI AFTER GANDHI

Gandhi was killed in 1948. His legacy survived. What was his contribution? Is Gandhi relevant? These are the questions one needs to ask to ascertain whether the Gandhian legacy is still meaningful even in the context of a globalizing society.

Gandhi's contribution to the human civilization is articulated in his alternative 'visions' particularly of 'nation' and 'state'. While challenging many forms of 'domination', whether ancient or modern, in the sub-continent, he developed a comprehensive theory that transcends national boundaries about the basic contours of 'a good society' and the importance of 'non-violence'. Drawing upon 'ethnicity', 'religion' and other India-specific socio-economic characteristics, the Mahatma sought to articulate a distinctive 'cultural' vision of nationhood, which is a powerful critique of urban-industrial civilization. The model which he sought to develop is based on an interrogation of history and contestations of assumptions about modernity, modernization and nation state. Refusing to accept the definitional catholicity of these ideas due to their Western-centric intellectual roots, Gandhi, as an activist-theoretician, sought to redefine them, both in ideological terms and in the domain of praxis, by constantly problematizing what is often thought to be settled today. The ideas that Gandhi nurtured in his battle for freedom clearly identify a definite domain of nationalist thought, which, though different, had its root in post-enlightenment philosophy of nationalism. Given the public nature of *Harijan*, the views that Gandhi expressed, were carefully drafted and the Mahatma therefore appeared to be less ambiguous here than anywhere else. Seeking to integrate what was worth salvaging in modern civilization within the framework of Indian civilization, Gandhi went beyond the conventional approach to 'nationalist' thought where the so-called Indian vision was always uncritically glorified to champion 'a sectarian' political thought. As shown, *Hind Swaraj* is Gandhi's creative response to the theoretical basis of Western civilization. Drawn on the civilizational resources of Hindu religion and its tradition, he put forward a new theoretical framework to conceptualize both colonialism and industrial capitalism. Perhaps the most controversial Gandhian economic formulation was his theory of trusteeship which he developed as a counter to both capitalism and socialism. The thesis drew on the assumption that the capitalists would hold their wealth as trustees for the service of society. Trusteeship was thus viewed as 'a moral compact' between wealthy and society at large. The thesis provoked vehement critique. But in the context of globalized capitalism when the command economy in retreat, Gandhi's trusteeship seems to have raised a relevant question by underling the need for a moral and ethical basis for business.

Gandhi was an activist-theoretician who was involved in India's struggle for independence. He was a revolutionary offering a radical critique of the oppressive and unjust status quo. His definition of violence was not restricted to physical violence. He spoke about structural violence and violence of status quo that is hardly recognized on the surface. Several designs for 'affirmative action' either in developed or developing countries seem to have been drawn on this Gandhian assumption. The Gandhian welfare design underlining 'distributive justice' is at the core of the Part IV of the Constitution of India, entitled *Directive Principles of State Policy,* which, for instance, is a significant influence in some of the major policy shifts in contemporary India. Furthermore, Gandhi's notion of democratic decentralization is both a critique of bureaucracy and a device of participative governance. By according constitutional guarantee to grassroots democracy or *panchayati raj*, as Gandhi described, the Indian policy makers put into practice the Gandhian formula. Last and not the least, Gandhi's emphasis on *dharma* (by that he meant 'sensitivity and responsiveness') in governance seeking to redefine bureaucracy seems to have articulated a modern concern that remains at the core administrative innovations – with focus on reinventing government, or downsizing bureaucracy – in contemporary world. Apart from underlining the importance of *dharma*, Gandhi suggested the overhauling of the governmental structure by introducing the idea of 'oceanic circle'. In his words,

> Life will not be pyramid with the apex sustained by the bottom.

> But it will be an oceanic circle whose centre will be the individual always ready to perish for the village, the latter ready to perish for the circle of villages, till at last the whole becomes one composed of individuals, never aggressive in their arrogance but ever humble, sharing the majesty of the oceanic circle of which they are an integral part.[8]

The model, drawn on the oceanic circle that Gandhi sought to develop may not appear to be realistic given the brutal nature of contemporary civilization especially in the wake of globalization. Two ideas seem pre-eminent here: first, for him, a circle of inter-dependent villages remained perhaps the most viable unit for sustained and equitable economic growth for any society. Secondly, perhaps more importantly, systematic economic well-being would certainly make the individuals within the circle self-reliant and thus confident. His basic objective of installing 'a sense of self respect' among the Indians would thus be realized in the oceanic circle of villages. However, his uncritical appreciation of 'village' as a socio-economic phenomenon provoked, as discussed earlier, severe critique from his nationalist colleagues, including B.R. Ambedkar. Nonetheless, one cannot dismiss the theoretical importance of this model which by insisting on mass participation in activities, meaningful and beneficial to the people at large, undoubtedly marks a serious search for transcendental civilizational alternative visions.

---

1 NAI, Home-Poll53/1921, Weekly Report of Director, Intelligence Bureau, 10 March, 1921 – quoted in Judith M. Brown, *Gandhi:*

Prisoner of Hope, Oxford University Press, Delhi, 1990, p. 168.

2 Judith M Brown, 'The Mahatma and modern India', *Modern Asian Studies*, 111, (1969), p. 337.

3 IOR, Mss. Eur. F 93(5), Willingdon, the Madras Governor to Reading, the Viceroy, 3 April, 1921.

4 Jawaharlal Nehru, *The Discovery of India,* Oxford University Press, Delhi, 1989, p. 358.

5 Susanne Hoeber Rudolph and Lloyd I. Rudolph, *Gandhi: The Traditional Roots of Charisma*, Orient Longman, 1987, p. 5.

6 Monash University Library, Melbourne, microfilm collection of declassified State Department documents, Counselor, American Embassy in Calcutta to the Secretary of State, 27 August, 1947.

7 Shahid Amin, 'Gandhi as Mahatma: Gorakhpur district, eastern Uttar Pradesh', in R. Guha, *Subaltern Studies*, Vol. III, OUP, Delhi, 1984, p. 55.

8 Gandhi's interview in the press, *CWMG*, vol.85, p.33.

GLOSSARY

Adhikar: A right, a right that is earned or deserved
Advaita: Non-dualism, monism
Anasakti: Non-attachment
Ashram: A commune of spiritual aspirants organized around a guru
Atman: Soul or spirit
Bania: Of the class of traders and moneylender
Brahmacharya: Celibacy, chastity
Buddhi: Intelligence
Chetana: Consciousness
Dalits: Those previously described as untouchables. The untouchables were people considered so low to be placed outside the pale of normal physical contact with those who are considered ritually superior.
Dharma: Duty, moral law, characteristic activity of a class of objects or beings
Dharna: A form of sit-down strike
Duragraha: Stubborn persistence
Ekpraja: A sense of belonging to a single community
Fakir: Muslim ascetic or mendicant
Goonda: Ruffian/hooligan
Harijan: Untouchables; literally, people of God

Karma: Action, law of moral retribution
Lathi: Stick
Lokshakti: People's power, power generated by people's collective action
Mahatma: Great soul. An honorific title conferred on Gandhi by Rabindranath Tagore
Maitri: Friendliness
Manas: Mind
Moksha: Liberation, release from the cycle of rebirth
Nishkam dharma: Disinterested action
Panchayat: Originally a committee or council of five members, now a small local council
Sabha: Assembly, society
Sadbhava: Goodwill, a wish to see someone flourish
Sanatani: A strict follower of ancient Vedic religion, orthodox
Satya: Truth
Shakti: Energy or power
Swadeshi: Belonging to or made in one's country
Swaraj: Self rule, individual or collective autonomy
Tapasya, Tapas: Religious penance, austerity, sacrifice
Ulema: Muslim theologian
Varna: Caste
Varnashrama: Four-fold division of Hindu society
Yajna: Any activity undertaken in the spirit of sacrifice to a deity
Yantravad: Mechanization as an end in itself or for its own sake.
Yogi: One who practises yoga
Zamindar: Landlord

BIBLIOGRAPHY

Alavi, Hamza, 'Misreading partition road signs', *Economic and Political Weekly*, November, 2-9, 2002.

Alavi, Hamza, 'Social forces and ideology in the making of Pakistan', *Economic and Political Weekly*, October, 21, 2002

Ali Chaudhuri, Muhammad, *The Emergence of Pakistan*, Columbia University Press, New York, 1967.

Ambedkar, B. R., 'Thoughts on Pakistan' in Mushirul Hasan (ed.), *Inventing Boundaries: Gender, Politics and Partition of India*, Oxford University Press, Delhi, 2000.

Ambedkar, B.R., *What Congress and Gandhi done to the Untouchables*, Thacker & Co., Bombay, 1946.

Amin, Shahid, 'Gandhi as Mahatma: Gorakhpur district, eastern UP, 1021-2', in Ranajit Guha (ed.), *Subaltern Studies: Writings on South Asian Studies*, Vol. III, Oxford University Press, Delhi, 1984.

Amin, Shahid, *Event, Metaphor, Memory: Chauri Chaura, 1922-92*, Oxford University Press, New Delhi, 1995.

Ananthanathan, A.K., 'The significance of Gandhi's interpretation of Gita', *Gandhi Marg,* 13 (3), October, 1991.

Bagchi, Amiya, *Private Investment in India, 1900-39*, Cambridge University Press, Cambridge, 1972.

Bakshi, Rajni, *Bapu Kuti: Journeys in Rediscovery of Gandhi*, Penguin, New Delhi, 1998.

Bandyopadhyaya, Jayantuja, *Social and Political thought of Gandhi*, Allied Publishers, Bombay, 1969.

Bhalla, Alok (ed.), *Stories about the Partition of India*, Penguin, New Delhi, 1994.

Bhattacharya, Sabyasachi (edited and compiled), *The Mahatma and the Poet: Letters and Debates between Gandhi and Tagore, 1915-1941*, National Book Trust, New Delhi, 1997.

Bose, N.K., *My Days with Gandhi*, Orient Longman, Calcutta, 1974.

Bose, Nirmal Kumar, *Studies in Gandhism*, India Associated Publishing Co., Calcutta, 1962.

Bose, Subhas Chandra, *The Indian Struggle, 1920-42*, Asia Publishing House, London, 1964.

Bose, Sugata, 'Nation, reason and religion: India's independence in international perspective', *Economic and Political Weekly*, August 1, 1998

Bose, Sugata and Ayesha Jalal, *Modern South Asia: History, Culture, Political Economy*, Oxford University Press, Delhi, 1998.

Brown, Judith, 'The Mahatma and modern India', *Modern Asian Studies*, 3(4), 1969.

Brown, Judith, *Gandhi and Civil Disobedience: The Mahatma in Indian Politics, 1928-1934*, Cambridge University Press, Cambridge, 1977.

Brown, Judith, *Gandhi: Prisoner of Hope*, Oxford University Press, Delhi, 1990.

Brown, Judith, *Gandhi's Rise to Power: Indian Politics, 1915-1922*, Cambridge University Press, Cambridge, 1972.

Brown, Judith, *Modern India: The Origins of an Asian Democracy*, Oxford University Press, Delhi, 1985.

Brown, Judith, *Nehru: Political Life*, Oxford University Press, New Delhi, 2004.

Chakrabarty, Bidyut, 'Peasants and the Bengal Congress, 1928-38, *South Asia Research*, 5(1) May, 1985.

Chakrabarty, Bidyut, *Subhas Chandra Bose and Middle Class Radicalism: A Study in Indian Nationalism, 1928-40*, Oxford University Press, 1990.

Chakrabarty, Bidyut, *Local Politics and Indian Nationalism: Midnapur, 1919-1944*, Manohar, 1997.

Chakrabarty, Bidyut, *Biplabi: A Journal of the 1942 Open Rebellion*, K.P. Bagchi, Calcutta, 2002.

Chakrabarty, Bidyut, 'Religion, Colonialism and Modernity: Relocating "self" and "collectivity"', *Gandhi Marg*, 23 (3), 2002.

Chakrabarty, Bidyut (ed.), *Communal Identity in India: Its Construction and Articulation in the Twentieth Century*, Oxford University Press, Oxford University Press, Delhi, 2003.

Chakrabarty, Bidyut, *The Partition of Bengal and Assam, 1932-47: Contour of Freedom*, Routledge Curzon, London & New York, 2004.

Chatterjee, Margaret, *Gandhi's Religious Thought*, Macmillan, London, 1983.

Chatterjee, Partha, 'Gandhi please stand up?', *Illustrated Weekly of India*, 15-21 January, 1984.

Chatterjee, Partha, 'The Nation in Heterogeneous Time', *Indian Economic and Social History Review*, 38, 4, 2001.

Chatterjee, Partha, *A Princely Impostor? The Kumar of Bhawal and the Secret History of Indian Nationalism*, Permanent Black, New Delhi, 2002.

Chaudhuri, Nirad C, *The Autobiography of an Unknown Indian*, University of California Press, Berkeley, 1968.

Chaudhuri, Nirad C, *Thy Hand Great Anarch: India, 1921-52*, Chatto and Windus, London, 1987.

Choudhury, Khaliquzzaman, *Pathway to Pakistan*, Longmans, Lahore, 1961.

Dalton, Dennis, *Non-Violence in Action: Gandhi's Power*, Oxford University Press, Delhi, 1998.

Darling, Malcolm Lyall, *At Freedom's Dawn*, Oxford University Press, London, 1949.

Das, Durga (ed), *Vallabhbhai Patel Correspondence, 1945-50*, Vol. IV, Ahmedabad, 1972.

Dasgupta, Ajit K., *Gandhi's Economic Thought*, Routledge, London & New York, 1996.

Datta, V. N, 'Iqbal, Jinnah and India's Partition', *Economic and Political Weekly*, December, 14-20, 2002.

Dutt, R. Palme, *India Today*, Victor Gollancz Ltd, London, 1940.

Erickson, E., *Gandhi's Truth: On the Origins of Militant Non-violence*, Faber & Faber, New York, 1970.

Fisher, Louis, *The Life of Mahatma Gandhi*, Harper and Row, New York, 1981.

Fisher, Louis, *Gandhi: His Life and Message for the World*, New American Library, New York, 1982.

Fox, Richard, *Gandhian Utopia: Experiments with Culture*, Beacon Press, Boston, 1989.

Frank, Andre Gunder, 'Gandhi, the Philosopher', *Economic and Political Weekly*, 38 (43), 2003.

Freitag, Sandria B, *Collective Action and Community: Public Arenas and the Emergence of Communalism in North India*, Oxford University Press, Delhi, 1990.

Gier, Nicholas, 'Gandhi, Ahimsa and Self', *Gandhi Marg*, 15 (1), 1993

Gopal, S, *Jawaharlal Nehru*, 3 vols, Jonathan Cape, London, 1973-84.

Gore, M.S., *The Social Context of an Ideology: Ambedkar's Political and Social Thought*, Sage, New Delhi, 1993.

Griffiths, Percival, *To Guard My People: The History of the Indian Police*, Ernest Benn, London, 1971.

Guha, Ranajit, *Dominance without Hegemony: History and Power in Colonial India*, Oxford University Press, Delhi, 1998.

Haksar, Vinit, *Rights, Communities and Disobedience: Liberalism and Gandhi*, Oxford University Press, New Delhi, 2001.

Hardiman, David, *Peasants Nationalists of Gujarat: Kheda District, 1917-34*, Oxford University Press, Delhi, 1981.

Hardiman, David, *Gandhi in his Times and Ours*, Permanent Black, New Delhi, 2003.

Hardy, P, *The Muslims of British India*, Cambridge University Press, Cambridge, 1972.

Hasan, Mushirul (ed.), *India Partitioned: The other Face of Freedom*, vol. 1, Roli Books, New Delhi, 1995.

Hasan, Mushirul, *Legacy of a Divided Nation: India's Muslims since Independence*, Oxford University Press, Delhi, 1997.

Hasan, Mushirul (ed.), *Inventing Boundaries: Gender, Politics and the Partition of India*, Oxford University Press, New Delhi, 2000.

Hashim, Abul, *In Retrospection*, Mowla Brothers, Dhaka, 1974.

Hodosn, H. V., *The Great Divide: Britain – India – Pakistan*, Hutchinson of London, London, 1969.

Horsburgh, H.J.N., *Non-violence and Aggression: A study of Gandhi's Moral Equivalent of War,* Oxford University Press, London, 1968.

Iyer, Raghavan, *The Moral and Political thought of Mahatma Gandhi*, Oxford University Press, Delhi, 1973.

Iyer, Raghavan (ed.), *The Moral and Political Writings of Mahatma Gandhi*, Clarendon Press, Oxford, Vols. 1 & 2, 1986 and Vol. 3, 1987.

Jha, Sadan, 'Charkha, "Dear forgotten friend", of widows: Reading the erasures of symbols', *Economic and Political Weekly*, 39 (28), 2004.

Jinnah, Muhammad Ali, *Speeches,* Pakistan Publications, Karachi, 1963.

Juergensmeyer, Mark, *Fighting with Gandhi*, Harper and Row, San Francisco, 1984.

Juergensmeyer, Mark, *Gandhi's Way: A Handbook of Conflict Resolution*, Oxford University Press, New Delhi, 2003.

Khilnani, Sunil, 'Gandhi and History', *Seminar*, No. 461 (Annual), January, 1998

Kripalani, Krishna, *Gandhi: A Life*, National Book Trust, New Delhi, 1968.

Kripalani, Sucheta, *An Unfinished Biography*, Navajivan Publishing House, Ahmedabad, 1978.

Kumar, R, *Essays on Gandhian Politics: The Rowlatt Satyagraha of 1919*, Clarendon Press, Oxford, 1971.

Mahajan, Sucheta, *Independence and Partition: The Erosion of Colonial Power*, Sage, New Delhi, 2000.

Mansergh, Diana (ed.), *Independence Years: The Selected Indian and Commonwealth Papers of Nicholas Mansergh*, Oxford University Press, Delhi, 1999.

Markovits, Claude, *The un-Gandhian Gandhi: The Life and Afterlife of the Mahatma,* Permanent Black, New Delhi, 2003.

Menon, Dilip, 'Religion and colonial modernity: Rethinking belief and identity', *Economic and Political Weekly*, April 27, 2002.

Menon, V. P., *The Transfer of Power in India*, Orient Longman, Madrars, 1993 (reprint), Appendix X.

Mitra, Ashok, *The New India, 1948-1955: Memoirs of an Indian Civil Servant*, Popular Prakashan, Bombay, 1991.

Moon, Penderel, *The British Conquest of Dominion of India*, Duckworth, London, 1989.

Moore, Barrington Jr., *Social Origins of Dictatorship and Democracy: Lord and Peasant in the Making of the Modern World*, Beacon Press, Boston, 1966.

Morris-Jones, W.H., 'Mahatma Gandhi: Political philosopher', *Political Studies*, Vol. VIII (1), February, 1960.

Mukherjee, Hiren, *Gandhi: A Study*, People's Publishing House, New Delhi, 1991 (reprint).

Mukherjee, Rudrangshu, *The Penguin Gandhi Reader*, Penguin, New Delhi, 1993.

Mukherjee, Subrata, *Gandhian Thought: Marxist Interpretation*, Deep & Deep, New Delhi, 1997.

Mukherjee, Subrata and Sushila Ramaswamy (ed.), *Economic and Social Principles of Mahatma Gandhi,* Deep & Deep, New Delhi, 1998.

Mukherjee, Subrata and Sushila Ramaswamy (ed.), *Ethics, Religion and Culture*, Deep & Deep, New Delhi, 1998.

Mukherjee, Subrata and Sushila Ramaswamy (ed.), *Non-violence and Satyagraha*, Deep & Deep, New Delhi, 1998.

Namboodiripad, E.M.S., *The Mahatma and the Ism*, People's Publishing House, New Delhi, 1959.

Nanda, B.R., *The Nehrus: Motilal and Jawaharlal*, George & Allen, London, 1962.

Nanda, B.R., *Gandhi and his Critics*, Oxford University Press, Delhi, 1985.

Nanda, B.R., *In Search of Gandhi: Essays and Reflections*, Oxford University Press, New Delhi, 2004.

Nanda, B.R., *Mahatma Gandhi: 125 Years*, New Age International Publishers, New Delhi, 1995.

Nanda, B.R., *Mahatma Gandhi*, Oxford University Press, Delhi, 1996 (reprint).

Nandy, Ashis, *The Illegitimacy of Nationalism: Rabindranath and the Politics of Self*, Oxford University Press, Delhi, 1994.

Nandy, Ashis, *The Intimate Enemy: Loss and Recovery of Self under Colonialism*, Oxford University Press, Delhi, 1983.

Narayan, R.K., *Waiting for the Mahatma,* Indian Thought Publications, Chennai, 2003 (reprint).

Nehru, Jawaharlal, *Jawaharlal Nehru: An Autobiography*, John Lane The Bodley Head, London, 1941.

Nehru, Jawaharlal, *The Discovery of India*, Oxford University Press, Delhi, (centenary edition), 1985,

Orwell, G, 'Reflections on Gandhi', *Partisan Review*, 16 January, 1949.

Pandey, Gyanendra, 'The prose of otherness', *Subaltern Studies*, Vol. VIII, Oxford University Press, Delhi, 1994.

Pandey, Gyanendra, *Hindus and Others: The Question of Identity in India Today*, Viking, New Delhi, 1997.

Pandey, Gyanendra, *Remembering Partition: Violence, Nationalism and History in India*, Cambridge University Press, Cambridge, 2001.

Pantham, Thomas and Kenneth L. Deutsch, *Political Thought in Modern India*, Sage, New Delhi, 1986.

Pantham, Thomas, 'Gandhi: Swaraj, Sarvadaya and Satyagraha', in Thomas Pantham, *Political Theories and Social Reconstruction: A Critical Survey of the Literature on India*, Sage, New Delhi, 1995.

Pantham, Thomas, 'Thinking with Mahatma Gandhi: Beyond Liberal Democracy', *Political Theory*, 11 (2), 1983.

Parekh, Bhikhu, *Gandhi's Political Philosophy*, University of Notre Dame Press, Notre Dame, IN, 1989.

Parekh, Bhikhu, 'Nehru and the national philosophy of India', *Economic and Political Weekly*, 26 (182), 1991.

Parekh, Bhikhu, *Gandhi*, Oxford University Press, Oxford, 1997.

Parekh, Bhikhu, *Colonialism, Tradition and Reform: An Analysis of Gandhi's Political Discourse*, Sage, New Delhi, 1999.

Parel, Anthony J (ed.), *Gandhi, Freedom and Self-rule*, Vistaar, New Delhi, 2000.

Parel, Anthony J, (ed.), *Hind Swaraj and other Writings*, Cambridge University Press, Cambridge, 1997.

Pouchepadas, Jacques, *Champaran and Gandhi: Planters, Peasants and Gandhian Politics*, Oxford University Press, New Delhi, 1999.

Prasad, Bimal, *Pathway to India's Partition: The Foundations of Muslim Nationalism*, Vol. I, Manohar, Delhi, 1996.

Ray, Rajat K. (ed.), *Mind, Body and Society: Life and Mentality in Colonial Bengal*, Oxford University Press, Calcutta, 1995.

Ray Sibnarayan (ed.), *Selected Works of M.N. Roy*, Vol. I (1917-1922), Oxford University Press, New Delhi, 2000.

Ray, Sibnarayan (ed.), *Selected Works of M.N. Roy*, Vol. II (1923-1927), Oxford University Press, New Delhi, 2000.

Richards, G, *The Philosophy of Gandhi: A Study of his Basic Ideas,* Curzon Press, Surrey, 1982.

Rodrigues, Valerian (ed.), *The Essential Writings of B.R. Ambedkar*, Oxford University Press, New Delhi, 2004.

Rolland, Romain, *Mahatma Gandhi*, Allen and Unwin, London, 1924.

Rudolph, L.I. and S.H., *Postmodern Gandhi and other Essays: Gandhi in the World and at Home,* Oxford University Press, New Delhi, 2006.

Sethi, J.D., *Gandhi Today*, Carolina Academic Press, Durham, 1978.

Settar, S and Indira B. Gupta (ed.), *Pangs of Partition: The Human Dimension*, Vol. II, Manohar, New Delhi, 2002.

Settar, S. and Indira B. Gupta (ed.), *Pangs of Partition: The Parting of Ways*, Vol. I, Manohar, New Delhi, 2002.

Shaikh, Farzana, 'Muslims and political representation in colonial India: The making of Pakistan', *Modern Asian Studies*, 20, 3, 1986.

Singh, Anita Inder, *The Origins of Partition of India, 1936-47*, Oxford University Press, Delhi, 1987.

Sitaramayya, B. Pattabhi, *History of the Indian National Congress*, Vol. II, (1935-47), S. Chand & Co, Delhi, 1969.

Spear, Percival, *The Oxford History of Modern India, 1740-1947*, Clarendon Press, Oxford, 1965.

Tai, Yong Tan and Gynesh Kudaisya, *The Aftermath of Partition in South Asia,* Routledge, London, 2000.

Taneja, Anup, *Gandhi, Women and the National Movement, 1920-47*, Har-Anand, New Delhi, 2005.

Tarchek, Ronald J, *Gandhi: Struggling for Autonomy*, Vistaar, New Delhi, 1998.

Tendulkar, D.G., *Mahatma: The Life of M.K. Gandhi*, Ministry of Information and Broadcasting, Government of India, New Delhi, 1961.

Weber, Thomas, *Conflict Resolution and Gandhian Ethics*, The Gandhi Peace Foundation, New Delhi, 1991.

Wolpert, S, *Nehru: A Tryst with Destiny*, Oxford University Press, New York, 1996.

Zaidi, A. M. and S. G. Zaidi (ed.), *The Encyclopaedia of the Indian National Congress*, Vol. 12, S. Chand & Co, New Delhi, 1981.

Ziegler, P, *Mountbatten: The Official Biography*, Collins, Glasgow, 1985.

INDEX